N. York. March 18th 1787

for you the peccan nuts have all been

when I recd. by the post about a dozen

by a French gentleman in a vessel bound

can himself to Paris, or consign them to

despair of being able to possess myself of

my endeavours have been equally un-

maple, notwithstanding the different plans

begun a letter to you of some length which I

short notice I had of it, the tediousness of

nable interruptions make it doubtful

The Founding Fathers

Engraving after a painting by Gilbert Stuart

The Founding Fathers

JAMES MADISON

A Biography in His Own Words

VOLUME 1

Edited by
MERRILL D. PETERSON

With an Introduction by
ROBERT A. RUTLAND
Editor, *The Papers of James Madison*

JOAN PATERSON KERR
Picture Editor

NEWSWEEK
New York

We dedicate this series of books to the memory of
Frederick S. Beebe
friend, mentor, and "Founding Father" of Newsweek Books

James Madison, A Biography in His Own Words,
has been produced by the Newsweek Book Division:

Joseph L. Gardner, Editor

Janet Czarnetzki, Art Director

Judith Bentley, Copy Editor

Susan Storer, Picture Researcher

S. Arthur Dembner, Publisher

This book is based on *The Papers of James Madison*
edited by William T. Hutchinson and William M. E. Rachal (Vols. 1-7)
and by Robert A. Rutland and William M. E. Rachal (Vol. 8),
sponsored by The University of Virginia, published by
The University of Chicago Press, and copyright The University of Chicago.
The texts of all documents in this edition from the Madison Papers
have been supplied by Mr. Rutland.
Permission to reproduce excerpts has been granted through the courtesy
of The University of Chicago Press.
Other sources are acknowledged on page 408.

Contents

VOLUME 1

Introduction   6

Chronology of Madison and His Times   10

1   A Revolutionary Vocation   13

2   Congressman at War   45

3   Radical Reformer   82

  A PICTURE PORTFOLIO: Man from Montpelier   111

4   Father of the Constitution   130

5   First Man in Congress   166

VOLUME 2

6   To the Revolution of 1800   209

7   Secretary of State   235

8   Gathering Storm Clouds   273

  A PICTURE PORTFOLIO: Mr. Madison's War   303

9   Second War for Independence   322

10   Last of the Fathers   365

  Selected Bibliography   408

  Acknowledgments   408

  Index   410

Introduction

by Robert A. Rutland
Editor, The Papers of James Madison

When John F. Kennedy accepted the first two volumes of *The Papers of James Madison* in 1962, he remarked with some earnestness that in his judgment Madison was probably "the most underrated of our Founding Fathers." President Kennedy was acknowledging the public's dim perception of Madison as Father of the Constitution, a view overlooking the rest of his long life and public career. Modern scholarship has sought to revive Madison as a total participant in the nation's birth and development, however; and the basis for a reevaluation lies in the papers he wrote or received, which he guarded at Montpelier until the end of his days and which now belong to the nation he usually alluded to as "our beloved Country."

In our age of instantaneous communications, an impersonalization of the written and spoken word has become so common that citizens are skimming and skipping, half listening or barely watching a great deal of the time. What a contrast with James Madison's world, where the pace of life was not dependent upon person-to-person telephone calls or vast electronic networks of programmed and stereotyped mass communications. Indeed, the scholar who delves into the papers of the Founding Fathers is invariably impressed by both the wisdom imparted and the sheer bulk of their writings. Surely Madison must have spent a good part of many days at Montpelier, Richmond, Philadelphia, Washington—wherever family or public duties took him—at the writing desk. The personal effort required, the thought processes involved, and the time consumed all make his correspondence, and that of all our early leaders, a monumental accomplishment.

The preservation of that achievement has become a public concern and a significant historical endeavor. Much of the record of history in Western society has been saved from the flames or insects only by chance. Public record keeping was still an infant art when the first Englishmen claimed their foothold on American soil, yet official records of that period abound. On the other hand, the survival of the colonists' diaries, personal letters, and family records was rather haphazard. By the time of the Revolution, however, American leaders often realized the importance of what they were doing and their unique position in history.

In the intellectual climate of the revolutionary era, Madison's generation brought together the elements for what has become an exemplary situation in world history. Never before was a nation created through joint efforts of pen and sword, with the chief participants fully conscious of the usefulness of both weapons. Burdened with such a sense of history, they carefully rewrote sentences, painstakingly called back letters written to departed colleagues, and guarded personal secrets by instructing surviving spouses to burn certain letters.

Fortunately for the nation they helped found, three Virginians—Washington, Jefferson, and Madison—were particularly aware of their role in history and anxious to preserve their niche by augmenting the memories of others with their own collections of personal papers. Their motives were not solely altruistic. Washington's vanity and a certain punctiliousness doubtless motivated him to collect and save the papers of a life that was to demand worldwide attention. Jefferson's epistolary activities were in part a protective shield to explain both his triumphs and his failures. Madison, probably in imitation of Jefferson's example, began to save papers as his public career developed and as he grew to recognize the magnitude of the revolutionary movement in which he was a participant.

Until Madison began to perceive his role in the American Revolution he was an indifferent collector of letters, although he was a young and eager spectator at the beginnings of the resistance. From his first writings in a commonplace book until his last letters were penned from Montpelier, Madison's seriousness is apparent. Many citizens — particularly Jefferson and Washington — were struck with the giant intellect of this small Virginian. His probity, logic, and tenacious pursuit of a national goal are discernible in so much of Madison's literary legacy that we are disappointed we know little of the other side of his personality. From such observers as Mrs. Samuel Harrison Smith and Harriet Martineau we learn that Madison could be jovial and even jocular on the right occasion, but the image most often projected in history books and fixed in the mind's eye is more to the turn of Washington Irving's unfortunate phrase, "Jemmy Madison — ah! poor Jemmy! He is but a withered little apple-John." The publication of Madison's papers, however, is bringing a more balanced view of a far different kind of person.

For most of his life Madison wrote with some reserve, but his letters to fellow Princetonian William Bradford between 1772 and 1775 reveal unguarded moments when the youthful Madison took solace in his collegiate attachments. "Friendship like all Truth delights in plainness and simplicity," Madison wrote "Dear Billey" from his "Obscure Corner" of the world. As young Whigs, they yearned to share in the excitement of the protest against British policies. Soon Madison moved from the role of a passive spectator to that of a drill-field marksman, and finally into more stirring action at Williamsburg.

After serving in the Virginia Convention of 1776 and participating in the Revolution as a privy councilor in Virginia, Madison entered the Continental Congress at Philadelphia in 1780 and began to save letters, memoranda, notes for speeches, and drafts of important documents made while the young nation struggled for its existence. His note-taking in Congress and later at the Federal Convention would in itself have assured Madison a special niche among the preservers of history; but Madison seems to have sensed the necessity for saving every scrap of paper related to his public career, either for its archival value or as an aid in writing a projected history of the Revolution (which he eventually abandoned).

Madison accumulated a great bulk of papers as he moved from the state legislature to Congress, advised President Washington, maintained his close ties with Jefferson, and became a leading figure in national politics. Except for a brief interval from 1797 to 1799, Madison remained active in the political life of his state and nation until his retirement from the Presidency on March 4, 1817. He lived another nineteen years, most of it spent at Montpelier, and during much of that time he was engaged in preparing his Federal Convention notes and other papers for eventual publication. His expenses were great and his income dwindled, but Madison believed that in his legacy of the primary sources of history he was securing a comfortable settlement for his devoted wife, Dolley.

Madison's plan to preserve history and secure needed income for his family was only partially successful. Interest in the Federal Convention of 1787 was great, as Madison realized, and the sparse information contained in the official journals released by the government in 1819 only whetted the public's expectations. Madison thought that the posthumous publication of his notes would bring his widow twelve thousand dollars and at the same time leave the nation with an accurate account of that historic conference. He hoped to set the record aright and provide future historians with a unique body of information. Not content to collect materials by recalling letters from the estates of important correspondents who had died, Madison began to revise his letters and documents in ways that have invariably obscured the record. In some instances, as with a coded letter to Jefferson concerning Lafayette, Madison attempted to alter and soften a contemporary judgment; but with other emendations, as in the Federal Convention notes, his tinkering caused doubts as to what was changed in 1787 for the sake of accuracy and what might have been altered much later as an outright distortion. Usually, the changes Madison made or caused his aides (Dolley Madison, her brother, and her son) to make can be easily discerned because of the ink or penmanship. But the fact that Madison, probably the most intellectual of the Founding Fathers, succumbed to the temptation to change the record tells us something about man's vanity. The full answer to why he did it is buried with Madison, of course, but his whole life was dedicated to making the American experiment in self-government succeed, and in his later years Madison was trying to erase old animosities and help secure the Union, which he perceived was in danger.

Madison died quietly on June 28, 1836. Dolley came into immediate possession of his papers, which she considered "Sacred, and no more to be infringed or altered than his last Will. He desired me to read them over and if any letter—line—or word struck me as being calculated to injure the feelings of any one or wrong in themselves that I would withdraw them or it." Thus the process of correcting and changing would continue "consonant to his wishes and directions, and made with my concurrence." Some of the personal letters between husband and wife were then destroyed or loaned out and later lost to history. Clerks made copies of the papers for a proposed edition of Madison's writings, but Mrs. Madison thought the publishers set too small a price on their worth. She figured the convention and congressional notes alone were worth one hundred thousand dollars—a stunning amount in that time—but finally accepted the thirty thousand Congress offered. These papers were published by Congress in three volumes in 1840, but meanwhile John C. Payne, Dolley's brother, had arranged additional papers and planned to offer a three or four-volume set from a commercial publisher. The original copies were deposited in a Washington bank while Mrs. Madison negotiated with the publishers, and during this period her impecunious son, John Payne Todd, had access to this treasure trove of early American history.

Todd drew on the papers to settle debts accumulated from his visits to the fleshpots in Washington. One of his chief creditors, James C. McGuire, ultimately came into the possession of hundreds of documents. Mrs. Madison herself displayed little evidence that she had much business acumen, and the sale of the rest of the papers became by 1848 a matter of some desperation. Four years of fruitless negotiations with a private firm had led to nothing, and in 1848 Congress offered Dolley Madison twenty-five thousand dollars for "all the unpublished papers" of her late husband still in her possession. The legislation was prudently conditioned on an immediate payment of five thousand dollars to Mrs. Madison's creditors and the establishment of a trust fund with the remaining money as an annuity for her.

As it developed, the Madison papers Dolley sold Congress were only a portion of those the aged Virginian had so carefully preserved. When Mrs. Madison died a year later, McGuire hauled trunkloads of papers from Montpelier to his Washington home as security for John Payne Todd's unpaid debts. Most of this material came to public attention when McGuire's collection was advertised for sale in 1892 and nearly three thousand letters to and from Madison were sold under the auctioneer's hammer. As late as 1903 some Madison documents, lent by Dolley Madison to a relative a short time before her death, were apparently burned by a descendant who wished to carry out a promise made by Anna C. Payne to the President's widow.

Despite the confusion and self-deception apparent in Dolley Madison's household, most of the Madison papers finally came to the Library of Congress in 1903. Important documents that had been plucked from the collection slowly returned to the main body through official channels, auction sales, and as gifts, while other valuable acquisitions were made by university and public libraries. Most of the twenty-two thousand Madison items are now found there, although some holdings remain in the Virginia State Library, Virginia Historical Society, the University of Virginia, the National Archives, and Princeton University. And although 125 years have elapsed since Dolley Madison thought she was turning the remnants of the President's papers over to a national custodian, a few major gaps remain. These important letters are in the hands of private manuscript collectors who guard their anonymity tenaciously, and their wishes are considered a sacred trust by some autograph dealers who regard an unpublished Madison letter as a tempting bit of merchandise. Perhaps several hundred Madison letters fall into this category. Eventually, they will reach the Library of Congress and rest in the manuscript depository of the James Madison Memorial annex to that storehouse of national scholarship.

The Library of Congress files are the basis of the ongoing *Papers of James Madison* project, which was jointly sponsored by the Universities of Chicago and Virginia from 1956 to 1970. Since 1971 the editorial offices have been at the University of Virginia and the publishing has continued at the University of Chicago. Following the scholarly guidelines laid down by Julian P. Boyd in *The Papers of Thomas Jefferson*, the editorial staff strives to produce accurate texts, duly annotated, of all the documents that affected the life of James Madison between 1759 and 1836. The previous editions of Madison's writings by Henry Gilpin (1840), William C. Rives and Philip R. Fendall (1865), and Gaillard Hunt (1900–10) all bore limitations that greatly restrict the modern scholar.

In this volume Merrill D. Peterson has brought together the panoramic view of Madison as a legislator, party leader, Cabinet officer, President, and senior statesman. From the files of his papers, Madison is presented in his own language as the dispassionate Founding Father whose chief interest in life was to prove that Americans had been chosen by Providence for an experiment to test man's capacity for self-government. The passion of James Madison's life was to make that experiment succeed.

Perhaps the reader of these excerpts will be able to make his own discovery as to the driving force in Madison's life. The consensus of biographers from Rives through Irving Brant, after they studied Madison's life with a sometimes microscopic eye, has been that Madison was primarily concerned with the survival of the American nation as a political unit. If the reader finds his own interpretation, then he will know the scholar's delight in uncovering new truths in the old repositories of knowledge.

EDITORIAL NOTE

Most of the Madison writings reprinted in this biography have been excerpted from the longer original documents being published in their entirety by the University of Chicago Press. Omissions at the beginning or ending of a document are indicated by ellipses only if the extract begins or ends in the middle of a sentence; omissions within a quoted passage are also indicated by ellipses. The original spellings have been retained; editorial insertions are set within square brackets.

Chronology of Madison and His Times

James Madison born in King George County, Virginia, March 16 (March 5, Old Style)	1751	
	1754	French and Indian War, 1754–63
	1760	Reign of George III of England, 1760–1820
Enrolled at Donald Robertson's school	1762	
	1765	Stamp Act
Studies with the Rev. Thomas Martin	1767	Parliament passes Townshend duties
Student at College of New Jersey in Princeton, 1769–72	1769	Nonimportation movement in Colonies
	1770	Townshend duties repealed; Boston Massacre; ministry of Lord North, 1770–82
Receives baccalaureate degree; continues study	1771	
Returns to Virginia; suffers from nervous disorder; letters to William Bradford	1772	
Legal studies begin	1773	Boston Tea Party
Visits Philadelphia; elected to Orange County Committee of Safety	1774	Coercive Acts; First Continental Congress; Louis XVI rules France, 1774–92
Colonel in Orange County militia	1775	Second Continental Congress; Battles of Lexington and Concord
Delegate to Virginia Convention and General Assembly	1776	Virginia Declaration of Rights; Declaration of Independence
Defeated in race for assembly, but chosen for Council of State, 1778–79	1777	Battle of Saratoga
Delegate to Continental Congress: investigates Lee's charges against Franklin, supports western lands motion, prepares instructions for Jay on Mississippi navigation	1780	Fall of Charleston; mutiny at Morristown
	1781	Virginia cedes Ohio lands; Articles of Confederation ratified; British campaign in Virginia; Battle of Yorktown
Urges impost unsuccessfully	1782	Preliminary peace treaty signed in Paris
Drafts new impost plan; end of engagement to Kitty Floyd; retires from Congress	1783	Congress ratifies peace treaty; British West Indies closed to American trade
Trip to Fort Stanwix with Lafayette; fight for religious liberty in Virginia assembly	1784	
"Memorial . . . against Religious Assessments"	1785	Congress moves to New York
Enactment of Virginia Statute for Religious Freedom; attends Annapolis Convention	1786	Shays' Rebellion
Returns to Continental Congress; supports a strong government at Federal Convention; contributes to *The Federalist*	1787	Adams's *A Defence of the Constitutions of Government of the United States . . .*
Fights for ratification at Virginia convention	1788	Constitution ratified
Elected to House of Representatives; sponsors Bill of Rights	1789	George Washington inaugurated as President; beginning of French Revolution
Compromise on funding and location of capital	1790	Hamilton's first *Report on the Public Credit*
Argues unconstitutionality of a national bank; tours the North with Jefferson; writes for Freneau's *National Gazette*	1791	*Report on Manufactures*; French Legislative Assembly, 1791–92; Thomas Paine's *The Rights of Man*
Leader of Republican opposition in Congress	1792	Hamilton and Jefferson feud in Philadelphia press; reelection of Washington
"Helvidius" essays; Citizen Genêt affair	1793	Execution of Louis XVI; France declares war on Britain; Proclamation of Neutrality

Seeks commercial restrictions against Britain; marries Dolley Payne Todd	1794	Jay mission to London; Whisky Rebellion
Opposes Jay's Treaty in House	1796	Washington's Farewell Address
Declines mission to France; voluntary retirement to Montpelier	1797	John Adams begins term as President; XYZ Affair
Virginia and Kentucky Resolutions; Address to the People	1798	Undeclared war with France; Alien and Sedition Acts
Elected to state legislature	1799	Adams sends new mission to Paris
Virginia Report on the Alien and Sedition Acts	1800	Federal capital moved to Washington; Spain cedes Louisiana to France
Secretary of State, 1801–9	1801	Electoral tie ends with selection of Jefferson as President; Tripolitan War, 1801–5
	1802	Peace of Amiens; Spain closes Mississippi
Louisiana Purchase	1803	Renewal of Napoleonic wars
	1804	William Pitt returns to power; Napoleon Bonaparte, Emperor of France, 1804–14
Investigates illegality of *Essex* decision	1805	Formation of the Third Coalition against France; Jefferson begins second term
Monroe-Pinkney Treaty	1806	Berlin Decree; Napoleon's Continental System
Chesapeake-Leopard affair; Embargo Act	1807	British orders in council
Inauguration as President with George Clinton as Vice President; Erskine agreement; nonintercourse with Britain	1809	Nonintercourse Act; repeal of embargo
Macon's Bill No. 2; resumption of French trade; annexation of West Florida	1810	Rambouillet Decree authorizes French seizure of American ships
Names Monroe Secretary of State	1811	Battle of Tippecanoe; Bank of the United States ends; War Hawks in Congress
War message to Congress	1812	Attempted invasion of Canada; capitulation of Detroit
Second inaugural with Elbridge Gerry as Vice President	1813	Britain blockades coast; Battles of Lake Erie and the Thames; Detroit retaken
Accepts British negotiations; Cabinet reorganization; end of embargo measures; flees Washington before British attack	1814	Napoleon abdicates; Congress of Vienna; Battle of Lake Champlain; Hartford Convention; Treaty of Ghent
Vetoes national bank; State of the Union message	1815	Battle of Waterloo; Battle of New Orleans; Congress ratifies peace treaty
	1816	Second Bank of the United States; peacetime tariff
Bonus bill veto; retires to Montpelier; president of Albemarle Agricultural Society; founder of American Colonization Society	1817	Presidency of James Monroe, 1817–25; Rush-Bagot Convention
	1820	Missouri Compromise
Refuses to publish Federal Convention notes	1821	
Lafayette visits Montpelier	1824	
Last visit with Jefferson	1825	University of Virginia opens; Presidency of John Quincy Adams, 1825–29
Succeeds Jefferson as rector of University of Virginia	1826	
Virginia constitutional convention	1829	Presidency of Andrew Jackson, 1829–37
Rebuts Hayne in *North American Review*	1830	Webster-Hayne debate; nullification controversy, 1830–33
	1831	Nat Turner insurrection
Resignation as rector; "Advice to My Country"	1834	
James Madison dies at Montpelier, June 28	1836	Establishment of Republic of Texas

For his unique contribution in drafting it, Madison was known as the Father of the Constitution.

Chapter 1

A Revolutionary Vocation

During the summer of 1769, James Madison, then a young gentleman of eighteen, left his home in the Virginia Piedmont to pursue his education at the College of New Jersey in Princeton. He traveled on horseback with two companions and a Negro servant, probably by the lowland route easterly from his native Orange County through Fredericksburg, Annapolis, and New Castle to the colonial metropolis of Philadelphia, thence across the Delaware to the sleepy village that was the seat of the college. The three-hundred-mile journey took perhaps a dozen days, and the Virginia uplander, who knew nothing of the bustle of towns and trade, must have marveled at the sights and sounds en route. All along the coast that summer, merchants were joining a nonimportation movement against Britain in retaliation for the hated Townshend Acts, which sought to raise revenue in America by imposing duties on certain goods imported by the Colonies. "No taxation without representation" was the cry, and in the provincial capitals through which the young Virginian passed—Annapolis, New Castle, Philadelphia—the agitation was especially warm. The education Madison was seeking lay at the end of the road in Princeton, but in the course of reaching it he was introduced to the spectacle of the American Revolution that would henceforth control his destiny.

The life of James Madison, more than the lives of his illustrious compatriots, was inseparable from the history of the revolutionary nation founded in 1776. There is virtually no accounting for him or of him apart from the great events of his time. Any chapter in the early life of the Republic is more important to his story than any chapter of merely personal history. And at the end, until his death in 1836, he stood as the lonely last sentinel of the Founding Fathers. Near the end, turning aside beseechers of autobiography, Madison said: "It has been remarked that the biography of an author must be a history of his writings. So must that of one whose whole life has in a manner been a public life, be gathered from

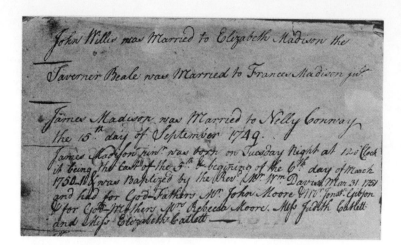

Part of a page from the Madison family Bible recording the birth of James Madison, Jr., on March 5, 1750 (March 16, 1751, New Style)

his official transactions, and his manuscript papers on public subjects...." There was for him no life apart from his public career. He did, it is true, finally dictate a hurried sketch of that career, "the merest skeleton" as he observed; and predictably, this so-called "autobiography" draws a veil over the person of James Madison. He devoted only two hundred words to his life before the eighteenth year. (Until then the record of his papers is a blank.) In retrospect, life began when he went to college, opened his mind to the world of learning, and then, by measured steps, entered into the actions and passions of his time.

He was born March 16, 1751, at his maternal grandparents' home in King George County, but was at once taken inland to the Madison home, Montpelier as he would later name it, in the deep-wooded, rolling hill country of Orange. His great-grandfather, James Taylor II, had explored this wilderness and beyond to the Blue Ridge in 1716 as a member of Governor Spotswood's land-surveying expedition, the "Knights of the Golden Horseshoe." Some years later he patented 13,500 acres on the Rapidan River in what would become Orange County. A substantial portion of this land descended to his eldest daughter, Frances Taylor, the wife of Ambrose Madison. The Madisons traced their Virginia ancestry back two generations to John Maddison, a ship's carpenter who came from England about the middle of the seventeenth century. They, like the Taylors, had prospered and, like many of the Tidewater gentry in the early part of the eighteenth century, cast their gaze and their fortunes westward to the virgin red lands of the Virginia Piedmont. Not long after the death of James Taylor II in 1729, Ambrose Madison settled his family in Orange. His eldest son, James Madison, was then only a child, but he grew up with the country, became one of its first citizens, and managed an estate of some four thousand acres. In 1749 he married Nelly Conway, the seventeen-year-old daughter of a planter in the low country. James Madison, Jr., was the first of twelve children born to them; only seven survived infancy.

Looking back two centuries from the lovely hills of Orange today, one imagines an idyllic rural boyhood for young Madison. He never lacked companionship. Not only were there brothers and sisters to play with and look after, but the country rapidly filled with families as large and often as comfortable as his own, and the network of cousinship extended well beyond the boundaries of Orange. Doubtless, with other Virginia boys, he liked to ride and to shoot, though in these favored pastimes he was neither physically nor temperamentally to the manner born. He was baptized and raised in the Anglican faith, the established religion of the colony. The nearest church, Brick Church, of which his father was a vestryman, lay six miles east of Orange Court House. These two places, church and court, were prominent landmarks in the youth's meagerly provisioned world.

Orange was no longer on the frontier, and Indians were about as rare as buffalo; yet the unusual interest that the upland planters felt in the land beyond the mountains was enough to raise apprehensions during the French and Indian War. Neighbors went off to fight and rumors of Indian attack spilled over the Blue Ridge. The West thus early became a fixture of Madison's consciousness. The war ended gloriously in British conquest to the Mississippi; nearer home and recurrent were the plagues of drought and disease, especially smallpox which reached epidemic proportions when Madison was about ten. His family must have suffered, along with most Virginia planters, from the frequently short crops and the depression of tobacco prices in the 1760s. This reversal of fortunes put a heavy strain on the province's relationship with the mother country. Yet with all these

Page of an autobiographical sketch written by Madison in later life, describing his schoolmaster Donald Robertson as having a "warm temper"

difficulties over several years, Madison's father built a spacious new mansion at Montpelier. The rectangular brick dwelling, simple but graceful in design, beautifully situated and offering the vista of the Blue Ridge, would become Madison's home for the rest of his life.

At about this time, in 1762, the lad was sent to a celebrated school kept by Donald Robertson in King and Queen County some seventy miles from home. Robertson had been educated in Scotland. His most famous pupil remembered him fondly as "a man of extensive learning, and a distinguished Teacher." To the small stock of rudimentary education acquired at Montpelier, Madison now added Latin and Greek, French, algebra and geometry, geography, and "miscellaneous literature." In 1767, after five years at the Robertson school, he returned home for further study under the tutelage of the Reverend Thomas Martin, newly appointed rector of Brick Church, who lived with the family and taught Madison's younger brothers and sisters as well. A recent graduate of the College of New Jersey, Martin seems to have steered Madison in that direction. Most college-bound Virginians went to William and Mary in the capital at Williamsburg. But the Madisons, father and son, feared the miasmal climate of the Tidewater, and they had doubtless heard stories about the rowdyism of students and the debauchery of Anglican professors at William and Mary. In contrast to the sinking reputation of William and Mary, they received glowing

LIBRARY OF CONGRESS

accounts from Martin, himself an exemplary model of piety and learning, of the young College of New Jersey.

Founded in 1746 under Scottish Presbyterian auspices, the college had just come under the dynamic leadership of Dr. John Witherspoon, the learned divine who had risen to eminence in the Church of Scotland before accepting the call from the academic citadel of Presbyterianism in the New World. Without in any way diverting the institution from its religious mission, Witherspoon gave to the college an equally vital civil character. As the American Revolution came on, Princeton was imbued with the patriot cause in which many of its graduates, together with its president, would distinguish themselves. Under Witherspoon, aided by such earnest alumni as Thomas Martin, the reputation of the college spread far beyond the reaches of the Delaware. Still, in 1769 Madison was among the first southern youths to attend Princeton—part of the vanguard of a virtual army to come —and being both Virginian and Anglican he must have felt somewhat out of place. It was a venturesome step, and it paid off not simply in the standard currency of education but in the education of a man whose personal identifications were neither Virginian nor Anglican, but American.

One massive building, Nassau Hall, its long, cold gray walls crowned by a sky-piercing tower, contained the entire college. Here, spread over four floors, were student rooms, classrooms, dining hall, library, and chapel

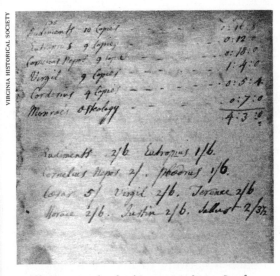

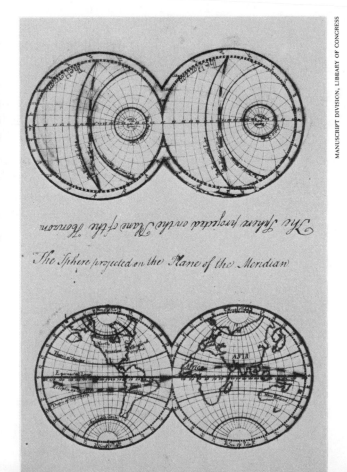

The sphere projected on the Plane of the Meridian

The account book of James Madison, Sr., for December 11, 1755 (left) listed expenses "To building a house...," probably referring to his mansion (far left, as sketched at a later date). In Donald Robertson's school young "Jamie" began his study of Latin and bought a number of the books listed above in Robertson's ledger. He also made the astronomical drawings seen at right.

—all the essentials for the care and instruction of some one hundred young men. Classes were in session when Madison arrived in midsummer. Discovering that he was a year or two older and also better prepared than most entering students, he commenced his studies at once in hopes of catching up with the freshman class, though final examinations were only a few weeks away. "The near approach of examination occasions a surprising application to study on all sides, and I think it very fortunate that I entered College immediately after my arrival," Madison wrote to Martin in August—the earliest letter from his pen that has survived. He passed the freshman examinations in English, Latin and Greek, mathematics, and the New Testament and was to finish the ordinary college course in two years. Following the commencement in September, the youth wrote to his father.

Nassau-Hall, September 30th. 69.

Hond. Sir,

I received your letter by Mr. Rosekrans, and wrote an Answer; but as it is probable this will arrive sooner which I now write by Doctor Witherspoon, I shall repeat some circumstances to avoid obscurity.

On Wednesday last we had the annual commencement. Eighteen young gentlemen took their Batchelors' degrees, and a considerable number their Masters Degrees; the Degree of Doctor of Law was bestowed on Mr. Dickenson the Farmer [author of *Letters From a Farmer in Pennsylvania*] and Mr. Galloway, the Speaker of the Pennsylvania Assembly, a distinguishing mark of Honour, as there never was any of that kind done before in America. The Commencement began at 10 O'Clock, when the President walked first into the Church, a board of Trustees following, and behind them those that were to take their Master's degrees, and last of all, those that were to take their first Degrees; After a short Prayer by the President, the Head Oration, which is always given to the greatest Scholar by the President & Tutors, was pronounced in Latin by Mr. Samuel [Stanhope] Smith son of a Presbyterean Minister in Pennsylvania. Then followed the other Orations, Disputes and Dialogues, distributed to each according to his merit, and last of all was pronounced the Valedictory Oration by Mr. John Henry son of a Gentleman in Maryland. This is given to the greatest *Orator*. We had a very great Assembly of People, a considerable number of whom came from N. York. Those at Philidelphia were most of them detained by Racis [horse races] which were to follow on the next day.

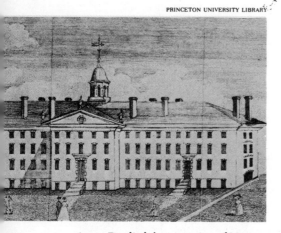

Amos Doolittle's engraving of Nassau Hall at Princeton, New Jersey

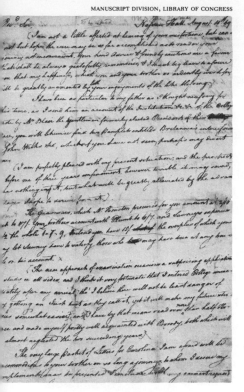

*Earliest surviving letter from
Madison's pen was to Thomas Martin.*

David Rittenhouse's orrery

Since Commencement the Trustees have been sitting about Business relative to the College, and have chose for Tutors the ensuing year, for the junior class Mr. Houston from N. Carolina in the room of Mr. Periam, for the Freshman class Mr. Reeves (a gentleman who has for several years kept a School at Elizabeth Town) in the room of Mr. Pemberton: the Sophomore Tutor Mr. Thomsom still retains his place, remarkable for his skill in the sophomore Studies having taken care of that class for several years past. Mr. Halsey was chosen Junior Tutor but refused. The Trustees have likewise appointed Mr. Caldwel, a Minister at Elizabeth Town, to take a journey through the Southern Provinces as far as Georgia to make collections by which the College Fund may be inabled to increase the Library, provide an apparatus of mathematical and Philosophical Instruments & likewise to support Professors which would be a great addition to the advantages of this College. Doctr. Witherspoon's business to Virginia is nearly the same as I conjecture and perhaps to form some acquaintance to induce Gentlemen to send their sons to this College.

I am very sorry to hear of the great drought that has prevailed with you, but am in some hopes the latter part of the year may have been more seasonable for you[r] crops. Your caution of frugality on consideration of the dry weather shall be carefully observed; but I am under a necesity of spending much more than I was apprehensive, for the purchasing of every small trifle which I have occasion for consumes a much greater sum than one wou[ld] suppose from a calculation of the necessary expences....

I recollect nothing more at present worth relating, but as often as opportunity and any thing worthy your attention shall occur, be assured you shall hear from your

Affectionate Son

JAMES MADISON

The letter is full of information, some of it faintly familiar. The poor collegian, then as now, pleads with his father for money. The poor college president, then as now, goes off on a fund-raising tour. (Witherspoon's southern tour was remarkably successful; part of the proceeds purchased David Rittenhouse's ingenious orrery, from which Madison learned the Newtonian wonders of the solar system.) Honorary degrees are conferred on the great men of the day, in this case on the Whig patriots John Dickinson and Joseph Galloway, the first honorary doctorates of laws conferred in America. (John Hancock, the Massachusetts hero, received an honorary A.M., though Madison does not mention him.) And the scholar of the class discourses in Latin. Samuel Stanhope Smith, whom Madison would come to know as a tutor and friend, later founded Hampden-Sydney College in Virginia, distinguished himself in natural history, and eventually became president of Princeton.

Madison was a diligent scholar. Witherspoon later remarked that he never knew him to do anything wrong. In the Presbyterian confines of Nassau Hall, shielded from the vices and follies of the world, young men found little opportunity to do wrong. Discipline, if not severe, was rigorous. Beginning with the five o'clock bell, followed by chapel at six, the daily schedule was carefully prescribed. The curriculum was classical and also Christian, as was customary, but Princeton had gone further than most academies in introducing newer liberal studies, such as natural science, modern philosophy, and modern literature, including French. If Princeton aimed to discipline the mind and strengthen character, it also aimed to cultivate reason and critical inquiry. "In the instruction of youth," said one account of the college, "care is taken to cherish a spirit of liberty, and free enquiry; and not only to permit, but even to encourage their right of private judgment, without presuming to dictate with an air of infallibility...." Learning this, Madison learned the best that Princeton had to teach. The ascendant intellectual spirit was that of the Scottish Enlightenment. In the culminating course of the senior year, moral philosophy, as taught by President Witherspoon himself, Madison read the Scottish luminaries— Francis Hutcheson, Adam Ferguson, Lord Kames, and others—who affirmed the natural reasonableness and benevolence of mankind. The persistent Scottish strain in Madison's education, curiously mixing Calvinistic Presbyterianism with Enlightenment liberalism, shaped a mental outlook in which the recognition of man's potentiality for virtuous freedom never lost sight of his potentiality for evil.

Madison's education as a political thinker came later, though he formed an early acquaintance with the tradition of political theory from Plato and Aristotle to the moderns, especially Locke and the English Whigs of the late-seventeenth and eighteenth centuries. Equally significant in this respect were the lively extracurricular debates on public issues. Studious, painfully shy, and averse to the platform, Madison nevertheless entered into the round of collegiate activities, both the frivolous and the serious. As a member of the Whig Society, a literary fellowship, he penned many sheets of harsh sophomoric doggerel for the "paper war" on the rival Cliosophic Society. Judging by the theses Princeton graduates expounded at commencement exercises, the libertarian issues in the Anglo-American controversy stirred the minds of the students. Resistance to tyranny, religious toleration, promotion of American manufactures, and nonimportation were among the theses defended in 1770. The despised Townshend Acts were repealed in the spring, but apparently the young Princetonians favored continued agitation. Writing to his father in July, mainly of trivial matters but also of his journey home during the coming fall vacation, Madison expressed his political feelings.

One of Madison's poems for Whig Society was "Clio's Proclamation."

Nassau Hall. July 23d. 1770

Inclosed are the measures of my Neck & rists. I believe my Mother need not hurry herself much about my shirts before I come for I shall not want more than three or four at most. I should chuse she would not have them ruffled 'till I am present myself. I have not yet procured a horse for my Journey, but think you had better not send me one as I cant wait long enough to know whether or not you'll have an opportunity without losing my chance, most of the horses being commonly engaged by the Students sometime before vacation begins. If I should set off from this place as soon as I expect you may look for me in October perhaps a little before the middle if the weather should be good. We have no publick news but the base conduct of the Merchants in N. York in breaking through their spirited resolutions not to import, a distinct account of which I suppose will be in the Virginia Gazete before this arrives. their Letter to the Merchants in Philadelphia requesting their concurrence was lately burnt by the Students of this place in the college Yard, all of them appearing in their black Gowns & the bell Tolling. The number of Students has increased very much of late; there are about an hundred & fifteen in College & the Grammar School, twenty two commence this Fall, all of them in American Cloth.

At the time of Madison's graduation a year later, in September, 1771, nonimportation had collapsed everywhere and the political waters were calm again. He refrained from any public part in the commencement exercises. The audience heard a rousing patriotic poem, "The Rising Glory of America," by two of his classmates, Philip Freneau and Hugh Henry Brackenridge.

And here fair freedom shall forever reign.
I see a train, a glorious train appear,
Of Patriots plac'd in equal fame with those
Who nobly fell for Athens or for Rome.
The sons of Boston, resolute and brave,

21

> The firm supporters of our injur'd rights,
> Shall lose their splendours in the brighter beams
> Of patriots fam'd and heroes yet unborn.

The long poem was a hymn to the New World, a testament to the "spirit of liberty" abroad at Princeton, and a leitmotiv to the young men who would make their careers as poets, ministers, soldiers, and statesmen of the new nation. Brackenridge would become one of the first American novelists; Freneau the first patriot poet as well as a partisan journalist closely associated with Madison. Several of his classmates later served valiantly in the Revolutionary War, and one of them, Gunning Bedford, Jr., of Delaware, would reappear in the Federal Convention of 1787. The paths of other college friends, though not of the Class of '71 — Henry Lee ("Light-horse Harry" of Revolutionary War fame) and Aaron Burr — would cross and re-cross Madison's own.

Not knowing what to do when he graduated and reluctant to exchange the exuberant intellectual life of Nassau Hall for the doldrums of Virginia, Madison stayed on at Princeton for six months to study Hebrew and theology under Dr. Witherspoon's direction. In poor health at this time, he grew worse after returning home in April, 1772. Madison and his friends traced the illness to the "doubled labour" of taking the bachelor's degree in two years. Whatever may have been the cause of the disease, he suffered from a severe nervous disorder that threw a pall over his future. In this distressed state of mind, he continued his course of study mainly along theological lines; then, as the melancholy cloud of eternity lifted, he shifted to the study of law without, however, any determination to become a lawyer. Indeed Madison's illness only complicated further the youthful ordeal of finding a proper vocation in life. The choices were few in eighteenth-century Virginia. In view of his education under Witherspoon's guiding hand, he must have considered the ministry for a time. Its charms soon passed, however. The law appealed to his reason, but he found the reading "coarse and dry" and dropped any thought of a career at the bar.

During this personal "time of troubles" Madison entered into correspondence with his former college friend William Bradford of Philadelphia. Bradford, whose father published the widely read *Pennsylvania Journal*, initiated this remarkable exchange of letters in October, 1772, on a soul-sick note that was more than reciprocated by Madison's despondency. "The value of a college-life like most other blessing[s] is seldom known but by its loss," the Pennsylvanian began. After Nassau Hall, he expected no happiness, only "trouble & anxiety," and he knew not what business to pursue in life. Madison replied in kind.

Orange Virginia Novr. 9th. 1772

My dear Billey,

  You moralize so prettily that if I were to judge from some parts of your letter of October 13 I should take you

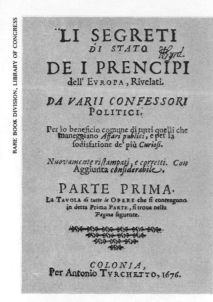

Few books from Madison's extensive library are known to have survived; this 1676 volume is among them.

William Bradford by St. Mémin

for an old Philosopher that had experienced the emptiness of Earthly Happiness. And I am very glad that you have so early seen through the romantic paintings with which the World is sometimes set off by the sprightly imaginations of the Ingenious. You have happily supplied by reading and observation the want of experiment and therefore I hope you are sufficiently guarded against the allurements and vanities that beset us on our first entrance on the Theatre of Life. Yet however nice and cautious we may be in detecting the follies of mankind and framing our Oeconomy according to the precepts of Wisdom and Religion I fancy there will commonly remain with us some latent expectation of obtaining more than ordinary Happiness and prosperity till we feel the convincing argument of actual disappointment. Tho I will not determine whether we shall be much the worse for it if we do not allow it to intercept our views towards a future State, because strong desires and great Hopes instigate us to arduous enterprizes fortitude and perseverance. Nevertheless a watchful eye must be kept on ourselves lest while we are building ideal monuments of Renown and Bliss here we neglect to have our names enrolled in the Annals of Heaven. These thoughts come into my mind because I am writing to you and thinking of you. As to myself I am too dull and infirm now to look out for any extraordinary things in this world for I think my sensations for many months past have intimated to me not to expect a long or healthy life, yet it may be better with me after some time tho I hardly dare expect it and therefore have little spirit and alacrity to set about any thing that is difficult in acquiring and useless in possessing after one has exchanged Time for Eternity. But you have Health Youth Fire and Genius to bear you along through the high tract of public Life and so may be more interested and delighted in improving on hints that respect the temporal though momentous concerns of man. . . .

As you seem to require that I should be open and unreserved (which is indeed the only proof of true friendship) I will venture to give you a word of advice though it be more to convince you of my affection for you than from any apprehension of your needing it. Pray do not suffer those impertinent fops that abound in every City to divert you from your business and philosophical amuse-

*Madison's opening correspondence
with his friend William Bradford*

ments. You may please them more by admitting them to the enjoyment of your company but you will make them respect and admire you more by shewing your indignation at their follies and by keeping them at a becoming distance. I am luckily out of the way of such troubles, but I know you are cirrounded with them for they breed in Towns and populous places, as naturally as flies do in the Shambles, because there they get food enough for their Vanity and impertinence.

I have undertaken to instruct my brothers and Sisters in some of the first rudiments of literature, but it does not take up so much of my time but I shall always have leisure to receive and answer your letters which are very grateful to me I assure you, and for reading any performances you may be kind enough to send me whether of Mr. Freneau or any body else. I think myself happy in your correspondence and desire you will continue to write as often as you can as you see I intend to do by the early and long answer I send you. You are the only valuable friend I have settled in so public a place and must rely on you for an account of all literary transactions in your part of the world. . . .

And now my friend I must take my leave of you, but with such hopes that it will not be long before I receive another epistle from you as make me more cheerfully conclude and Subscribe myself Yr. Sincere and Affecte. friend

JAMES MADISON JUNR.

Your Direction [address] was right however the addition of Junr. to my name would not be improper.

Another letter to Bradford, written nearly a year later, reveals Madison's growing inclination toward the study of law.

[Orange, Virginia,] Septr. 25th 1773
Since you first hinted to me your suspense as to the settled business of your life, I have partook of your anxiety & [though it] has been often in my thoughts I feel a backwardness to offer my opinion in so critical a matter and the more so for the weight you are pleased to give it. I have too much esteem and affection for you and am too conscious of my want of capacity and experience to direct in so important an Affair. I must therefore premise that it is my earnest request that you would act the

candid open friend as well as in rejecting as in asking advice; for I consult nothing but your real interest, and am sensible of my insufficiency to be a counsellor much more a preceptor. You forbid any recommendation of Divinity by suggesting that you have insuperable objections therefore I can only condole with the Church on the loss of a fine Genius and persuasive Orator. I cannot however suppress thus much of my advice on that head that you would always keep the Ministry obliquely in View whatever your profession be. This will lead you to cultivate an acquaintance occasionally with the most sublime of all Sciences and will qualify you for a change of public character if you should hereafter desire it. I have sometimes thought there could not be a stronger testimony in favor of Religion or against temporal Enjoyments even the most rational and manly than for men who occupy the most honorable and gainful departments and are rising in reputation and wealth, publicly to declare their unsatisfatoriness by becoming fervent Advocates in the cause of Christ, & I wish you may give in your Evidence in this way. Such Instances have seldom occurred, therefore they would be more striking and would be instead of a "Cloud of Witnesses.["] If I am to speak my Sentiments of Merchandize, Physic and Law I must say they are all honorable and usefull professions and think you ought to have more regard to their Suitableness to your Genius than to their comparative Excellence. As far as I know your endowments I should pronounce Law the most eligeble. It alone can bring into use many parts of knowledge you have acquired and will still have a taste for, & pay you for cultivating the Arts of Eloquence. It is a sort of General Lover that wooes all the Muses and Graces. This cannot be said so truly of commerce and Physic & therefore less Learning & smaller understanding will do for them. The objection founded on the number of Lawyers should stimulate to Assiduity rather than discourage the Attempt. I greatly commend your determined adherence to probity and Truth in the Character of a Lawyer but fear it would be impracticable. Misrepresentation from a client or intricacy in a cause must often occasion doubt and ignorance till the matter has been considerably debated at the bar; Though it must be allowed there are a thousand cases in which your rule would be safe and highly commend-

The London Coffee House, where Madison had stopped en route to Princeton, and the bookstore next door were both operated by the family of William Bradford.

able. I must add after all that if you should enter on a mercantile State (to which peculiar reasons for ought I know may advise) I should be loth to disapprove.

Madison closed this letter with mention of the hardships caused by "a very great scarcity of circulating cash" in Virginia, then abruptly broke off, "I do not meddle with Politicks." In truth he had not and would not for several months yet. However, the course of legal study soon led him into the great questions of freedom and self-government thrown up by the onrushing tide of the American Revolution; and as his mind took hold of these questions and as his health slowly mended as well, Madison's spirits revived and the youthful melancholy disappeared to be replaced by vigorous and life-fulfilling purpose.

Madison's political feelings were most aroused, oddly enough, not by the imperial issues of trade and taxation, but by the repressions and abuses of the Anglican Church in Virginia. Schooled at Princeton in the dissenting tradition and straitlaced Presbyterian morality, he was shocked by the corruptions of the Anglican clergy and the persecuting intolerance of the established church toward nonconforming sectarians in his own neighborhood. Although by 1774 he could denounce the Tea Act and cheer the Boston mob, it was the union of Church and State that set him on fire. The cause of religious freedom became Madison's passport to revolution, as is evident in his letters to Bradford.

[Orange, Virginia,] Dec. 1. 1773.
I am glad you have rescued yourself from your anxiety and suspence and have come to a determination to engage in the study of the Law, which I hope you had better reasons for chusing than I could suggest. I intend myself to read Law occasionally and have procured books for that purpose so that you need not fear offending me by Allusions to that Science. Indeed any of your remarks as you go along would afford me entertainment and instruction. The principles & Modes of Government are too important to be disregarded by an Inquisitive mind and I think are well worthy [of] a critical examination by all students that have health & Leisure. I should be well pleased with a scetch of the plan you have fixed upon for your studies, the books & the order you intend to read them in; and when you have obtained sufficient insight into the Constitution of your Country and can make it an amusement to yourself send me a draught of its Origin & fundamental principals of Legislation; particularly the extent of your religious Toleration. Here

As a young man, Madison was often referred to as pale and sickly.

allow me to propose the following Queries. Is an Ecclesiastical Establishment absolutely necessary to support civil society in a supream Government? & how far it is hurtful to a dependant State? I do not ask for an immediate answer but mention them as worth attending to in the course of your reading and consulting experienced Lawyers & Politicians upon. When you have satisfied yourself in these points I should listen with pleasure to the Result of your reserches.

You recommend sending for the Reviews as the best way to know the present State of Literature and the Choicest Books published. This I have done and shall continue to do: but I find them loose in their principals [and] encourage[r]s of free enquiry even such as destroys the most essential Truths, Enemies to serious religion & extreamly partial in their Citations, seeking them rather to Justify their censures and Commendations than to give the reader a just specimen of the Authors genius. I can rely with greater confidence on you[r] judgment after you have read the Authors or have known their Character from you[r] judicious friends. I am meditating a Journey to Philada which I hope to accomplish early in the spring if no unforeseen hindrances stop me. I shall bring a brother with me to put to school somewhere there, perhaps at Mr. Smith's. I need not say how far the desire of seeing you and others is a powerful Inducement and that my imagination daily anticipates the pleasure of this Tour. Who were the authors of the Sermons you sent me? What is the exchange with you now & what is it likely to be in the spring? Write speedily & forgive my troublesome questions.

Writing to Bradford in January and April, Madison relayed developments in Virginia and commented on events in Philadelphia: citizens there had forced a ship laden with East India Company tea to return to sea, threatening otherwise to tar and feather the captain.

[Orange, Virginia,] Jan 24. 1774

I congratulate you on your heroic proceedings in Philada. with regard to the Tea. I wish Boston may conduct matters with as much discretion as they seem to do with boldness: They seem to have great Tryals and difficulties by reason of the obduracy...of their Governour. However Political Contests are necessary sometimes as well as military to afford exercise and practise and to instruct in the Art of defending Liberty and property. I verily believe the frequent Assaults that have been made on America Boston especially will in the end prove of real advantage. If the Church of England had been the established and general Religion in all the Northern Colonies as it has been among us here and uninterrupted tranquility had prevailed throughout the Continent, It is clear to me that slavery and Subjection might and would have been gradually insinuated among us. Union of Religious Sentiments begets a surprizing confidence and Ecclesiastical Establishments tend to great ignorance and Corruption all of which facilitate the Execution of mischievous Projects. But away with Politicks! Let me address you as a Student and Philosopher & not as a Patriot now. I am pleased that you are going to converse with the Edwards and Henry's & Charles &c&c who have swayed the British Sceptre though I believe you will find some of them dirty and unprofitable Companions unless you will glean Instruction from their follies and fall more in love with Liberty by beholding such detestable pictures of Tyranny and Cruelty. I was afraid you would not easily have loosened your Affections from the Belles Lettres. A Delicate Taste and warm imagination like yours must find it hard to give up such refined & exquisite enjoyments for the coarse and dry study of the Law: It is like leaving a pleasant flourishing field for a barren desert; perhaps I should not say barren either because the Law does bear fruit but it is sour fruit that must be gathered and pressed and distilled before it can bring pleasure or profit. I perceive I have made a very awkward Comparison but I got the thought by the end and had gone to far to quit it before I perceived that it was too much entangled in my brain to run it through. And so you must forgive it. I myself use to have too great a hankering after those amusing Studies. Poetry wit and Criticism Romances Plays &c captivated me much: but I begin [to] discover that they deserve but a moderate portion of a *mortal's* Time. and that something more substantial more durable more profitable befits a riper Age. It would be exceeding improper for a labouring man to have nothing but flowers in his Garden or to determine to eat nothing but sweet-meats and Confections. Equally absurd would it be for a Scholar and man

As Madison's correspondence with Bradford continued, he wrote in January, 1774, that it was "too far advanced to req[uire a]pologies for bad writing & [b]lots."

of Business to make up his whole Library with Books of Fancy and feed his Mind with nothing but such Luscious performances.

When you have an Opportunity and write to Mr. Brackinridge pray tell him I often think of him and long to see him and am resolved to do so in the Spring. George Luckey was with me at Christmas and we talked so much about old Affairs & Old Friends that I have a most insatiable desire to see you all. Luckey will accompany me and we are to set off on the 10th. of April if no disaster befalls either of us. I want again to breathe your free Air. I expect it will mend my Constitution & confirm my principles. I have indeed as good an Atmosphere at home as the Climate will allow: but have nothing to brag of as to the State and Liberty of my Country. Poverty and Luxury prevail among all sorts: Pride ignorance and Knavery among the Priesthood and Vice and Wickedness among the Laity. This is bad enough But It is not the worst I have to tell you. That diabolical Hell conceived principle of persecution rages among some and to their eternal Infamy the Clergy can furnish their Quota of Imps for such business. This vexes me the most of any thing whatever. There are at this [time?] in the adjacent County not less than 5 or 6 well meaning men in close Goal [gaol] for publishing their religious Sentiments which in the main are very orthodox. I have neither patience to hear talk or think of any thing relative to this matter, for I have squabbled and scolded abused and ridiculed so long about it, [to so lit]tle purpose that I am without common patience. So I [leave you] to pity me and pray for Liberty of Conscience [to revive among us.]

I expect to hear from you once more before I see you if time will admit: and want to know when the Synod meets & where: What the Exchange is at and as much about my friends and other Matters as you can and think worth notice. Till I see you Adieu.

JM

NB Our Correspondence is too far advanced to req[uire a]pologies for bad writing & [b]lots.

April 1st. 1774. Virginia Orange Cy. Our Assembly is to meet the first of May When It is expected something will be done in behalf of the Dissenters: Petitions I hear are already forming among the

The closing of the port of Boston was pictured in a British cartoon showing the caged Bostonians being fed codfish by their sympathizers.

Persecuted Baptists and I fancy it is in the thoughts of the Presbyterians also to intercede for greater liberty in matters of Religion. For my part I can not help being very doubtful of their succeeding in the Attempt. The Affair was on the Carpet during the last Session; but such incredible and extravagant stories were told in the House [of Burgesses, the lower house of the assembly] of the monstrous effect of the Enthusiasm prevalent among the Sectaries and so greedily swallowed by their Enemies that I believe they lost footing by it and the bad name they still have with those who pretend too much contempt to examine into their principles and Conduct and are too much devoted to the ecclesiastical establishment to hear of the Toleration of Dissentients, I am apprehensive, will be again made a pretext for rejecting their requests. The Sentiments of our people of Fortune & fashion on this subject are vastly different from what you have been used to. That liberal catholic and equitable way of thinking as to the rights of Conscience, which is one of the Characteristics of a free people and so strongly marks the People of your province is but little known among the Zealous adherents to our Hierarchy. We have it is true some persons in the Legislature of generous Principles both in Religion & Politicks but number not merit you know is necessary to carry points there. Besides the Clergy are a numerous and powerful body have great influence at home by reason of their connection with & dependence on the Bishops and Crown and will naturally employ all their art & Interest to depress their rising Adversaries; for such they must consider dissenters who rob them of the good will of the people and may in time endanger their livings & security.

You are happy in dwelling in a Land where those inestimable privileges are fully enjoyed and public has long felt the good effects of their religious as well as Civil Liberty. Foreigners have been encouraged to settle amg. you. Industry and Virtue have been promoted by mutual emulation and mutual Inspection, Commerce and the Arts have flourished and I can not help attributing those continual exertions of Gen[i]us which appear among you to the inspiration of Liberty and that love of Fame and Knowledge which always accompany it. Religious bondage shackles and debilitates the mind and unfits it for every noble enterprize every expanded prospect. How far this is the Case with Virginia will more clearly appear when the ensuing Trial is made.

I am making all haste in preparing for my Journey.

The journey took Madison to Philadelphia, where he was visiting with college friends when news arrived of the act closing the port of Boston. The first of Parliament's Coercive Acts in retaliation upon Massachusetts for the Boston Tea Party of December 16, 1773, the act inflamed the continent and led to demands from one colonial capital to another for a continental congress and for the revival of economic coercion against the mother country. Madison returned from the ferment in Philadelphia full of eagerness for the movement that had suddenly acquired a national dimension. In Virginia the House of Burgesses, having been dissolved by Governor Dunmore, had gone into business for itself and, among other forward actions, called for the election of delegates to a revolutionary convention to meet in Williamsburg in August. Madison was now obsessed by politics. He devoured the pamphlets Bradford sent him from Philadelphia and rejected counsels of caution such as he detected in the proceedings of the Pennsylvania assembly. A few months earlier he could exclaim, with charming insouciance, "But away with Politicks!" and break into discourse on the pleasures of belles lettres. No longer. His only regret now was that he had not put off his northern journey until September, when the leading patriots of all the colonies were to assemble in Philadelphia. Excerpts from additional letters to Bradford chart his course.

Another British cartoon showed Virginia Loyalists being forced to sign resolutions drawn up by the 1774 convention in Williamsburg.

[Orange, Virginia,] July 1. 1774.

I am once more got into my native land and into the possession of my customary enjoyments Solitude and Contemplation, though I must confess not a little disturbed by the sound of War blood and plunder on the one Hand and the Threats of Slavery and Oppression on the Other. From the best accounts I can obtain from our Frontiers The Savages are determined in the extirpation of the Inhabitants, and no longer leave them the alternative of Death or Captivity....

As to the Sentiments of the people of this Colony with respect to the Bostonians I can assure [you] I find them generally very warm in their favour. The Natives are very unanimous and resolute, are making resolves in almost every County and I believe are willing to fall in with the Other Colonies in any expedient measure, even if that should be the universal prohibition of Trade. It must not be denied though that the Europeans especially the Scotch and some interested Merchants among the

Madison wrote to Bradford that the naming of Joseph Galloway to the Pennsylvania assembly "seems to forebode difficulties."

Carpenters' Hall in Philadelphia

natives discountenance such proceedings as far as they dare alledging the Injustice and perfidy of refusing to pay our debts to our Generous Creditors at Home. This Consideration induces some honest moderate folks to prefer a partial prohibition extending only to the *Importation* of Goods.

[Orange,] Virginia August 23. 1774

I have seen the instructions of your committee to your representatives & greatly admire the wisdom of the advice & the elegance and cogency of the diction. In the latter especially they are vastly superior to what has been done by our convention. But do you not presume too much on the generosity & Justice of the crown, when you propose deffering all endeavours on our part till such important concessions & novel regulations are obtained; Would it not be advisable as soon as possible to begin our defence & to let its continuance or cessation depend on the success of a petition presented to his majesty. Delay on our part emboldens our adversaries and improves their schemes; whilst it abates the ardor of the Americans inspired with recent Injuries and affords opportunity to our secret enemies to disseminate discord & disunion. But I am mounting into the sphere of the general Congress to whose wisdom and Judgment all private opinions must give place. This Colony has appointed seven delegates to represent it on this grand occasion, most of them glowing patriots & men of Learning & penetration. It is however the opinion of some good Judges that one or two might be exchanged for the better. The Conduct of your Assembly in chusing [a conservative, Joseph] galloway & Humphries [Charles Humphreys, a Quaker] seems to forbode difficulties and divisions which may be strengthened by the deputees from N.Y. It also seems to indicate a prevalency of selfish Quakers in your House which frustrate the generous designs & manly efforts of the real friends to American Freedom. I assure you I heartily repent of undertaking my Journey to the North when I did. If I had it to perform now, the opportunity of attending the Congress would be an infinite addition to the pleasures of it. I cannot help congratulating you on your happy situation in that respect. I comfort myself however under the privation of such an happiness with the hope that you will befriend me in sending a brief account of whatever is singular and important in their proceedings that can not be gathered from the public papers. Indeed I could wish their Debates were to be published which might greatly illuminate the minds of the thinking people among us and I would hope there would be sufficient abilities displayed in them to render us more respectable at Home.

Madison had found his vocation in the American Revolution. Bradford reported from Philadelphia that the city had "become another Cairo; with this difference that the one is a city swarming with Merchants, the other with politicians & Statesmen." Congress sat behind the closed doors of Carpenters' Hall, one room of which housed the city library supposed to be much used by the delegates, "by which we may conjecture that their measures will be wisely plan'd since they debate on them like philosophers; for by what I was told Vattel, Barlemaqui Locke & Montesquie seem to be the standar[d]s to which they refer either when settling the rights of the Colonies or when a dispute arises on the Justice or propriety of a measure." Madison, if he had not already read these philosophers, and others of lesser fame, would soon do so. The demiphilosophers in Philadelphia repudiated the authority of Parliament, called upon the people to arm, and adopted the system of nonintercourse. Madison heartily approved these bold measures. In December, 1774, he was elected to the Orange County Committee of Safety, which was charged to enforce the economic boycott — the Continental Association — and which quickly became the revolutionary local government. Of the eleven members, his father being chairman, Madison was much the youngest. Some months later the provincial committee of safety in Williamsburg commissioned him a colonel in the Orange County militia. But for his uncertain health, he might have taken to the field in 1775. As it was, although the honorific "Colonel" clung to him for many years, his only military service was on the parade ground, and that briefly. Of Orange and Virginia events, of his hopes and his fears, Madison wrote in letters to Bradford.

[Orange,] Virginia Nov: 26. 1774.

The pamphlets & letters you sent me were safely delivered about ten days after the date of them....

The proceedings of the Congress are universally approved of in this Province & I am persuaded will be faithfully adheared to. A spirit of Liberty & Patriotism animates all degrees and denominations of men. Many publickly declare themselves ready to join the Bostonians as soon as violence is offered them or resistance thought expedient. In many counties independent companies are forming and voluntaraly subjecting themselves to military discipline that they may be expert & prepared against a time of Need. I hope it will be a general thing thro'ought this province. Such firm and provident steps will either intimidate our enemies or enable us to defy them. By an epistle from the yearly meeting of the Quakers in your City to their bretheren & friends in our Colonies I observe they are determined to be passive on this Critical occasion from a regard to their religious principles mixed I presume with the Leaven of civil policy.

If america & Britain should come to an hostile rupture I am afraid an Insurrection among the slaves may & will be promoted. In one of our Counties lately a few of those unhappy wretches met together & chose a leader who was to conduct them when the English Troops should arrive—which they foolishly thought would be very soon & that by revolting to them they should be rewarded with their freedom. Their Intentions were soon discovered & proper precautions taken to prevent the Infection. It is prudent such attempts should be concealed as well as suppressed.

Madison's commission as a colonel in the Orange County militia

Virginia Orange County Jany 20. 1775

We are very busy at present in raising men and procuring the necessaries for defending ourselves and our friends in case of a sudden Invasion. The extensiveness of the Demands of the Congress and the pride of the British Nation together with the Wickedness of the present Ministry, seem, in the Judgment of our Politicians to require a preparation for extreme events. There will by the Spring, I expect, be some thousands of well trained High Spirited men ready to meet danger whenever it appears, who are influenced by no mercenary Principles, bearing their own expences and having the prospect of no recompence but the honour and safety of their Country. I suppose the Inhabitants of your Province are more reserved in their behaviour if not more easy in their Apprehensions, from the prevalence of Quaker principles and politics. The Quakers are the only people with us who refuse to accede to the Continental Association.... When I say they refuse to accede to the Association my meaning is that they refuse to Sign it, that being the method used among us to distinguish friends from foes and to oblige the Common people to a more strict observance

A 1775 cartoon showing George III in his carriage being driven to destruction by his advisers while America burns in the background

The logo of Rivington's Gazetteer

of it: I have never heard whether the like method has been adopted in the other governments.

[Orange, Virginia, *c.* March 10, 1775] We had a report here a few days [ago] that the New Yorkers had again given way & that the assembly had voted the proceedings of the Congress illegal. It raised a surprizing spirit of indignation & resentment which however Subsided on the report's being contradicted. The intimation you gave me of the state of affairs there prepared me to hear it without Surprize.

I lately saw in one of our Gazettes a pamphlet in answer to the friendly address [a tract by an Anglican clergyman] &c: by what you informed me I conjecture it to have been written by Genl. [Charles] Lee. It has much Spirit and Vivacity & contains some very sensible remarks. Some of our old bigots did not altogether approve the Strictures on the Clergy & King Charles; but it was generally, nay with this exception, universally, applauded. I wish most heartily we had [James] Rivington [a Tory newspaper editor] & his ministerial Gazetteers for 24. hours in this place. Execrable as their designs are, they would meet with adequate punishment. How different is the Spirit of Virginia from that of N York? A fellow was lately tarred & feathered for treating one [of] our county committees with disre[s]pect;

in N Y. they insult the whole Colony and Continent with impunity!

[Orange,] Virginia May 9th. 1775

We have lately had a great alarm here about the Governor's removing a large quantity of powder from our magazine and conveying it on board a ship of war: Not less [than] 600 men well armed and mounted assembled at Fredg. on this occasion, with a view to proceed to Wmsburg. [to] recover the powder & revenge the insult: The propriety of such a step was warmly agitated and weighty arguments aduced both for & against it: At length the advice of Peyton Randolph, Edm. Pendleton, Richd. H. Lee, and George Washington Esqrs. delegates for the Congress, to return home was complied with. The reasons however that induced these Gentlement to give this advice did not appear satisfactory to Patrick Henry Esqr. another of our delegates whose sentiments were not known at Fredg. This Gentleman after the dispersion of the troops at the above named place under the authority of the committee of his County and at the head of an Independant Company undertook to procure redress, which he resolutely accomplished by taking of the King's Quit-rents as much money as would replace the powder which had been removed so far that it could not be come at. This affair has prevented his appearing at the [Second Continental] Congress as early as his Colleagues, and has afforded me this opportunity of sending you a few lines [via Henry]. I expect his conduct as contrary to the opinion of the other delegats will be disapproved of by them, but it [has] gained him great honor in the most spirited parts of the Country and addresses of thanks are already presenting to him from different Quarters: The Gentlemen below [planters along the lower reaches of the York and James rivers] whose property will be exposed in case of a civil war in this Colony were extremely alarmed lest Government should be provoked to make reprisals. Indeed some of them discovered a pusilanimity little comporting with their professions or the name of Virginian.

I sent last fall to England for a few books, among which was priestly's treatise on Government. The present state of our affairs seems to threaten that it may be a long time before our commercial intercourse will be renewed: If

Historical Collections of Virginia BY HENRY HOWE, 1856

The Old Magazine in Williamsburg from which Lord Dunmore, the royal governor, had powder removed

this sd. appear to you to be the Case (& the session of the Congress will enable you to form a good guess) and it should be convenient in other respects, I should be glad you would send me the above treatise by the return of Mr. S. Smith.

On April 19, 1775, the first skirmishes of the American Revolution took place at Lexington and Concord. A few weeks later, American militiamen led by Ethan Allen captured Fort Ticonderoga and Crown Point in upper New York. Rumors of further encounters flew through the Colonies. Two days after the defeat of American forces at Bunker Hill, a report had reached Virginia of a great American victory in Boston. The rumor later proved unfounded, as Madison suspected it would.

[Orange, Virginia,] June 19th. 1775

A rumour is on the wing that the provincials have stormed Boston & with the Loss of 7,000 have cutt off or taken Gage & all his men. It is but little credited. Indeed the fact is extremely improbable: but the times are so remarkable for strange events; that improbability is almost become an argument for their truth.

Our friend Mr Wallace I hear is well & has entered into the Connubial state with one Miss McDowell, daughter of one of the representatives of Bottatourt County. Since I wrote last a Dysentry hath made an Irruption in my father's family. It has carried off a little sister about seven & a brother about four years of age. It is still among us but principally among the blacks. I have escaped hitherto, & as it is now out of the house I live in, I hope the danger is over. It is a disorder pretty incident to this Country & from some symptoms I am afraid will range more generally this year than common. Our Burgesses from the County are not yet returned from Willmsbg. where they hold their Assembly. So I cannot give you any particulars of their proceedings. The news papers will do that I expect: I understand Lord Dunmore by deserting his Palace & taking Sanctuary on board the Ship of War, under pretence of the fear of an Attack on his person, has surprized & incensed them much, As they thought it incredible he should be actuated on that occasion by the Motive he alledges. It is judged more likly to have proceeded from some intelligence or Instructions he has received from his friends or superiors to the North. It is said the Governor of N Carolina has treated

While minutemen in Massachusetts participated in battles such as Lexington, Colonel Madison was becoming a marksman in Orange.

his Assembly nearly in the same manner. Some will have it that Lord Dunmore removed from Wmsbg. & pretended danger that he might with more force & consistency misrepresent us to the ministry. His unparralled malice to the people of this Colony since the detection of his false & wicked letters, sent home at the time he was professing an ardent friendship for us must lead us to suppose he will do us all the Injury in his power. But we defy his power as much as we detest his Villany. We have as great unanimity & as much of the Military Ardor as you can possibly have in your government; & the progress we make in discipline & hostile preparations is as great as the Zeal with which these things were undertaken. The strength of this Colony will lie chiefly in the rifle-men of the Upland Counties, of whom we shall have great numbers. You would be astonished at the perfection this art is brought to. The most inexpert hands recon on it an indifferent shot to miss the bigness of a man's face at the distance of 100 Yards. I am far from being among the best & should not often miss it on a fair trial at that distance. If we come into an engagement, I make no doubt but the officers of the enemy will fall at the distance before they get withing 150 or 200 Yards. Indeed I believe we have men that would very often hit such a mark 250 Yds. Our greatest apprehensions proceed from the scarcity of powder but a little will go a great way with such as use rifles. It is imagined our Governor has been tampering with the Slaves & that he has it in contemplation to make great Use of them in case of a civil war in this province. To say the truth, that is the only part in which this Colony is vulnerable; & if we should be subdued, we shall fall like Achilles by the hand of one that knows that secret. But we have a good cause & great Courage which are a great support. I shall just add that among other incouragement we have a prospect of immense crops of Grain.

Lord Dunmore

Virginia Orange: July 28 — 1775
Our convention is now sitting, and I believe intends to strike a considerable sum of money & to raise 3 or 4,000 men as an Army to be in immediate pay. The independants [minutemen], who I suppose will be three times that number will also have their pay commence as soon as they are called to action. The Preparations for War are

every where going on in a most vigorous manner. But the Scarcity of Ammunition is truly alarming. Can you tell how they are supplied in N England and what steps are taking to procure a sufficiency for the time to come. I was a little induced from the confident assertion of the Congress that foreign Assistance if necessary was ["] *undoubtedly* attainable," to think & hope that some secret Overtures had been made to them. If so I imagine they are wrapped up in impenetrable secresy as yet. . . .

A Letter to Mr Smith is in company with this. It is directed to him at Princeton to the care of Plum. If he should be in Philada. at the time you get this I should be glad you would give him notice of it. Or if by going to Princeton you think it will miss of him in that case you would oblige me by taking it out of the office and conveying it to him. I have requested him to bring me two pamphlets "An apology for the Church of England as by Law Established" &c by Josiah Tucker — and An Essay on Toleration with a particular view to the late Application of the Dissenting Ministers to Parliament &c. by Phil. Furneaux. If he should not be in Town after he recieves this & you could procure them and send them to him with Priestly before he sets off for Virginia you would lay me under another Obligation.

A Scotch Parson in an adjoining County refused to observe the fast or preach on that day [a day designated for "public humiliation, Fasting and prayer" by the Continental Congress]. When called on he pleaded Conscience, alledging that it was his duty to pay no regard to any such appointments made by unconstitutional authority. The Committee it seems have their Consciences too: they have ordered his Church doors to be shut and his salary to be stopped, and have sent to the convention for their advice. If the Convention should connive at their proceedings I question, should his insolence not abate if he does not get ducked in a coat of Tar & surplice of feathers and then he may go in his new Canonicals and act under the lawful Authority of Gen. Gage if he pleased. We have one of the same Kidney in the parish I live in. He was sometime ago published in the Gazette for his insolence and had like to have met with sore treatment; but finding his protection to be not so much in the law as the favor of the people he is grown very supple & obsequious.

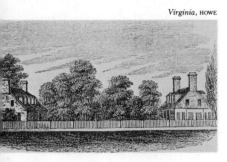

Virginia, HOWE

Nineteenth-century engraving of the site of Lord Dunmore's Palace

The war was a year old; Lord Dunmore and his Loyalist band had been driven to sea; and the movement for independence had made great strides when, on April 25, 1776, the twenty-five-year-old colonel of militia was elected by the freeholders of Orange to the Virginia Convention in Williamsburg. Early in the next month, he set out on his first journey to the capital village a hundred miles away. A stranger to the town, he found familiar faces in the convention, which was the revolutionary successor to the House of Burgesses. Among the delegates were kinsmen and friends of the family who helped smooth the way for Madison. Several of the celebrated Virginia patriots—George Washington, Richard Henry Lee, Thomas Jefferson—were on other errands; but Patrick Henry—the most celebrated of them all—and Edmund Pendleton, the presiding officer, were not only among Madison's relations, but among the great men of Virginia in the convention. On May 15, the delegates instructed the Virginians in Congress to propose a united declaration of independence. Without waiting for the formalities to be completed in Philadelphia, the convention at once set to work to form a new government for Virginia.

Pendleton named Madison to the committee that was to prepare a constitution and a declaration of rights. George Mason, a wealthy planter from Fairfax who was well versed in Whig theory, was the dominant force in the committee. The new constitution, adopted in convention on June 28, bore no traces of Madison's hand, and he would later join with Jefferson in efforts to reform it in democratic directions. But toward the proposed declaration of rights the freshman delegate overcame his reserve and offered an important amendment to Mason's article on religion. Madison recalled

the episode in an account written years later, in which he referred to himself in the third person.

"Autobiographical Notes," 1832

Certificate of election (above) of James Madison, Jr., and William Moore to the convention that met at Williamsburg in the second capitol (left, below), built in 1751

Being young & in the midst of distinguished and experienced members of the Convention he [Madison] did not enter into its debates; tho' he occasionally suggested amendments; the most material of which was a change of the terms in which the freedom of Conscience was expressed in the proposed Declaration of Rights. This important and meritorious instrument was drawn by Geo. Mason, who had inadvertently adopted the word *"toleration"* in the article on that subject. The change suggested and accepted, substituted a phraseology which —declared the freedom of conscience to be a *natural* and absolute right.

This account merits some elaboration. Mason had proposed "the fullest Toleration in the Exercise of Religion." The concept of toleration, as in the English Toleration Act previously in force in the colony and in Locke's celebrated *Letter Concerning Toleration,* assumed an official and preferred religion along with the right of the State to grant or to withhold favor from "dissenting" religions. Perhaps one-half the inhabitants of Virginia were dissenters from the Anglican Church in 1776. Some sectarians, especially the Baptists, had been persecuted; all had been regulated, and they demanded not merely toleration but equality. Having earlier championed their cause at home, Madison now attempted to push it to conclusion in Williamsburg. For Mason's words he proposed to substitute a clause stating that "all men are equally entitled to the full and free exercise of [religion] according to the dictates of Conscience." This was not all. It followed from the first principle "therefore that no man or class of men ought, on account of religion to be invested with peculiar emoluments or privileges." The second principle looked to the separation of Church and State and, of course, threatened to dethrone the Anglican clergy. Madison prevailed upon Patrick Henry to introduce the amendment on the floor. It failed mainly because it struck at the established Church. Seeing that he might win one point without permanently jeopardizing the other, Madison took the road to compromise—a road he would travel often during his long career. He revised the amendment, dropping the directive toward separation but maintaining the latitude of the principle of religious freedom. In this form it was adopted. The Virginia Declaration of Rights became a model for the new American states, and indeed for revolutionary peoples everywhere. The right of religious freedom enunciated by James Madison acquired the force of authority it had never had before. In Virginia the victory was the first in a long campaign—Madison always at the fore—climaxed in 1786 with the passage under his leadership of Thomas Jefferson's Statute for Religious Freedom.

Madison returned to Williamsburg for the October, 1776, session of the general assembly, the legislative body established by the new Virginia Constitution. But he was defeated—his first and last defeat at the polls— in the ensuing April election. There was a special reason for his defeat, as he explained many years later.

Madison's handwritten amendment on his copy of the printed broadside of Virginia Declaration of Rights

"Autobiographical Notes," 1832

Previous to the Revolution the election of County Representatives, was as in England, septennial, and it was as there the usage for the candidates to recommend themselves to the voters, not only by personal solicitation, but by the corrupting influence of spirituous liquors, and other treats, having a like tendency. Regarding these as equally inconsistent with the purity of moral and of republican principles; and anxious to promote, by his example, the proper reform, he [Madison] trusted to the new views of the subject which he hoped would prevail with the people; whilst his competitors adhered to the old practice. The consequence was that the election went against him; his abstinence being represented as the effect of pride or parsimony.

$\mathbb{F}$ortunately for Madison, the assembly valued his services and promptly elected him to the Council of State. Headed by the governor, who also received his office from the all-powerful legislature, the eight-man council was the executive power under the new constitution. Since it met daily the year around, except during the "sickly season" in the Tidewater, Madison took up residence with his second cousin, the Reverend James Madison, president of William and Mary, who occupied a charming Georgian house in the college yard. Before long the young councilor wrote to his father.

Williamsburg Jany. 23rd. 1778

Virginia, HOWE

Hond Sir

I got safe to this place on Tuesday following the day I left home, and at the earnest invitation of my Kinsman Mr. Madison have taken my lodgings in a Room of the Presidents house, which is a much better accomdation than I could have promised myself. It would be very agreeable to me if I were enabled by such rarities as our part of the County furnishes, particularly dried fruit &tc which Mr. Madison is very fond of to make some

The College of William and Mary

The Reverend James Madison

little returns for the Culinary favours I receive. Should any opportunity for this purpose offer I hope they will be sent. You will see by the inclosed Acct. of Sales what money you have in Mr. Lee's hands [William Lee, his business agent], and if you chuse to draw for it, you can transmit me your Bills for Sale. You will be informed in due time by Advertisement from the Governor what is proper to be done with the Shoes &tc. collected for the Army. You will be able to obtain so circumstantial an Acct. of public affairs from Majr. Moore that I may spare myself the trouble of anticipating it. Majr. Moore also has for my Mother 4 Oz. of Bark [quinine]. The other Articles wanted by the family are not at present to be had. Whenever I meet with them I shall provide and transmit them. I hope you will not forget my parting request that I might hear frequently from home and whenever my brother returns from the Army I desire he may be informed I shall expect he will make up by letter the loss of intelligence I sustain by my removal out of his way. With the sincerest affection for yourself & all others whom I ought particularly to remember on this occasion,

I am Dear Sir Your Affecte. son

JAMES MADISON JNR.

What Madison himself contributed to the council's work cannot be determined, but it must have given him a liberal education in the hardships and frustrations of wartime government. Problems of taxation and finance, of recruitment, trade, Indian affairs, public works, the navy, supply and logistics, and so on, were constantly on the council's agenda, and they grew more difficult with the passage of time. Patrick Henry was governor, as he had been since 1776. Madison worked hand-in-glove with Henry; only in later years would they become political enemies. Thomas Jefferson succeeded Henry in June, 1779, just after the first of several British invasions by way of Hampton Roads. Government became a task of Sisyphus as the enemy converged on the defenseless state from the Carolinas and the Chesapeake. Madison was not around for the finish in 1780–81. Having been elected a Virginia delegate to the Continental Congress in December, 1779, he had moved on to a larger theater. But the invasion devastated Jefferson, who was left to cope almost single-handedly with the war.

The fifty-year friendship between these two Virginians, Jefferson and Madison, is the most remarkable in the annals of statesmanship. Madison first knew Jefferson as a member of the assembly, where he was equally ardent in his support of the war and in his advocacy of liberal reforms for Virginia. Not until they labored together as governor and councilor, however, did they become political intimates. In some respects they were much alike. They came from the same part of the country—Monticello was only thirty miles from Madison's home—belonged to the same class, responded to the same intellectual currents, and shared the same republican principles. Yet they were men of fundamentally different personal styles and temperaments, and from this, rather than from their similarities, stemmed the creative genius of their partnership. Jefferson, the older man by eight years, was tall, angular, and robust; Madison, slight of build—five feet six inches tall—frail, with soft features and a bleached skin that resembled parchment. Jefferson was the bolder thinker, easily caught up in philosophical speculation, looking less to the *is* than to the *ought to be*. Madison's was the tougher, more probing, persistent, and sagacious mind: he helped keep his friend's feet on the ground: Jefferson had the gift of brilliant rhetoric, which Madison lacked, though it was John Marshall who said that if eloquence included the unadorned power of reasoned persuasion, Madison was "the most eloquent man I ever heard." Both men were reticent in social intercourse; some observers thought them cold, stiff, and aloof. Jefferson, nevertheless, radiated political magnetism, and Madison, without this aura, shone in caucuses and committees. He genuinely liked politics and thought it a worthy vocation. Jefferson soon came to consider politics a curse and would have gladly thrown it off for the pleasures of the arts and sciences if he could have.

In 1780, while Jefferson struggled with the discouraging problems of the Virginia magistracy, Madison entered the continental stage where the problems were different but no less intractable. Each in his own station would be the eyes and ears and helping hand to the other, and this great collaboration would endure, with scarcely a ripple between them, as long as they lived.

Royal arms of colonial Virginia

Chapter *2*

Congressman at War

M adison was delighted to exchange Williamsburg for Philadelphia. The city on the Delaware was not only the political but also the cultural and intellectual capital of the new nation. The Quaker imprint remained strong. Philadelphia was enlightened, wealthy, moral, and staid. The neatly patterned and treelined streets with their rows of sedate, red brick and white-trimmed houses expressed the city's sober charm. Benjamin Franklin once said that if there existed an atheist in the universe he would be converted on seeing Philadelphia—everything was so well arranged. In this aspect, certainly, the city appealed to the earnest young Virginian. Arriving in March after unusually heavy snows had melted in Virginia, he took up residence in Mrs. House's boardinghouse at Fifth and Market streets, only a block from the State House where Congress met. Madison served in Congress continuously, almost never away from his seat, for three and a half years. And Philadelphia, not Montpelier, not Virginia, would be the principal seat of his life for the next twenty years.

The early months of 1780 were the gloomiest of the war. No one could remember a harsher winter. For the soldiers of the Continental Army encamped at Morristown, New Jersey, conditions were worse than at Valley Forge the year before; supplies ran low, rations were cut, and money, so far as the soldiers saw any, was as worthless as oak leaves. Mutiny broke out in May and was quickly crushed. Between the opposing armies in the North, things were at a stalemate. Unable to destroy General Washington's army, the British commander in chief, Sir Henry Clinton, pursued a more promising strategy: "to unravel the thread of rebellion from the southward." Georgia had already fallen to the British, and Charleston was under siege when Madison entered Congress. It would fall on May 12, the darkest day of the war. Weak, broke, and bitterly divided, Congress was unable to rally the country. Although twelve states had at last, after two years, ratified the Articles of Confederation, Maryland still balked on the ground that the western lands claimed by several of the states should become the property of the Union. Much of the discord in Congress flowed from the French alliance. The acrimonious dispute between Silas Deane and Arthur Lee, commissioners with Franklin in negotiating the alliance, had been dumped into the lap of Congress in 1778, and the political forces that formed around these rivals led to pro-French and anti-French factions which kept Congress in turmoil until peace came. France had drawn her ally Spain into the war in 1779, and she would soon deliver on the promise of an army to fight alongside the Americans. Without France the war could not be won; her power, accordingly, was bound to be felt for good or ill in the peace. Peace was a dim prospect, yet Congress had, some months before Madison's arrival, hammered out preliminary terms and sent John Adams to Europe to negotiate whenever the time grew ripe.

Money was the fundamental problem facing Congress. From the beginning the war had been floated on a sea of paper money. Depreciation set in early and it ran rampant in 1780. As the Continental presses printed more and more money, the more and more worthless it became. The state currencies were caught in the same dizzy spiral. Government could not pay its bills, credit was undermined, and disaffection spread among soldiers and civilians alike. Alert to the problem, Madison, while snowbound at Montpelier, had made a study of public finance and recorded his views in a little essay called "Money." Attacking the quantity theory of money as

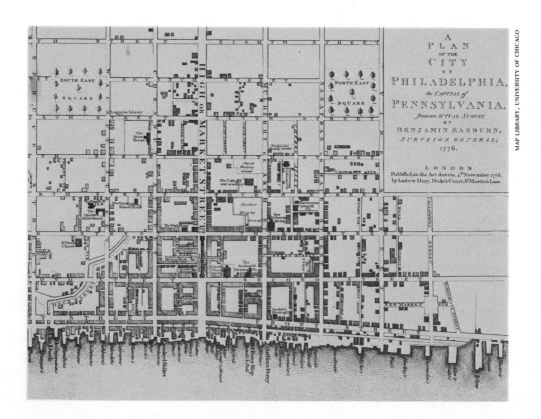

expounded by David Hume, he argued that the value of money depended not on its quantity but on public confidence in the issuing authority, in this case the government. To create that confidence he recommended a loan of specie from abroad, increased taxes, rigorous economy, and the kind of leadership that would raise the public's faith in the ability of the government to meet its obligations.

Congress was ready to act, though not exactly along the lines of Madison's thought. On the day he arrived in Philadelphia it adopted a bold "new plan of finance." Congress printed no more money; the dollar was devalued to two and a half cents; as the states retired the old currency through tax collections, they would issue new paper which Congress pledged to redeem in coin after five years. Another part of the plan substituted supplies in kind from the states for requisitions of money. It was a hazardous experiment. Congress surrendered the one real power it had over its own affairs—the power of issuing money—and threw the responsibility of supporting the continent, including the Continental Army, upon the states. Madison was apprehensive for the plan's success. He expressed his views in two letters to Governor Jefferson.

A plan of the city of Philadelphia published in 1776 (left), and James Madison's credentials as a delegate to the Continental Congress which was meeting there in 1780

Philadelphia March 27th. 1780

Among the various conjunctures of alarm and distress which have arisen in the course of the revolution, it is with pain I affirm to you Sir, that no one can be singled out more truly critical than the present. Our army threatened with an immediate alternative of disbanding or living on free quarter; the public treasury empty; public credit exhausted, nay the private credit of purchasing Agents employed, I am told, as far as it will bear, Congress complaining of the extortion of the people; the people of the improvidence of Congress, and the army of both; our affairs requiring the most mature & systematic measures, and the urgency of occasions admitting only of temporizing expedients, and those expedients generating new difficulties. Congress from a defect of adequate Statesmen more likely to fall into wrong measures and of less weight to enforce right ones, recommending plans to the several states for execution and the states separately rejudging the expediency of such plans, whereby the same distrust of concurrent exertions that has damped the ardor of patriotic individuals, must produce the same effect among the States themselves. An old system of finance discarded as incompetent to our necessities, an untried & precarious one substituted, and a total stagnation in prospect between the end of the former & the operation of the lat-

For the NATIONAL GAZETTE.

MONEY.

[OBSERVATIONS *written posterior to the circular* ADDRESS *of* CONGRESS *in Sept.* 1779; *and prior to their Act of March,* 1780.]

IT has been taken for an axiom in all our reasonings on the subject of finance, that supposing the quantity and demand of things vendible in a country to remain the same, their price will vary according to the variation in the quantity of the circulating medium; in other words, that the value of money will be regulated by its quantity. I shall submit to the judgment of the public some considerations which determine mine to reject the proposition as founded in error. Should they be deemed not absolutely conclusive, they seem at least to shew that it is liable to too many exceptions and restrictions to be taken for granted as a fundamental truth.

If the circulating medium be of universal value as specie, a local increase or decrease of its quantity, will not, whilst a communication subsists with other countries, produce a correspondent rise or fall in its value. The reason is obvious. When a redundancy of universal money prevails in any one country, the holders of it know their interest too well to waste it in extravagant prices, when it would be worth so much more to them elsewhere. When a deficiency happens, those who hold commodities, rather than part with them at an undervalue in one country, would carry them to another. The variation of prices, in these cases, cannot therefore exceed the expence and insurance of transportation.

Suppose a country totally unconnected with Europe, or with any other country, to possess specie in the same proportion to circulating property that Europe does; prices there would correspond with those in Europe. Suppose that so much specie were thrown into circulation as to make the quantity exceed the proportion of Europe tenfold, without any change in commodities, or in the demand for them: as soon as such an augmentation had produced its effect, prices would rise tenfold; or which is the same thing, money would be depreciated tenfold. In this state of things, suppose again, that a free and ready communication were opened between this country and Europe, and that the inhabitants of the former, were made sensible of the value of their money in the latter; would not its value among themselves immediately cease to be regulated by its quantity, and assimilate itself to the foreign value?

Madison's essay "Money," written in 1780, was published in the National Gazette *in 1791.*

ter: These are the outlines of the true picture of our public situation. I leave it to your own imagination to fill them up. Believe me Sir as things now stand, if the States do not vigorously proceed in collecting the old money and establishing funds for the credit of the new, that we are undone; and let them be ever so expeditious in doing this still the intermediate distress to our army and hindrance to public affairs are a subject of melancholy reflection. Gen Washington writes that a failure of bread has already commenced in the army, and that for any thing he sees, it must unavoidably increase. Meat they have only for a short season and as the whole dependance is on provisions now to be procured, without a shilling for the purpose and without credit for a shilling. I look forward with the most pungent apprehensions.

Philada. May 6th. 1780

I am sorry I can give you no other account of our public situation than that it continues equally perplexed & alarming as when I lately gave you a sketch of it. Our army has as yet been kept from starving, and public measures from a total stagnation, by draughts on the States for the unpaid requisitions. The great amount of these you may judge of, from the share that has fallen to Virginia. The discharge of debts due from the purchasing departments has absorbed a great proportion of them, and very large demand still remain.... A punctual compliance on the part of the States with the specific supplies will indeed render much less money necessary than would otherwise be wanted, but experience by no means affords satisfactory encouragement that due and unanimous exertions will be made for that purpose not to mention that our distress is so pressing that it is uncertain whether any exertions of that kind can give relief in time. It occurs besides, that as the ability of the people to comply with the pecuniary requisitions is derived from the sale of their commodities, a requisition of the latter must make the former proportionally more difficult and defective: Congress have the satisfaction however to be informed that the legislature of Connecticut have taken the most vigorous steps for supplying their quota both of money & commodities; and that a body of their principal merchants have associated for supporting the credit of the new paper, for which purpose they have in a public address pledged their faith to the Assembly to sell their merchandise on the same terms for it as if they were to be paid in specie. A Similar vigor throughout the Union may perhaps produce effects as far exceeding our present hopes as they have heretofore fallen short of our wishes.

It is to be observed that the situation of Congress has undergone a total change from what it originally was. Whilst they exercised the indefinite power of emitting money on the credit of their constituents they had the whole wealth & resources of the continent within their command, and could go on with their affairs independently and as they pleased. Since the resolution passed for shutting the press, this power has been entirely given up and they are now as dependent on the States as the King of England is on the parliament. They can neither enlist pay nor feed a single soldier, nor execute any other pu[r]pose but as the means are first put into their hands. Unless the legislatures are sufficiently attentive to this change of circumstances and act in conformity to it, every thing must necessarily go wrong or rather must come to a total stop. All that Congress can do in future will be to administer public affairs with prudence vigor and oeconomy. In order to do which they have sent a Committee to Head Quarters with ample powers in concert with the Commander in chief and the Heads of the departments to reform the various abuses which prevail and to make such arrangements, as will best guard against a relapse into them. . . .

With great regard, I am Dr Sir Yr Obt Servt

JAMES MADISON JNR.

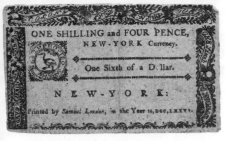

Examples of the paper money issued by the state of New York during the Revolutionary War

M adison's fears proved justified. The new currency was cheapened before it could be launched in the states, and the system of specific supplies encountered massive logistical problems. In October, Madison penned a grim analysis for his good friend in Virginia, Joseph Jones, and urged harsh measures by the state's legislature, of which Jones was a member. If the people would not voluntarily support the cause of liberty and union, Madison would force them to it.

Philada. Octr. [24,] 1780

We continue to receive periodical alarms from the Commissary's & Quarter Master's departments. The season

Madison's good friend, Joseph Jones

The southeast corner of Third and Market streets in Philadelphia, two blocks from Madison's lodgings

is now arrived when provision ought to be made for a season that will not admit of transportation, and when the monthly supplies must be subject to infinite disappointments even if the States were to do their duty. But instead of Magazines being laid in our army is living from hand to mouth, with a prospect of being soon in a condition still worse. How a total dissolution of it can be prevented in the course of the winter is for any resources now in prospect utterly inexplicable, unless the States unanimously make a vigorous & speedy effort to form Magazines for the purpose. But unless the States take other methods to procure their specific supplies than have prevailed in most of them, their utmost efforts to comply with the requisitions of Congress can be only a temporary relief....

As you are at present a *legislator* I will take the liberty of hinting to you an idea that has occurred on this subject. I take it for granted that taxation alone is inadequate to our situation. You know as well as I do how far we ought to rely on loans to supply the defect of it. Specific taxes as far as they go are a valuable fund but from local and other difficulties will never be universally and sufficiently adopted. Purchase with State money or certificates will be substituted. In order to prevent this evil and to insure the supplies therefore I would propose, that they be diffused and proportioned among the people as accurately as circumstances will admit, that they be *impress*[ed] with vigor and impartiality, and paid for in certificates not transferrible & be redeemable at some period subsequent to the war at specie value and bearing an intermediate interest. The advantage of such a scheme is this, that it would anticipate during the war the future revenues of peace, as our Enemies and all other modern nations do. It would be compelling the people to lend the public their commodities, as people elsewhere lend their money to purchase commodities. It would be a permanent resourse by which the war might be supported as long as the earth should yield its increase. This plan differs from specific taxes only in this that as an equivalent is given for what is received much less nicely would be requisite in apportioning the supplies among the people, and they might be taken in places where they are most wanted. It differs from the plan of paying for supplies in state emissions or common certificates in this, that the latter produce all the evils of a redundant medium, whereas the former not being transferrible can not have that effect, and moreover do not require the same degree of taxes during the war.

The financial crisis continued for months, even years, but disaster was eventually averted by the vigorous efforts of Robert Morris, the Philadelphia merchant-capitalist who was appointed Superintendent of Finance by Congress in 1781. Charges of "dictator" and "profiteer" were thrown at Morris, but Madison supported him. Meanwhile, in all matters, Madison won a place of leadership in Congress. The eminence which distinguished that body in its birth was no longer present, and Madison, though at age twenty-nine the youngest member, put his head for legislative business and his nationalist ardor to good use. Amidst the turbulence of congressional politics, which sickened and disgusted so many, Madison seemed to flourish. In the fall of 1780 the Lee-Deane affair surfaced again, this time with malicious intent to destroy the chief American architect of the French alliance in Paris, Benjamin Franklin. Madison was named chairman of a committee to investigate Lee's charges. The committee rebuffed Lee, and in the ensuing turmoil Madison did what he could to sustain Franklin and the alliance. He thus allied himself with the pro-French faction, which included Morris and other leading Middle State men as well as most Virginians, against the anti-Gallicans led by the Massachusetts brace of Adamses, John and Samuel, the Virginia Lees, and prominent South Carolinians. The commitment colored Madison's position on all the great issues before Congress during the next three years.

One of these issues concerned western lands. Of the seven states boasting western lands, Virginia's claim above the Ohio River and to the Mississippi was by far the largest. The Articles of Confederation left these virgin lands with the states. The so-called "landless states" were unhappy with this arrangement and one of them, Maryland, held out against ratification. They argued that the lands should be ceded to Congress for the "common benefit." Behind this mask of high-mindedness was the speculative greed of private land companies, especially powerful in Maryland and Pennsylvania, which sought to validate old titles allegedly obtained from the Crown or from Indian tribes. In the final analysis, of course, the future of the Transappalachian West hung on the outcome of the war. To win this stake the Confederation must be completed, Congress strengthened, and the jealousies of the states sunk in the common cause. Among Virginians in 1780 these political realities overcame the niceties of the state's legal title; on the strength of that claim, however, Virginia set conditions to the western cession that would annihilate the pretensions of the speculators. In September, Congress called upon Virginia to cede without conditions.

Joseph Jones, then a Virginia delegate to Congress, countered with a motion seconded by Madison stipulating the conditions. The Ohio lands would be carved into separate and independent states; Virginia would be secured in her remaining territory, which included Kentucky; she would be reimbursed for the costs of defending her "back lands"; and all the company claims would be denied. Later, when Jones was called home, Madison became the Virginia spokesman on this question. Writing in September to Edmund Pendleton, a prominent figure in Virginia politics, Madison advocated, with unwarranted optimism, Virginia's cession of its western land claims.

Phila. Sepr. 12th. 1780

Congress have also at length entered seriously on a plan for finally ratifying the confederation. Convinced of the necessity of such a measure, to repress the hopes with which the probable issue of the campaign will inspire our Enemy, as well as to give greater authority & vigor to our public councils, they have recommended in the most pressing terms to the States claiming unappropriated back lands, to cede a liberal portion of them to the general benefit. As these exclusive claims formed the only obstacle with Maryland there is no doubt that a compliance with this recommendation will bring her into the confederation. How far the States holding the back lands may be disposed to give them up cannot be so easily determined. From the sentiments of the most intelligent persons which have come to my knowledge, I own I am pretty sanguine they will see the necessity of closing the union in too strong a light to oppose the only expedient that can accomplish it.

A month later Madison reported to Jones the outcome of their motion. Congress adopted the Virginia principle of erecting new republican states in the West and agreed to assume the defense expenses incurred by the ceding states; but Congress refused to guarantee their remaining territory or to slam the door on the speculators.

Philada. Oct. 17th. 1780

Congress have at length been brought to a final consideration of the clause relating to Indian purchases. It was debated very fully and particularly, and was in the result lost by a division of the house. Under the first impression of the chagrin I had determined to propose to my colleagues to state the whole matter to the [Virginia General] Assembly with all the circumstances and reasonings of the opponents to the measure. But on cooler reflection I think it best to leave the fact in your hands to be made use of as your prudence may suggest. I am the rather led to decline the first determination because I am pretty confident that whatever the views of particular members might be it was neither the wish nor intention of many who voted with them to favor the purchasing companies. Some thought such an assurance from Congress unnecessary because their receiving the lands from the States as vacant & unappropriated excluded all individual claims, and because they had given a general assurance that the cession should be applied to the common benefit. Others supposed that such an assurance might imply that without it Congress would have a right to dispose of the lands in any manner they pleased, and that it might give umbrage to the states claiming an exclusive jurisdiction over them. All that now remains for the Ceding States to do is to annex to their cessions the express condition that no private claims be complied with by Congress. Perhaps it would not be going too far, by Virginia who is so deeply concerned to make it a condition of her grant that no such claims be admitted even within the grants of others, because when they are given up to Congress she is interested in them as much as others, and it might so happen, that the benefit of all other grants except her own might be transferred from the public, to a few land mongers. I can not help adding however that I hope this incident in Congress will not discourage any measures of the Assembly which would otherwise have been taken for ratifying the Confederation. Under the cautions I have suggested, they may still be taken with perfect security.

Fort Franklin, below Lake Erie, was typical of the frontier outposts in the western part of America.

A t the beginning of the new year, the Virginia assembly voted to cede the unappropriated Ohio lands with the original conditions. It was enough to complete the Confederation: Maryland ratified in March, 1781. But rather than acknowledge the Virginia claim Congress spurned her gift. Madison vented his irritation to Jefferson.

Philada: Jany. 15th. 1782

The machinations which have long been practised by interested individuals agst. this claim are well known to you. The late proceedings within the walls of Congress in consequence of the territorial cessions produced by their recommendations to the States claiming the Western Country were many weeks ago transmitted for the Legislature by a Capt. Irish. By the same conveyance I wrote to you on the subject. We have the mortification to find by our latest letters from Richmond that this Gentleman had not at the date of them appeared there. As it is uncertain whether that information may not have totally miscarried it will be proper to repeat to you that the States besides Virga. from which the cessions came were Connecticut & N York. The cession of the former consisted of all her claim west of N. York as far as the Missippi. That of the latter of all her claims beyond a certain western limit drawn on the occasion. The cession of Con[necticu]t extended to the soil only expressly reserving the jurisdiction. That of N.Y. made no reservation. These cessions with that of Virga. & sundry memorials from the Ind[ian]a & other land Companies were referred to a Committee composed of a Member from N.H. R.I. N.J. Pa. & Maryld. The ingredients of this composition prepared us for the complexion of their proceedings. . . . The upshot of the whole was a report to Congress rejecting the Cessions of Virga. & Cont. and accepting that of N.Y.; disallowing also, the claims of the Companies N.W. of the Ohio but justifying that of the Inda. Compy. The report seems to distrust the doctrine hitherto maintained, of territorial rights being incident to the U.S. Collectively which are not comprehended within any individual State; substituting the expedient of recognizing the title of N.Y. stretching it over the whole country claimed by the other ceding States, & then accepting a transfer of it to the U.S. In this state the business now rests, the report having never been taken into consideration, nor do we wish it should, till it shall have undergone the consideration of Virga.

In whatever light the policy of this proceeding may be viewed it affords an additional proof of the industry & perseverance with which the territorial rights of Virga. are persecuted, & of the necessity of fortifying them with every precaution which their importance demands. As a very obvious & necessary one we long since recommended to the State an accurate & full collection of the documents which relate to the subject. . . . we have no hope at present of being enabled from any other sources than the voluntary aids of individuals to contradict even verbally the misrepresentations & calumnies which are

Thomas Paine opposed Virginia's western land claims in this 1780 pamphlet entitled Public Good.

daily levelled agst. the claims of Va. & which can not fail to prepossess the public with errors injurious at present to her reputation & which may affect a future decision on her rights. Col. Masons industry & kindness have supplied us with some valuable papers & remarks. Mr. Jones has also recd. from Mr. Pendleton some judicious remarks on the subject. We are still notwithstandg. far from possessing a complete view of it. Will you permit me to ask of you such information as your researches have yielded, with the observations which you have made in the course of them. I would not obtrude such a request on you if the subject were not of public importance & if it could have been addressed with equal prospect of advantage elsewhere. Indeed if you cd. prevail on yourself to spare as much time as would Survey the whole subject, beginning with the original charter, pursuing it thro' the subsequent charters & other public acts of the crown thro' the Govs. of Virga., & referring to all the transactions with the Indians which have been drawn into the question, the public utility I am persuaded wd. sufficiently reward you for the labor.

Jefferson declined this task. Unable to muster either the troops or the finances needed to fight off the British invasion of Virginia, he had finally resigned as governor and, wanting nothing more to do with public life, had retired to Monticello. As the western land affair dragged on in Congress, it became associated with other sensitive issues, among them that of Vermont. The Vermonters demanded statehood against the competing claims made on their territory by Massachusetts, New Hampshire, and New York. New England congressmen purposely delayed resolution of the western land problem in hopes of logrolling Maryland and Pennsylvania votes on Vermont. Virginia opposed independence for Vermont because it would set a precedent for dismembering large states and, of course, add to northeastern political power in the Union. For his own edification Madison wrote an analysis of the intricate political issue.

May 1st. 1782.

The two great objects which predominate in the policies of Congress at this juncture are I. Vermont. II. Western territory.

I The independence of Vermont and its admission into the Confederacy are patronised by the Eastern States (N. Hampshire excepted)   1. from ancient prejudice agst. N York: 2. the interest which Citizens of those

55

The first American map of the United States was made by Abel Buell in 1784. He extended the southern states to the Mississippi.

States have in lands granted by Vermont. 3. but principally from the accession of weight they will derive from it in Congress. N. Hampshire having gained its main object by the exclusion of its territory East of Connecticut River from the claims of Vermont, is already indifferent to its independence, and will probably soon combine with other Eastern States in its favor.

The same patronage is yielded to the pretensions of Vermont by Pennsylvania & Maryland with the sole view of reinforcing the opposition to claims of Western territory particularly those of Virginia and by N. Jersey & Delaware with the additional view of strengthening the interest of the little States. Both of these considerations operate also on Rhode Island in addition to those above mentioned.

The independence of Vermont and its admission into the Union are opposed by N. York for reasons obvious & well known.

The like opposition is made by Virginia N. Carolina

S. Carolina, and Georgia. The grounds of this opposition are. 1. an habitual jealosy of a predominance of Eastern Interests. 2. the opposition expected from Vermont to Western claims. 3. the inexpediency of admitting so unimportant a State, to an equal vote in deciding on peace & all the other grand interests of the Union now depending. 4. the influence of the example on a premature dismemberment of other States. These considerations influence the four States last mentioned in different degrees. The 2. & 3. to say nothing of the 4. ought to be decisive with Virginia.

II The territorial claims, particularly those of Virginia are opposed by Rhode Island, N. Jersey, Pennsylvania Delaware & Maryland. Rhode Island is influenced in her opposition by 1. a lucrative desire of sharing in the vacant territory as a fund of revenue. 2. by the envy & jealousy naturally excited by superior resources & importance. N.J. Penna: Delaware, Maryland, are influenced partly by the same considerations; but principally by the intrigues of their Citizens who are interested in the claims of land Companies. The decisive influence of this last consideration is manifest from the peculiar, and persivering opposition made agst. Virginia within whose limits those claims lye.

The Western claims, or rather a final settlement of them, are also thwarted by Massachusetts and Connecticut. This object with them is chiefly subservient to that of Vermont, as the latter is with Pennsylvania & Maryland to the former. The general policy and interests of these two States are opposed to the admission of Vermont into the Union, and if the case of the Western territory were once removed, they would instantly divide from the Eastern States in the case of Vermont. Of this Massachusetts & Connecticut are not insensible, and therefore find their advantage in keeping the territorial Controversy pending. Connecticut may likewise conceive some analogy between her claim to the Western Country & that of Virginia, and that the acceptance of the cession of the latter, would influence her sentiments in the controversy between the former & Pennsylvania.

The Western claims are espoused by Virga. N & S. Carolinas, Georgia & N. York, all of these States being interested therein S. Carolina is the least so. The claim of N. York is very extensive, but her title very flimsy. She

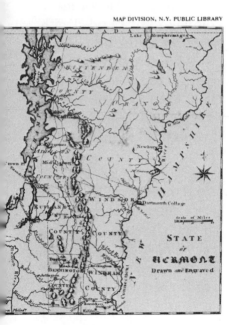

Vermont did not become a state until 1791, almost ten years after Madison wrote his analysis.

urges it more with the hope of obtaining some advantage, or credit, by its cession, than of ever maintaining it. If this Cession should be accepted, and the affair of Vermont terminated, as these are the only ties which unite her with the Southern States, she will immediately connect her policy with that of the Eastern States; as far at least, as the remains of former prejudices will permit.

The vexing question of western lands would be settled at last in 1784, more or less on Virginia's terms. The Virginia empire became the foundation of American empire. Coveting the West, the Virginians also coveted the navigation of the Mississippi, without which the Transappalachian lands would be next to worthless. Spain ruled west of the Mississippi and sought the return of the Floridas from Britain. Aiming at this conquest, Spain had no intention of spoiling it by inviting the imperious Americans to navigate the Mississippi through New Orleans to the Gulf. France sided with Spain. It was a clear case of conflicting ambitions between the new nation and its allies. The United States needed Spanish help in the war, but must the Mississippi be sacrificed to obtain it? In August, 1779, when Congress drew up preliminary peace terms, the answer had been no. The United States demanded free navigation of the Mississippi, and John Jay, the American Minister to Spain, was so instructed. Jay quickly ran into trouble at Madrid. Spain would not throw herself into the war unless the Americans receded on the Mississippi. In August, 1780, Jay wrote to Congress asking for clarification of his instructions. Madison came into the affair at this point. He steered through Congress a report that had been written by his colleague Jones reaffirming the American ultimatum. Then, in October, Madison drafted new instructions to Jay. The first of many important diplomatic papers from his pen, it was also a landmark statement of American policy on the Mississippi. He took up the matter of navigation and commerce after making a defense of the American territorial claim to the 31st parallel, the northern boundary of the Floridas.

[October 17, 1780]

The next object of the instructions is the free navigation of the Mississippi for the citizens of the United States in common with the subjects of his C M [Catholic Majesty].

On this subject the same inference may be made from Art: 7 of the Treaty of Paris [1763] which stipulates this right in the amplest manner to the King of G. Britain, and the devolution of it to the United States as was applied to the territorial claims of the latter. Nor can Congress hesitate to believe that even if no such right could be inferred from that treaty that the generosity of his C. M.

would suffer the inhabitants of these States to be put into a worse condition in this respect by their alliance with him in the character of a sovereign people, than they were in when subjects of a power who was always ready to turn their force against the Majesty; especially as one of the great objects of the proposed alliance is to give greater effect to the common exertions for disarming that power of the faculty of disturbing others.

Besides, as the United States have an indisputable right to the possession of the East bank of the Mississippi for a very great distance, and the navigation of that river will essentially tend to the prosperity and advantage of the Citizens of the United States that may reside on the Mississippi or the waters running into it, it is conceived that the circumstance of Spain's being in possession of the banks on both sides near its mouth, cannot be deemed a natural or equitable bar to the free use of the river. Such a principle would authorize a nation disposed to take advantage of circumstances to contravene the clear indications of nature and providence, and the general good of mankind.

The Usage of nations accordingly seems in such cases to have given to those holding the mouth or lower parts of a river no right against those above them, except the right of imposing a moderate toll, and that on the equitable supposition that such toll is due for the expence and trouble the former may have been put to.

"An *innocent passage* (says Vattel) [a Swiss jurist] is due to all nations with whom a State is at peace; and this duty comprehends troops equally with individuals." If a right to a passage by land through other countries may be claimed for troops which are employed in the destruction of Mankind; how much more may a passage by water be claimed for commerce which is beneficial to all nations.

Here again it ought not to be concealed that the inconveniences which must be felt by the inhabitants on the waters running westwardly under an exclusion from the free use of the Mississippi would be a constant and increasing source of disquietude on their part, of more rigorous precautions on the part of Spain, and of an irritation on both parts, which it is equally the interest and duty of both to guard against.

But notwithstanding the equitable claim of the United

CULVER PICTURES, INC.

Early view on the upper Mississippi

*First page of the new instructions
Madison drafted for Jay in Madrid
on navigation of the Mississippi*

States to the *free* navigation of the Mississippi and its great importance to them, Congress have so strong a disposition to conform to the desires of his C. M that they have agreed that such equitable regulations may be entered into as may be a Requisite security against contraband; provided the point of right be not relinquished and *a free port or ports below the 31st: degree of N. L. and accessible to Merchant ships be stipulated to them.*

The reason why a port or ports as thus described was required must be obvious. Without such a stipulation the free use of the Mississippi would in fact amount to no more that a free intercourse with New Orleans and the other ports of Louisiana. From the rapid current of this river it is well known that it must be navigated by vessels of a peculiar construction and which will be unfit to go to sea. Unless therefore some place be assigned to the U.S. where the produce carried down the river and the merchandis [a]rriving from abroad may be reposited till they can be respectively taken away by the proper vessels there can be no such thing as a foreign trade.

There is a remaining consideration respecting the navigation of the Mississippi, which deeply concerns the maritime powers in general but more particularly their most Christian and Catholic Majesties. The Country watered by the Ohio with its large branches having their sources near the lakes on one side, and those running N. Westward and falling into it on the other sides will appear from a single glance on a map to be of vast extent. The circumstance of its being so finely watered, added to the singular fertility of its soil and other advantages presented by a new country, will occasion a rapidity of population not easy to be conceived. The spirit of emigration has already shewn itself in a very strong degree, notwithstanding the many impediments which discourage it. The principal of these impediments is the war with Britain which can not spare a force sufficient to protect the emigrants against the incursions of the Savages. In a very few years after peace shall take place this Country will certainly be overspread with inhabitants. In like manner as in all other new settlements, agriculture, not manufactures will be their employment. They will raise wheat corn Beef Pork tobacco hemp flax and in the southern parts perhaps, rice and indigo in great quantities. On the other hand their consumption of foreign manufactures will be in proportion, if they can be exchanged for the produce of their soil. There are but two channels through which such commerce can be carried on—the first is down the river Mississippi—the other is up the rivers having their sources near the lakes, thence by short portages to the lakes or the rivers falling into them, and thence through the lakes and down the St. Lawrence. The first of these channels is manifestly the most natural and by far the most advantageous. Should it however be obstructed, the second will be found far from an impracticable. If no obstructions should be thrown in its course down the Mississippi, the exports from this immense tract of Country will not only supply an abundance of all necessaries for the W. Indies Islands, but serve for a valuable basis of general trade, of which the rising spirit of commerce in France & Spain will no doubt particularly avail itself. The imports will be proportionally extensive and from the climate as well as other causes will consist in a great degree of the manufactures of the same countries. On the other hand should obstructions in the Mississippi force this trade into a contrary direction through Canada, France and Spain and the other maritime powers will not only lose the immediate benefit of it to themselves, but they will also suffer by the advantage it will give to G. Britain. So fair a prospect would not escape the commercial sagacity of this nation. She would embrace it with avidity; she would cherish it with the most studious care; and should she succeed in fixing it in that channel, the loss of her exclusive possession of the trade of the United States might prove a much less decisive blow to her maritime preeminence and tyranny than has been calculated.

These were brave words. But in the fall of 1780, when Cornwallis was marching through the Carolinas and Virginia lay defenseless before the enemy, the United States could not place the future interests of the West ahead of survival. Theodorick Bland, the only other Virginian then in Congress, broke with Madison on the Mississippi question. The two men were frequently at odds; they belonged to different factions. In this case Bland was responding to fears that peace would be negotiated by the Russian-led League of Armed Neutrality on the basis of *uti possidetis*, that is, a peace in which the belligerents would retain the territories they held at the time the agreement was signed. Accordingly, Georgia and South

Theodorick Bland

Carolina would remain British colonies. Bland urged the Virginia legislature to drop the Mississippi demand in exchange for military assistance from Spain, which was urgently needed. Of this discouraging development Madison wrote to Jones.

Philada. Novr. 25th. 1780

I informed you some time ago that the instructions to Mr. Jay had passed Congress in a form which was entirely to my mind. I since informed you that a Committee was preparing a letter to him explanatory of the principles & objects of the instructions. This letter also passed in a form equally satisfactory. I did not suppose that any thing further would be done on the subject, at least till further intelligence should arrive from Mr. Jay. It now appears that I was mistaken. The Delegates from Georgia & South Carolina, apprehensive that a *Uti possidetis* may be obtruded on the belligerent powers by the armed neutrality in Europe and hoping that the accession of Spain to the Alliance will give greater concert & success to the military operations that may be pursued for the recovery of these States, and likewise add weight to the means that may be used for obviating a *Uti possidetis*, have moved for a reconsideration of the Instructions in order to empower Mr. Jay in case of necessity to yield to the claims of Spain on condition of her guarantieng our independence and affording us a handsome subsidy. The expediency of such a motion is further urged from the dangerous negociations now on foot by British Emissaries for detaching Spain from the war. Wednesday last was assigned for the consideration of this motion and it has continued the order of the day ever since without being taken up. What the fate of it will be I do not predict; but whatever its own fate may [be] it must do mischief in its operation. It will not probably be concealed that such a motion has been made & supported, and the weight which our demands would derive from unanimity & decision must be lost. I flatter myself however that Congress will see the impropriety of sacrificing the acknowledged limits and claims of any State without the express concurrence of such State. Obsticles enough will be thrown in the way of peace, if [it] is to be bid for at the expence of particular members of the Union. The Eastern States must on the first suggestion take the alarm for their fisheries. If they will not support other States in their rights, they cannot expect to be supported themselves when theirs come into question.

In this important business, which so deeply affects the claims & interests of Virginia & which I know she has so much at heart, I have not the satisfaction to harmonise in Sentiment with my Colleague [Bland]. He has embraced an opinion that we have no just claim to the subject in controversy between us & Spain, and that it is the interest of Virginia not to adhere to it. Under this impression he drew up a letter to the Executive to be communicated to the Legislature, stating in general the difficulty Congress might be under, & calling their attention ,to a revision of their instructions to their Delegates on the subject. I was obliged to object to such a step, and in order to prevent it observed that the instructions were given by the Legislation of Virga. on mature consideration of the case, & on a supposition that Spain would make the demands she has done . . . that Mr. Jay's last despatches encouraged us to expect that Spain would not be inflexible if we wer[e] so, that [we] might every day expect to have more satisfactory information from him. that finally if it should be thought expedient to listen to the pretensions of Spain, it would be best before we took any decisive step in the matter to take the Counsel of those who best know the interests & have the greatest influence on the opinions of our Constituents, that as you were both a member of Congress & of the Legislature & were not with the latter, you would be an unexceptionable medium for effecting this, and that I would write to you for the purpose, by the first safe conveyance.

These objections had not the weight with my Colleague which they had with me. He adhered to his first determination & has I believe sent the letter above mentioned by Mr. Walker who will I suppose soon forward it to the Governour. You will readily conceive the embarrassments this affair must have cost me. All I have to ask of you is that if my refusing to concur with my Colleague in recommending to the legislature a revision of their instructions should be misconstrued by any, you will be so good as to place it in its true light, and if you agree with me as to the danger of giving express power to concede, or the inexpediency of conceding at all, that you will consult with gentlemen of the above description and acquaint me with the result.

John Jay at the time of his mission to Spain, in a portrait by Caleb Boyle

For several weeks Madison held out against any change of policy. Early in the new year, however, amidst the devastation left by the traitor Arnold's invasion of the state, the Virginia assembly reversed itself, and Madison grudgingly shelved the Mississippi demand for the duration of the war. He did not yield the principle or the interest behind that demand. The right of navigation of the Mississippi was essential to the Union, in his opinion, and he would pursue that right until it was finally wrested from Spain in 1795. Cornwallis followed Arnold into Virginia. The state was terrorized from the Chesapeake to the Blue Ridge. Outraged by the enemy's "atrocities," Madison formed a consuming hatred of Great Britain. His report to Philip Mazzei, an Italian who had lived in Virginia, suggests the inflamed state of his feelings.

> Philada. July 7th. 1781
>
> No description can give you an adequate idea of the barbarity with which the Enemy have conducted the war in the Southern States. Every outrage which humanity could suffer has been committed by them. Desolation rather than conquest seems to have been their object. They have acted more like desperate bands of Robbers or Buccaneers than like a nation making war for dominion. Negroes, Horses, Tobacco &c not the standards and arms of their antagonists are the trophies which display their success. Rapes, murders & the whole catalogue of individual cruelties, not protection & the distribution of justice are the acts which characterize the sp[h]ere of their usurped Jurisdiction. The advantage we derive from such proceedings would, if they were purchased in other terms than the distresses of our Citizens, fully compensate for the injury occurring to the public. They are a daily lesson to the people of the U. States of the necessity of perseverance in the contest, and where ever the pressure of their local tyranny is removed the subjects of it rise up as one man to avenge their wrongs and prevent a repetition of them. Those who have possessed a latent partiality for them as their resentments are embittered by their disappointments generally feel most sensibly their injuries & insults and are the foremost in retaliating them. It is much to be regretted that these things are so little known in Europe. Were they published to the World in their true colours, the British nation would be hated by all nations as much as they have heretofore been feared by any, and all nations would be sensible of the policy of abridging a power which nothing else can prevent the abuse of.

Gallant action in Amelia County, Virginia, by Peter Francisco (above) who fought his way clear of British dragoons; French troops marching toward Yorktown (opposite)

Three months later, Madison asked Congress to issue a manifesto directing field commanders to retaliate for the firing of American towns and villages by executing enemy officers held as prisoners of war. Congress tabled the proposal, nor would Congress support his opposition to treaty provision for the restitution of property belonging to British subjects. The prospects of a "glorious peace"—a peace laid in victory—brightened in October, 1781, upon the surrender of Cornwallis at Yorktown. "With what hope or with what view can they [the British] try the fortunes of another campaign?" Madison asked, adding "it seems scarcely possible for them much longer to shut their ears against the voice of peace." In his posture toward the negotiation of peace, Madison adhered to the French alliance. In June, 1781, when victory was still a dream, Congress had instructed its peace commission to seek little more than the recognition of American independence and to be governed in all matters by French advice. A year later, as negotiations actually began in Paris, Congress not only raised its sights but spurned the indignity of subservience to France. The Lee-Adams faction led this anti-Gallic revolt. Arthur Lee himself, now a Virginia delegate, offered a resolution to revoke the clause placing the American commissioners on cue from Versailles. Opposed to revocation, Madison spoke against a milder substitute for Lee's motion. His remarks were recorded in Secretary Charles Thomson's notes of the debate.

> "Debates in the Congress" [August 8, 1782]
> Mr. Madison grants that the instructions given are a sacrifice of national dignity. But it was a sacrifice of dignity to policy. The situation of affairs and circumstances at the time rendered this sacrifice necessary. Nothing essential is given up, nor did it render our situation less precarious than it was before; nay he was per-

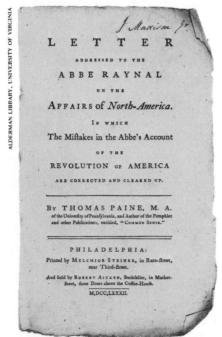

In October, 1781, Madison drafted a "Manifesto" (above) seeking retaliation against the British; below, a pamphlet on the Revolution that survives from his library

suaded that this mark of confidence gave an additional security to our interests as the Court of France must be sensible that the odium of unequal or hard conditions will now rest wholly on her. At least he was sure that the instructions given did not weaken that security. Our interests are as safe in her hands now as they were before or as if the ministers were left wholly to their discretion. Our ministers may still, notwithstanding the instructions given, state & assert our claims and contend with the utmost earnestness for our rights, and it is only in the last extremity when all their pleas, all their reasoning and all their most earnest endeavours prove ineffectual that they are ultimately to govern themselves by the advice and opinion of the Court of France; and must not this have been the case if the instructions had never been given? France has voluntarily bound herself by the treaties she has entered into with us to secure and guarantee our independence & sovereignty absolute and unlimited as well in matters of government as commerce. What indication has she given of any alteration of sentiment or conduct towards us? It is her interest as well as policy to secure the affections of the people of these States and forever separate us from G. Britain. She can never think us formidable to her while we continue absolutely independent, nor will she ever object to our enlarging our boundaries or increasing our commerce & naval power unless we give her reason to suspect a want of confidence in her and a disposition to reunite ourselves with her ancient enemy. In that case interest and policy will both unite and induce her to keep us as weak as possible. Whether withdrawing our confidence at this critical moment will not give just grounds of suspicion and jealousy he leaves gentlemen to determine. There was a passage in Mr Jay's letter lately read which made a strong impression on him; he did not know whether it made the same on others. He meant that passage which mentioned the fears and suspicions occasioned by the late change in the British administration, lest the men now in office who had always professed themselves friends to America and had in such severe terms condemned the war might influence the councils and conduct of the Americans. The withdrawing the instructions given on the 15th June, 1781 ... will increase that jealousy.

Let us consider how it will operate on Great Britain. Tired with the war and disappointed in all her attempts to separate us from France, there is reason to think there are serious thoughts of peace, but flushed with her late success [a defeat of the French Fleet in the West Indies] and flattered with the hopes of rising dissentions & jealousies between us & the other belligerent, will she not be encouraged to prosecute the war with new vigour & try by redoubled efforts to reduce us to her power?

But it is said our dignity is stained, and that we must revoke the instructions in order to wipe off that stain and restore its lustre. But will this do? Will it repair our loss of dignity in the eyes of the nations of Europe to convince them we are a people unstable in our councils & measures, governed wholly by circumstances, *abject & profuse* of promises when in distress and difficulties, but who veer about on a change of circumstances & on whose promises and professions no reliance can be placed? In a word, continued he, I am persuaded that a change in the instructions will not add to our security. I am persuaded that it will give umbrage to our ally, and by a seeming act of ingratitude or of diffidence awaken her suspicions and jealousies, and abate her zeal in our favour. I am persuaded that the umbrage and jealousy which this measure will excite will be prejudicial to us and will give encouragement to our enemy to prosecute

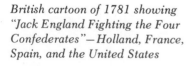

British cartoon of 1781 showing "Jack England Fighting the Four Confederates"—Holland, France, Spain, and the United States

the war. I am persuaded it is now too late to alter, and that withdrawing our confidence will not cure the wound given to our national dignity. For all these reasons I shall be against touching the instructions given. But if any member thinks that anything farther can be done to secure to the United States the several objects claimed, by them, I shall have no objections to that, it being well understood that no encroachment is to be made on the instructions given, but they are to remain in their full force. I shall therefore move that the motion before the house be postponed.

Madison prevailed. The motion was postponed, only to be renewed in December with the same result. Dispatches from two of the commissioners, Jay and Adams, had refueled the hostility to France in Congress. Like the third commissioner, Franklin, Madison was well aware of Versailles's concern to hold the Americans in check and to deny their claim to the Newfoundland fisheries and their ambitions in the West; but, again like Franklin, he felt that the country had placed its trust to France at a desperate time, that any withdrawal of confidence would risk the loss of French aid and support and draw down upon the new nation "the reproach of ingratitude," and, finally, that the United States was "more in danger of being seduced by Britain than sacrificed by France." If American and French interests did not perfectly coincide, as on the Mississippi, they

Instructions drafted by Madison to peace commissioners in 1782 (right); and the Department of Foreign Affairs where the Proclamation of Peace was drafted in 1783 (above)

*British cartoon of 1783 entitled
"Blessed are the Peace Makers"*

were not "diametrically opposed." In peace as in war Britain remained the enemy in Madison's eyes. For that reason alone it was necessary to maintain the French alliance.

News of the preliminary peace treaty with Great Britain reached Philadelphia in March, 1783. Madison thought the terms "extremely liberal." Britain recognized the independence of the United States, gave the Americans liberty to fish in Newfoundland waters, agreed to the Mississippi as the western boundary, and, so far as it was Britain's to grant, consented to the right of navigation of that great river. Madison was nevertheless disturbed. The American commissioners had been decoyed by their British counterparts into negotiating independently of the French ministry. "In this business," he wrote cryptically to a friend, "Jay has taken the lead & proceeded to a length of what you can form little idea. Adams has followed with cordiality. Franklin has been dragged into it." Moreover, the treaty contained a secret article on the Florida boundary that put the new nation in the dishonorable position of betraying its allies. (If in the treaty to come between Britain and Spain the former retained the Floridas, the boundary would be one hundred miles north of where it would be if the Floridas passed to Spain, as they did.) Madison and his friends cried "betrayal," but the treaty stood.

The nation had won its independence, but could it survive? Could it hold the West and secure its frontiers against the British to the north and the Spanish to the south? Could it recover old markets within the British commercial system or, excluded from that, find new markets for its products? Above all, could it create a government strong enough to bind the quarreling states and attend the national interest? Since his entrance into Congress, Madison had been a dedicated nationalist. He advocated financial independence of the Confederation from the member states; he advocated the reform of Congress and the creation of executive departments; he advocated vesting Congress with all the means necessary to carry out its powers.

Scarcely had the Articles of Confederation gone into effect than he proposed an amendment—which was never adopted—authorizing Congress to *enforce* obedience upon the states. Of this he wrote candidly to Jefferson.

Philada. April 16th. 1781

The necessity of arming Congress with coercive powers arises from the shameful deficiency of some of the States which are most capable of yielding their apportioned supplies, and the military exactions to which others already exhausted by the enemy and our own troops are in consequence exposed. Without such powers too in the general government, the whole confederacy may be insulted and the most salutary measures frustrated by the most inconsiderable State in the Union. At a time when all the other States were submitting to the loss and inconveniency of an embargo on their exports, Delaware absolutely declined coming into the measure, and not only defeated the general object of it, but enriched herself at the expense of those who did their duty.

The expediency however of making the proposed application to the States will depend on the probability of their complying with it. If they should refuse, Congress will be in a worse situation than at present: for as the confederation now stands, and according to the nature even of alliances much less intimate, there is an implied right of coer[c]io[n] against the delinquent party, and the exercise of it by Congress whenever a palpable necessity occurs will probably be acquiesced in.

It may be asked perhaps by what means Congress could exercise such a power if the States were to invest them with it? As long as there is a regular army on foot a small detachment from it, acting under Civil authority, would at any time render a voluntary contribution of supplies due from a State, an eligible alternative. But there is a still more easy and efficacious mode. The situation of most of the States is such, that two or three vessels of force employed against their trade will make it their interest to yield prompt obidience to all just requisitions on them. With respect to those States that have little or no foreign trade of their own it is provided that all inland trade with such states as supply them with foreign merchandize may be interdicted and the concurrence of the latter may be enforced in case of refusal by operations on their foreign trade.

There is a collateral reason which interests the States

Madison's committee report of June 19, 1782, which recommended suppressing "illicit and infamous" trade with the enemy

*Portion of Madison's expense
account as a delegate in Congress*

who are feeble in maritime resources, in such a plan. If a naval armament was considered as the proper instrument of general Government, it would be both preserved in a respectable State in time of peace, and it would be an object to mann it with Citizens taken in due proportio[ns] from every State. A Navy so formed and under the orders of the general Council of the States, would not only be a guard against aggression & insults from abroad; but without it what is to protect the Southern States for many years to come against the insults & aggressions of their N. Brethren.

Money became even more of a problem as the pressures of war lifted. The state legislatures, with problems enough of their own and no longer under compulsion to unite against a common enemy, repeatedly failed to meet the requisitions of Congress. This seeming indifference extended to the states' delegates in Philadelphia. Madison went months without pay, living on the funds advanced by the generous patriot Haym Salomon, as he explained in a letter to Edmund Randolph, Virginia's Attorney General.

September 30. 1782

The remittance to Col: Bland is a source of hope to his brethren. I am almost ashamed to reiterate my wants so incessantly to you, but they begin to be so urgent that it is impossible to suppress them. The kindness of our little friend in Front Street near the Coffee House is a fund which will preserve me from extremities, but I never resort to it without great mortification, as he obstinately rejects all recompense. The price of money is so usurious that he thinks it ought to be extorted from none but those who aim at profitiable speculations. To a necessitous Delegate he gratuitously spares a supply out of his private stock.

Madison was a leading member of the small cadre of nationalists that formed in Congress in 1781. Centered around Robert Morris, it was composed mainly of young men—men who had made their careers in Congress or the Continental Army—and it overlapped the "French party," just as the opposition to centralization overlapped the Lee-Adams faction. The paramount plank in the nationalists' platform was an independent revenue to be obtained by a uniform tax on imports. This "impost," as it was called, would enable Congress to pay the army, service the huge debt, and meet the other needs of the Confederation. Behind this fiscal necessity was a shrewd political calculation. By attaching the interests of creditors and soldiers to Congress, the central government would be strengthened at the expense of the states. The first attempt at an impost failed in November, 1782. Congress had asked the states to ratify an amendment to the Articles of Confederation empowering Congress to levy a duty of 5 percent ad valorem on imports. Twelve legislatures ratified; Rhode Island stubbornly refused. And the Articles could be changed only with unanimous consent. More decisive in the defeat, however, was Virginia's repeal in December, 1782, of what it had earlier approved. Bewildered and mortified, Madison expressed himself in letters to Randolph who, having just retired from Congress, took up the nationalist cause in Richmond.

Madison's notes on the debates in Congress for November 4, 1782

Philada. Novr. 26th. 1782

The obstinacy of Rhode Island in rejecting the Impost, is a subject of very general and pointed crimination not only among the public creditors and their friends who deem it equivalent to a denial of justice but among the most enlightened patrons of the foederal interests who pronounce it a blow to our credit abroad as well as our future credit at home And in truth who can combine this consideration with the paltry payments on the last re-requisition of Congress and not shudder at the prospect. This obstinacy on the part of R. I. is supposed, on good grounds, to be much cherished by the limited manner in which other states have acceded to the impost from which she infers a latent repugnance to the measure. Would it not then be prudent in Virginia to revise and enlarge her act of compliance? If her example should prove less efficatious than might be wished it would at least have a conciliating effect on other states and gain her general credit. I see no possible objection; unless indeed, she wishes the plan to be frustrated; in which case I can only give it as my firm opinion that a thorough knowledge of public affairs would speedily reconcile her to it. If your own ideas correspond with those here expressed, and the temper of the Legislature be not unfavorable, you will give such suggestions as may be best adapted to the object, and make them the subject of a future paragraph.

Philadelphia, January 22, 1783

The repeal of the impost act of Virginia is still considered as covered with some degree of mystery. . . . Many have surmised that the enmity of Doctor Lee against Morris is at the bottom of it. But had that been the case, it can scarcely be supposed that the repeal would have passed so quietly. By this time, I presume, you will be able to furnish me with its true history, and I ask the favor of you to do it. Virginia could never have cut off this source of public relief at a more unlucky crisis than when she is protesting her inability to comply with the continental requisitions. She will, I hope, be yet made sensible of the impropriety of the step she has taken, and make amends by a more liberal grant. Congress cannot abandon the plan as long as there is a spark of hope. Nay, other plans on a like principle must be added. Justice, gratitude, our reputation abroad, and our tranquility at home, require provision for a debt of not less than fifty millions of dollars, and I pronounce that this provision will not be adequately met by separate acts of the States. If there are not revenue laws which operate at the same time through all the States, and are exempt from the control of each—the mutual jealousies which begin already to appear among them all will assuredly defraud both our foreign and domestic creditors of their just claims.

The deputies of the army are still here, urging the objects of their mission. Congress are thoroughly impressed with the justice of time, and are disposed to do every thing which depends on them. But what can a Virginia Delegate say to them, whose constituents declare that they are unable to make the necessary contributions, and unwilling to establish funds for obtaining them elsewere?

Silhouette of James Madison, by Joseph Sansom, made in Philadelphia while he was a member of Congress

The nationalists at once renewed their campaign for a permanent revenue. The deputation from the army proved a powerful incentive, while Morris's threatened resignation evoked images of impending chaos. Creditors were turning to the state governments to receive their due, and, of course, if the states took over the debt, there would be no rock upon which to build a national government. Madison and his friends spoke of Congress becoming a mere "rope of sand," to which Arthur Lee replied, "he had rather see Congress a rope of sand than a rod of Iron." The debate raged for two months. Madison kept Randolph posted on its progress.

Philada. Feby. 25th. 1783.

Congress are still engaged on the subject of providing adequate revenues for the public debts, particularly that due to the army. The recommendation of the Impost will be renewed with perhaps some little variation, to which

Robert Morris

will be superadded probably a duty on a few enumerated articles. Master [John Francis] Mercer [another Virginia delegate] altho' he continues to be adverse to the measure declares now that he will not carry his opposition out of Congress. Whether any other general revenues will be recommended is very uncertain. A poll tax seems to be the only one sufficiently simple & equal for the purpose, and besides other objections to which even that is liable, the Constitution of Maryland which interdicts such a tax is an insuperable bar. The plan talked of by some for supplying the deficiency is to call on the States to provide each its proportion of a permanent revenue within itself, and, to appropriate it to the continental debt. The objections against this plan are that as the execution of it will depend on a unanimous & continued punctuality in the 13 States; it is a precarious basis for public credit—that the precariousness will be increased by mutual jealousies among the States that others may be sparing themselves exertions which they are submitting to; and that these jealousies will be still more increased by the mutual opinion which prevails that they are comparatively in advance to the U. States; an opinion which cannot be corrected without closing the accounts between all of them & the U. States; prerequisites to which are a valuation of the land, and a final discrimination of such parts of the separate expenditures of the States as ought to be transferred to the common mass, from such parts as ought in justice to fall on the particular States themselves. Some States also will contend and it would seem neither agst. the principles of justice nor the spirit of the Confederation, for a retrospective abatement of their share of the past debt according to their respective disabilities from year to year throughout the war. What will be the end of this complication of embarrassments time only can disclose. But a greater embarrassment than any is s[t]ill behind. The discontents and designs of the army are every day takeing a more solemn form. It is now whispered that they have not only resolved not to lay down their arms til justice shall be done them [but] that to prev[en]t surprize a public declaration will be made to that effect. It is added and I fear with too much certainty, that the influence of General [Washington] is rapidly decreaseing in the army insomuch that it is even in contemplation to substitute some less scrupulous guardian of their interests. . . .

You will suffer me to renew my exhortations to an exchange of your office [Attorney General] under the State for a seat in the Legislature. It depends much in my opinion on the measures which may be pursued by Congress & the several States within the ensuing period of 6 months whether prosperity & tranquility, or confusion and disunion are to be the fruits of the Revolution. The seeds of the latter are so thickly sown that nothing but the most enlightened and liberal policy will be able to stifle them. The easetern states particularly Massachusetts conceiv that compared with the Southern they are greatly in advance in the general account.

A respectable delegate from Massachusetts a few days ago being a little chafed by some expressions of Masters Lee and Mercer unfavorable to loan office creditors said that if notice was not to be obtained thro the general confederacy, the sooner it was known the better that some states might be forming other confederacys adequate to the purpose adding that some had suffered immensely from the want of a proportional compliance with deman[ds] for men & mon[ey] by others. However erroneous these ideas may be, do they not merit serious attention? Unless some amicable & adequate arrangements be speedily taken for adjusting all the subsisting accounts and discharging the public engagements, a dissolution of the union will be inevitable. Will not in that event the S[outhern] S[tates] which at sea will be opulent and weak, be an eascy prey to the easetern which will be powerful and rapacious? and particularly if supposed c[l]aims of justice are on the side of the latter will they not be a ready prete[x]t for reprisals? The consequence of such a situation would probably be that alliances would be sougt first by the weaker and then by the stronger party and this country be made subservi-[ent] to the wars and politics of Europe.

John Francis Mercer

Reluctantly, Madison was no longer insisting on the "whole loaf." In March he drafted a new impost plan more consistent with the character of the Confederation as a league of states. The tax would be limited to a period of twenty-five years and the revenue applied only to the principal and interest of the debt. Collectors would be appointed by the respective states which would retain the revenue until requisitioned by Congress. Madison's colleague from New York, Alexander Hamilton, scorned the compromise. It passed, however, as part of·a package containing a number of provisions in addition to the impost, and all this had now to run the gauntlet of the legislatures. In an artful address to the states, Madison explained the proposition in detail and concluded with an elevated appeal.

"Address to the States," April 26. 1783

The plan thus communicated and explained by Congress must now receive its fate from their Constituents. All the objects comprized in it are conceived to be of great importance to the happiness of this confederated republic, are necessary to render the fruits of the Revolution, a full reward for the blood, the toils, the cares and the calamities which have purchased it. But the object of which the necessity will be peculiarly felt, and which it is peculiarly the duty of Congress to inculcate, is the provision recommended for the national debt. Altho' this debt is greater than could have been wished, it is still less on the whole than could have been expected, and when referred to the cause in which it has been incurred, and compared with the burdens which wars of ambition and of vain glory have entailed on other nations, ought to be borne not only with cheerfulness but with pride. But the magnitude of the debt makes no part of the question. It is sufficient that the debt has been fairly contracted and that justice & good faith demand that it should be fully discharged. Congress had no option but between different modes of discharging it. The same option is the only one that can exist with the States. The mode which has after long & elaborate discussion been preferred, is, we are persuaded, the least objectionable of any that would have been equal to the purpose. Under this persuasion, we call upon the justice & plighted faith of the several States to give it its proper effect, to reflect on the consequences of rejecting it, and to remember that Congress will not be answerable for them.

If other motives than that of justice could be requisite on this occasion, no nation could ever feel stronger. For to whom are the debts to be paid?

To an Ally, in the first place, who to the exertion of his arms in support of our cause, has added the succours of his Treasurer; who to his important loans has added liberal donations; and whose loans themselves carry the impression of his magnimimity and friendship....

To individuals in a foreign country in the next place

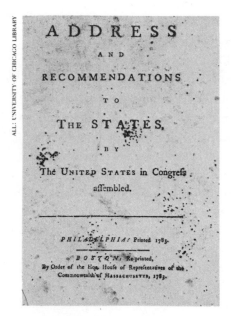

ADDRESS

AND

RECOMMENDATIONS

TO

THE STATES,

BY

The UNITED STATES in Congress assembled.

PHILADELPHIA: Printed 1783.

BOSTON: Re-printed,
By Order of the Hon. House of Representatives of the
Commonwealth of MASSACHUSETTS, 1783.

Madison's "Address to the States," printed in Philadelphia in 1783

who were the first to give so precious a token of their confidence in our justice, and of their friendship for our cause; and who are members of a republic which was second in espousing our rank among nations. . . .

Another class of Creditors is that illustrious & patriotic band of fellow Citizens, whose blood and bravery have defended the liberties of their Country, who have patiently borne, among other distresses the privation of their stipends, whilst the distresses of their Country disabled it from bestowing them; and who even now ask for no more than such a portion of their dues as will enable them to retire from the field of victory & glory into the bosom of peace & private citizenship, and for such effectual security for the residue of their claims as their Country is now unquestionably able to provide. . . .

The remaining class of Creditors is composed partly of such of our fellow Citizens as originally lent to the public the use of their funds or have since manifested most confidence in their Country by receiving transfers from the lenders; and partly of those whose property has been either advanced or assumed for the public service. To discriminate the merits of these several descriptions of creditors would be a task equally unnecessary & invidious. If the voice of humanity plead more loudly in favor of some than of others; the voice of policy, no less than of justice pleads in favor of all. A wise nation will never permit those who relieve the wants of their Country, or who rely most on its faith, its firmness and its resources, when either of them is distrusted, to suffer by the event.

Let it be remembered finally that it has ever been the pride and boast of America, that the rights for which she contended were the rights of human nature. By the blessing of the Author of these rights on the means exerted for their defence, they have prevailed against all opposition and form the basis of thirteen independant States. No instance has heretofore occurred, nor can any instance be expected hereafter to occur, in which the unadulterated forms of Republican Government can pretend to so fair an opportunity of justifying themselves by their fruits. In this view the Citizens of the U.S. are responsible for the greatest trust ever confided to a Political Society. If justice, good faith, honor, gratitude & all the other Qualities which enoble the character of a nation, and fulfil

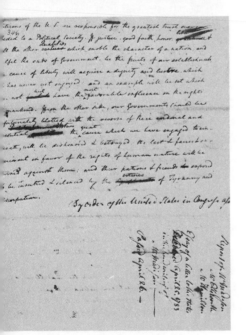

Two pages in Madison's handwriting of draft for "Address to the States"

*Elias Boudinot, president of
the Continental Congress*

the ends of Government, be the fruits of our establishments, the cause of liberty will acquire a dignity and
lustre, which it has never yet enjoyed; and an example
will be set which can not but have the most favorable
influence on the rights of mankind. If on the other side,
our Governments should be unfortunately blotted with
the reverse of these cardinal and essential Virtues, the
great cause which we have engaged to vindicate, will be
dishonored & betrayed: the last & fairest experiment in
favor of the rights of human nature will be turned against
them; and their patrons & friends exposed to be insulted
& silenced by the votaries of Tyranny and Usurpation.

Alas, the new plan—"the budget of Congress," as Madi-
son called it—would have no more success than the old. As peace came to
the United States, all incentive to tighten the continental belt seemed to
disappear. The Confederation became a work of futility, Congress a joke.
The ultimate disgrace struck on June 20 when a mutiny of soldiers drove
Congress from Philadelphia. Suddenly Madison found himself back in Princeton where the fleeing statesmen reconvened. His third annual term would
expire in November, and he had already planned to leave Congress. He had
not been home since March, 1780. He was tired. He was discouraged. The
nationalist cadre was breaking up. Hamilton was about to leave; Morris's
departure could be expected at any time. But Madison had an additional
reason: he had fallen in love. The young lady, only sixteen years old in
April, was Kitty (Catherine) Floyd, daughter of a New York delegate who
stayed under the same boardinghouse roof with Madison. Although there
was a rival for Kitty's affections in the person of a young medical student,
she and Madison quietly became engaged in the spring and expected to wed
at the end of the year, when Madison's term in Congress expired.

Jefferson, who encouraged this match, was also in Philadelphia, under
the same roof, during the early months of 1783. He had lost his wife the
previous September and, heeding the pleas of Madison and other friends to
return to service, had accepted congressional appointment as a peace commissioner. Peace came before he could embark for France, however. Stranded
in Philadelphia, he drew closer to Madison. The two men exchanged views
on many subjects, joined forces to reform the Virginia Constitution, and
concerted the first of several ciphers to be employed in their political correspondence. Jefferson was then preparing a catalogue of his personal library. From it and from other sources, Madison compiled a list of some three
hundred titles which he embodied in a report to Congress recommending
the establishment of a congressional library. He recorded the reasons for
this proposal and for its defeat in his notes of the congressional debate.

By His EXCELLENCY

Elias Boudinot, Esquire,

Prefident of the United States in Congrefs Affembled.

A PROCLAMATION.

WHEREAS a body of armed Soldiers in the fervice of the United States, and quartered in the Barracks of this City, having mutinoufly renounced their obedience to their Officers, did, on Saturday the Twenty-Fifth Day of this inftant, proceed, under the direction of their Serjeants, in a hoftile and threatning manner, to the Place in which Congrefs were affembled, and did furround the fame with Guards: And whereas Congrefs in confequence thereof, did on the fame Day, refolve," That the Prefident and Supreme Executive Council of this State " fhould be informed, that the authority of the United States having been, that Day, grofsly infulted by the " diforderly and menacing appearance of a body of armed Soldiers, about the Place within which Congrefs were affem- " bled; and that the Peace of this City being endangered by the motinous Difpofition of the faid Troops then in the " Barracks; it was, in the Opinion of Congrefs, neceffary, that effectual Meafures fhould be immediately taken for " fupporting the public Authority:" And alfo whereas Congrefs did at the fame Time appoint a Committee to confer with the faid Prefident and Supreme Executive Council on the practicability of carrying the faid Refolution into due effect: And alfo whereas the faid Committee have reported to me, that they have not received fatisfactory Affurances for expelling adequate and prompt exertions of this State for fupporting the Dignity of the federal Government: And alfo whereas the faid Soldiers ftill continue in a ftate of open Mutiny and Revolt, fo that the Dignity and Authority of the United States would be conftantly expofed to a repetition of Infult, whilft Congrefs fhall continue to fit in this City; I do therefore, by and with the Advice of the faid Committee, and according to the Powers and Authorities in me vefted for this Purpofe, hereby fummon the honourable the Delegates compofing the Congrefs of the United States, and every of them, to meet in Congrefs on Thurfday the Twenty Sixth Day of June inftant, at Princeton, in the ftate of New-Jerfey, in order that further and more effectual Meafures may be taken for fupprefling the prefent Revolt, and maintaining the Dignity and Authority of the United States, of which all Officers of the United States, civil and military, and all others whom it may concern, are defired to take Notice and govern themfelves accordingly.

GIVEN under my Hand and Seal at Philadelphia, in the ftate of Pennfylvania, this Twenty-Fourth Day of June, in the Year of Our Lord One Thoufand Seven Hundred and Eighty-Three, and of our Sovereignty and Independence the feventh.

ELIAS BOUDINOT.

Atteft,

SAMUEL STERETT, Private Secretary.

Philadelphia, Printed by DAVID C. CLAYPOOLE.

Boudinot issued this proclamation summoning congressmen to meet in Princeton after the mutiny of soldiers at Philadelphia.

"Notes on Debates," Thursday Jany. 23 [1783]

In favr. of the Rept. it was urged as indispensable that Congress sd. have at all times at command such authors on the law of Nations, treaties Negociations &c as wd. render their proceedings in such cases conformable to propriety; and it was observed that the want of this information was manifest in several important acts of Congress. It was further observed that no time ought to be lost in collecting every book & tract which related to American Antiquities & the affairs of the U.S. since many of the most valuable of these were every day becoming extinct, & they were necessary not only as materials for a Hist: of the U.S. but might be rendered still more so by future pretensions agst. their rights from Spain or other powers which had shared in the discoveries & possessions of the New World. Agst. the Report were urged 1st. the inconveniency of advancing even a few hundred pounds at this crisis; 2dly. the difference of expence between procuring the books during the war & after a peace. These objections prevailed, by a considerable majority. A motion was then made by Mr. Wilson 2ded. by Mr. Madison to confine the purchase for the present to the most essential part of the books. This also was negatived.

After Jefferson's return to Virginia, Madison informed him, bluntly, of the discouraging state of public affairs and, delicately, of the miscarriage of his personal affair with Miss Floyd, who had apparently had a change of heart in favor of the medical student.

Philada. Aug: 11th. 1783.

At the date of my letter in April I expected to have had the pleasure by this time of being with you in Virginia. My disappointment has proceeded from several dilatory circumstances on which I had not calculated. One of them was the uncertain state into which the object I was then pursuing had been brought by one of those incidents to which such affairs are liable. The result has rendered the time [of] my return to Virga. less material, as the necessity of my visiting the State of N.Jy: no longer exists. It would be improper by this communication to send particular explanations, and perhaps needless to [trou]ble you with them at any time.... My journey to Virga. tho' still somewhat contingent in point of time cannot now be very long postponed. I need not I trust renew my assur-

Motion, in Madison's handwriting, to appoint Jefferson a peace commissioner in November, 1782

ances that it will not finally stop on this side of Monticello.

The reserve of our foreign Ministers still leaves us the sport of misinformations concerning the def[initive]: Treaty.... Congs. remain at Princeton utterly undecided both as to their ultimate seat and their intermediate residence. Very little business of moment has been yet done at the new Metropolis, except a ratification of the Treaty with Sweeden. In particular nothing has been [d]one as to a foreign establishment. With regard to an internal peace [es]tablishment, though it has been treated with less inattention, it has undergone little discussion. The Commander cheif has been invited to Princeton with a view to obtain his advice and sanction to the military branches of it, and is every day expected [t]here. The Budget of Congs. is likely to have the fate of many of their other propositions to the States. Delaware is the only one among those which have bestowed a consideration on it that has acceded in toto. Several Legislatures have adjourned without giving even that mark of their [co]ndescension. In the Southern States a jealousy of Congressional usur[p]ations is likely to be the bane of the system: in the Eastern an aversion to the half-pay [pensions for veterans] provided for by it. New Jersey & Maryland have adopted the impost, the other funds recommended being passed for one year only by one of these States, and postponed by the other....Massts. has in the election of delegates for the ensuing year stigmatized the concurrence of those now in place in the provision for half-pay, by substituting a new representation; and has sent a Memorial to Congs. which I am told is pregnant with the most penurious ideas not only on that subject but on several others which concern the national honor & dignity. This picture of our affairs is not a flattering one; but we have been witnesses of so many cases in which evils & errors have been the parents of their own remedy, that we can not but view it with the consolations of hope.

Madison wrote to Jefferson (above) in April, 1783, in cipher (crossed-out passages in letter at left) to tell him of the progress of his romance with Catherine Floyd.

Jefferson was back in Philadelphia in October, this time to take a Virginia seat in Congress. That vagabond crew, it turned out, would next meet in Annapolis. Madison wound up his affairs in Philadelphia and, on his way home, accompanied Jefferson as far as the Maryland capital. Before leaving he presumably sold, in some form, his slave Billy who had been his personal servant for many years. Explaining his dilemma to his father, Madison revealed both his abhorrence of slavery and his complicity in the wretched system.

> Philada. Sepr. 8. 1783.
> On a view of all circumstances I have judged it most prudent not to force Billey back to Va. even if could be done; and have accordingly taken measures for his final separation from me. I am persuaded his mind is too thoroughly tainted to be a fit companion for fellow slaves in Virga. The laws here do not admit of his being sold for more than 7 years [of servitude]. I do not expect to get near the worth of him; but cannot think of punishing him by transportation merely for coveting that liberty for which we have paid the price of so much blood, and have proclaimed so often to be the right, & worthy the pursuit, of every human being.

Chapter *3*

Radical Reformer

A t home with his family, Madison seemed uncertain of what to do with himself. His father, hale and hearty, and his younger brother Ambrose looked after Montpelier; the long absent son was not needed in this work, and such was his distaste for slavery that he occasionally fancied removing himself altogether from Virginia. He resumed the study of law, thinking perhaps to attain independence through this profession; but, as before, his efforts were halfhearted. *Coke upon Littleton*, part of the great seventeenth-century work on English law, occupied the morning hours, he later recalled; in the afternoon, he "indulged in miscellaneous reading, which embraced among other works of philosophical cast, those of Buffon whose views of nature, however fanciful and even absurd in some instances were highly attractive in others, and especially by the fascinating eloquence which distinguishes them." Jefferson had put him on to Buffon and then engaged Madison in his campaign to demolish the great naturalist's theory of biological degeneracy in the New World. With Jefferson's help, too, Madison was building his own library, giving first place to political titles, though not omitting the scientific and the literary. The older man sympathized with Madison's isolation in Orange and, knowing well his own need for companionship, proposed that he come to live in the neighborhood of Monticello as two other young friends, James Monroe and William Short, had already planned to do. "With such a society," wrote Jefferson, "I could once more venture home and lay myself up for the residue of life, quitting all its contentions which grow daily more and more insupportable." Jefferson knew of a farm only two miles from Monticello, but Madison declined the invitation, while drawing upon Jefferson for books and other scarce items.

> Orange [Virginia,] March 16. 1784
> The winter has been so severe that I have never renewed
> my call on the library of Monticello, and the time is now
> drawing so near when I may pass for a while into a dif-

ferent scene, that I shall await at least the return to my studies. . . . I lately got home the Trunk which contained my Buffon, but have barely entered upon him. My time begins already to be much less my own than during the winter blockade. I must leave to your discretion the occasional purchase of rare and valuable books, disregarding the risk of duplicates. You know tolerably well the objects of my curiosity. I will only particularize my wish of whatever may throw light on the general Constitution and droit public of the several confederacies which have existed. I observe in Boinauds Catalogue [a listing from a Philadelphia bookstore] several pieces on the Du[t]ch, the German and the Helvetic. The operations of our own must render all such lights of consequence. Books on the Law of N. and N. [Nature and Nations] fall within a similar remark. The tracts of Bynkershoek which you mention I must trouble you to get for me and in french if to be had rather than latin. Should the body of his works come nearly as cheap, as these select publications perhaps it may [be] worth considering whether the whole would not be preferable. Is not Wolfius also worth having. I recollect to have seen at Pritchards a copy of Hawkin's Abridgt. of Co: Litt: I would willingly take it if it be still there and you have an opportunity. A copy of Deane's letters which were printed in New York and which I failed to get before I left Philada. I should also be glad of. I use this freedom in confidence that you will be equally free in consulting your own conveniency whenever I encroach upon it; I hope you will be so particularly in the request I have to add. One of my parents would be considerably gratified with a pair of good spectacles which can not be got here. The particular readiness of Dudley to serve you inclines me to think that an order from you would be well executed. Will You therefore be so good as to get from him one of his best pebble and double jointed pair, for the age of fifty five or thereabouts with a good case; and forward them by the first safe conveyance to me at Orange or at Richmond as the case may be.

PRES'T. MADISON'S LIBRARY, AT AUCTION.

AT Orange Court House, Virginia, on Tuesday the 27th day of June, prox., being the day after the County Court of Orange in that month; I shall sell at public auction, to the highest bidder, that part of the Library of the late James Madison, which, in a recent division of his books with the University of Virginia, fell to the share of my testator; and at the same time I will sell other books, the property of my said testator. In all there are some

SEVEN OR EIGHT HUNDRED VOLUMES,

among which are many very rare and desirable works, some in Greek, some in Latin, numerous others in French, and yet more in English, in almost all the departments of Literature; and a few of them being in this manner exposed to sale only because the University possessed already copies of the same editions. The sale beginning on the day above mentioned, will be continued from day to day till all the books shall have been sold, on the following terms:

Cash will be required of each purchaser whose aggregate purchases shall amount to no more than Five dollars; those whose purchases shall exceed that amount, will have the privilege either to pay the cash or to give bond with approved security, bearing interest from the date, and payable six months thereafter.

ELHANON ROW, Administrator, with the will annexed of John P. Todd, dec'd.

May 30, 1854.

Madison's library, collected over the years, was bequeathed in part to the University of Virginia. The remainder was sold to pay gambling debts of his stepson, John Todd.

Madison's retirement was mercifully short. In the spring of 1784 the freeholders of Orange elected him to the House of Delegates, the lower house of the general assembly. He was in Richmond for the May session, returned home briefly, and then embarked on a northerly tour. Falling in with the Marquis de Lafayette, the gallant Frenchman who was himself on tour, Madison journeyed all the way to old Fort Stanwix deep in the Mohawk Valley west of Albany, New York. He would never travel so far again. The Mississippi question weighed on Madison's mind—he had written to Jefferson at length on the subject—and he did not hesitate to press his views on Lafayette, as he reported to Jefferson, then a commissioner in France and soon to succeed Franklin as American minister.

Philada. Sepr. 7th. 1784.

Some business, the need of exercise after a very sedentary period, and the view of extending my ramble into the Eastern States which I have long had a curiosity to see have brought me to this place.... At Baltimore I fell in with the Marquis de la Fayette returning from a visit to Mount Vernon. Wherever he passes he receives the most flattering tokens of sincere affection from all ranks. He did not propose to have left Virginia so soon but Genl. Washington was about setting out on a trip to the Ohio, and could not then accompany him on some visits as he wished to do. The present plan of the Marquis is to proceed immediately to New York, thence by Rhode Island to Boston, thence through Albany to Fort Stanwix where a treaty with the Indians is to be held the latter end of this month, thence to Virginia so as to meet the Legislature at Richmond. I have some thoughts of making this tour with him, but suspend my final resolution till I get to N.Y. whither I shall follow him in a day or two.

The relation in which the Marquis stands to France and America has induced me to enter into a free conversation with him on the subject of the Mississippi. I have endeavored emphatically to impress on him that the ideas of America and of Spain irreconciliably clash, that unless the mediation of France be effectually exerted an actual rupture is near at hand, that in such an event the connection between France and Spain will give the enemies of the former in America the fairest opportunity of involving her in our resentments against the latter and of introducing Great Brit. as a party with us against both, that America can not possibly be diverted from her object and therefore France is bound to set every engine at work to divert Spain from hers and that France has besides a great interest in a trade with the western country thro the Missisipi. I thought it not unwise also to suggest to him some of the considerations which seem to appeal

While a delegate in Richmond, Madison signed this declaration by the short-lived Constitutional Society of Virginia, whose alleged purpose was to revise the state constitution.

84

to the prudence of Spain. He admitted the force of every thing I said, told me he would write in the most [approving?] terms to the Count de Vergennes [the French Minister of Foreign Affairs] by the packet which will probably carry this and let me see his letter at N. York before he sends it. He thinks that Spain is bent on excluding us from the Missisipi and mentioned several anecdotes which happened while he was at Madrid in proof of it.

The business at Fort Stanwix was a boundary settlement with the Iroquois. Congress had sent commissioners, including General Oliver Wolcott and Arthur Lee, to negotiate, but as it happened the Marquis upstaged the Americans and confounded the British, the old allies of the Six Nations. Lafayette reaped new glory and doubtless contributed to the eventual treaty. Upon his return to Philadelphia, Madison gave Jefferson an amusing as well as insightful account of the proceedings.

Philada. Octr. 17. 1784

It seems that most of the Indian tribes particularly those of the Iroquois retain a strong predilection for the French and most of the latter an enthusiastic idea of the marquis. This idea has resulted from his being a Frenchman, the figure he has made during the war and the arrival of several important events which he foretold to them soon after he came to this country. Before he went to Fort Schuyler [another name for Stanwix] it had been suggested, either in compliment or sincerity that his presence and influence might be of material service to the treaty. At Albany the same thing had been said to him by General Wolcot. On his arrival at Fort S. Mr. [Samuel] Kirkland [a missionary] recommended an exertion of his influence as of essential consequence to the treaty, painting in the strongest colours the attachment of the Indians to his person, which seemed indeed to be verified by their caresses and the artifices employed by the British partizans to frustrate the objects of the treaty, among which was a pretext that the alliance between the United States and France was insincere and transitory and consequently the respect of the Indians for the later ought to be no motive for their respecting the former. Upon these circumstances the M. grounded a written message to the Commissioners before they got up intimating his disposition to render the United States any service his small influence over the Indians might put in his power and

Bust of Lafayette by Houdon
VIRGINIA STATE CAPITOL BUILDING

Indian Tribes of the United States, BY HENRY R. SCHOOLCRAFT, 1851

Atotarho, a founder of the Iroquois League, appears at right as a Medusa-headed figure; the Indian at center wears a British redcoat.

Plan of Fort Stanwix

desiring to know what the Commissioners would chuse him to say. The answer in Mr. Lee's hand consisted of polite acknowledgments and information that the Commissioners would be happy in affording him an opportunity of saying what ever he might wish forbearing to advise or suggest what it would be best for him to say. The M. perceived the caution but imputed it to Lee alone. As his stay however was to be very short it was necessary for him to take provisional measures before the arrival of the commissioners and particularly for calling in the Oneida Cheifs who were at their town. It fell to my lot to be consulted in his dilemma. My advice was that he should invite the chiefs in such a way as would give him an opportunity of addressing them publicly, if on a personal interview with the Commissioners it should be judged expedient; or of satisfying their expectations with a friendly entertainment in return for the civilities his visit to their town had met with. This advice was approved; but the Indians brought with them such ideas of his importance as no private reception would probably have been equal to. When the Commissioners arrived the M. consulted them in person. They were reserved, he was embarrassed. Finally they changed their plan and concurred explicitly in his making a Speech in form. He accordingly prepared one, communicated it to the Commissioners and publicly pronounced it, the Commissioners premising such an one as was thought proper to introduce his. The answer of the sachems, as well as the circumstances of the audience denoted the highest reverence for the orator. The cheif of the Oneidas said that the words which he had spoken to them early in the war had prevented them from being misled to the wrong side of it. During this scene and even during the whole stay of the M. he was the only conspicuous figure. The Commissioners were eclipsed. All of them probably felt it. Lee complained to me of the immoderate stress laid on the influence of the M., and evidently promoted his departure. The M. was not insensible of it, but consoled himself with the service which he thought the Indian speech would witness that he had rendered to the United States. I am persuaded that the transaction is also pleasing to him in another view as it will form a bright column in the gazettes of Europe, and that he will be impatient for its appearance there without seeing any mode in which it can happen of course. As it is blended with the proceedings of the Commissioners, it will probably not be published in America very soon, if at all. The time I have lately passed with the M. has given me a pretty thorough insight into his character. With great natural frankness of temper he unites much address; with very considerable talents, a strong thirst of praise and popularity. In his politics he says his three hobbyhorses are the alliance between France and the United States, the Union of the latter and the manumission of the slaves. The two former are the dearer to him as they are connected with his personal glory. The last does him real honor, as it is a proof of his humanity. In a word, I take him to be as amiable a man as his vanity will admit, and as sincere an American as any Frenchman can be; one whose past services gratitude obliges us to acknowledge and whose future friendship prudence requires us to cultivate.

First page of the treaty concluded at Fort Stanwix in October, 1784

During the period Jefferson lived in France Madison was his tireless informant, not only of the great events in Richmond and Philadelphia but of the little events at home; and in the two-way exchange of knowledge between the continents Madison was both recipient and contributor. Jefferson supplied him with the fascinating curiosities of the French capital—phosphorous matches, a pedometer, the new Argand cylinder lamp—and news of recent balloon ascensions. But mostly he supplied him with books. Although the choices were often Jefferson's, he endeavored to meet his friend's requests, as Madison gratefully acknowledged.

Orange [Virginia,] April 27. 1785.

I have received your two favors of Novr. 11 and Decr. 8.

Along with the former I received the two pamphlets on animal magnetism and the last aeronautic expedition, together with the phosphoretic matches. These articles were a great treat to my curiosity. . . . I thank you much for your attention to my literary wants. All the purchases you have made for me, are such as I should have made for myself with the same opportunities. You will oblige me by adding to them the Dictionary [of Law] in 13 vol. 4°. by Felice and others, also de Thou in French. If the utility of [the historical dictionary by] Moreri be not superseded by some better work I should be glad to have him too. I am afraid if I were to attempt a catalogue of my wants I should not only trouble you beyond measure, but exceed the limits which other considerations ought to prescribe to me. I cannot however abridge the commission you were so kind as to take on yourself in a former letter, of procuring me from time to time such books as may be "either old and curious or new and useful." Under this description will fall those particularised in my former letters, to wit treatises on the ancient or modern foederal republics, on the law of Nations, and the history natural and political of the New World; to which I will add such of the Greek and Roman authors where they can be got very cheap, as are worth having and are not on the common list of School classics. Other books which particularly occur, are the translation [French] of the Historians of the Roman Empire during its decline by _____, Paschals provincial letters—Don Ulloa in the Original— Lynnaeus best edition—Ordinances Marines—Collection of Tracts in french on the Œconomies of different nations. I forget the full title. It is much referred to by Smith on the wealth of nations. I am told a Monsr. Amelot has lately published his travels into China, which if they have any merit must be very entertaining. Of Buffon I have his original work of 31 vol., 10 vol. of Supplemt. and 16 vol. on birds. I shall be glad of the continuation as it may from time to time be published. I am so pleased with the new invented lamp that I shall not grudge two guineas for one of them. I have seen a pocket compass of somewhat larger diameter than a watch and which may be carried in the same way. It has a spring for stopping the vibration of the needle when not in use. One of these would be very convenient in case of a ramble into the Western Country. In my walks for exercise or

A list of books that Jefferson bought in Paris for James Madison

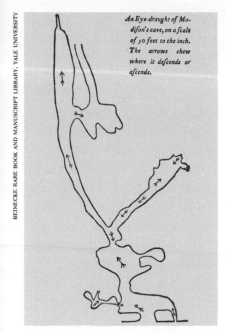

An Eye-draught of Madifon's cave, on a fcale of 50 feet to the inch. The arrows fhew where it defcends or afcends.

Jefferson's line drawing of a cave he described in Notes on Virginia

amusements, objects frequently present themselves, which it might be matter of curiosity to inspect, but which it is difficult or impossible to approach. A portable glass would consequently be a source of many little gratifications. I have fancied that such an one might be fitted into a Cane without making it too heavy. On the outside of the tube might be engraved a scale of inches &c. If such a project could be executed for a few Guineas I should be willing to submit to the price; if not, the best substitute I suppose will be a pocket-telescope, composed of several tubes so constructed as to slide the lesser into the greater. I should feel great remorse at troubling you with so many requests, if your kind and repeated offers did not stifle it in some measure. Your proposal for my replacing here advances for me without regard to the exchange is liable to no objection except that it will probably be too unequal in my favour. I beg that you will enable me as much as you can to keep those little matters balanced.

The balance was struck, imperfectly, by Madison's caring for Jefferson's nephews, the Carrs, and by dispatching American plants, seeds, specimens of animals, and other curiosities Jefferson wished to introduce to the Old World. To this enterprise, which was part of the vindication of American nature launched by Jefferson's *Notes on the State of Virginia*, Madison was a zealous friend. The two Virginians had often discussed the deficiencies and errors of the state constitution, and Madison upon entering the general assembly sought a convention for its reform. The people had had no vote in making the constitution; all power was concentrated in the legislative branch, which implied despotism on the theory of "separation of powers" derived from Montesquieu; representation was unequal, the court system inadequate, and fundamental personal liberties poorly protected. Unfortunately, as he had feared, Patrick Henry stood in "violent opposition," and reform was defeated. Henry held sway in the assembly. Because of his demagogic and parochial leadership, taxes were suspended, planters were secured from paying their prewar British debts, commerce languished, and Virginia retreated from her national responsibilities. Madison would emerge victorious in the end, but in the frustrating years 1785–87 he must have often felt, as Jefferson did, that the only thing to do was devoutly to pray for Henry's death.

Constitutional reform failing, Madison turned to statutory reform. He secured the printing of the *Report of the Committee of Revisors*, which Jefferson, George Wythe, and Edmund Pendleton had submitted to the legislature in 1779. Some of the revisors' reforms of colonial and English law had been enacted, but the original aim of a revised code had miscarried. Madison hoped to reverse this outcome or at least to see that the landmark bills of the revisal, "this mine of legislative wealth," became law. Among these were Jefferson's plan for establishing a public school system, his Bill for Proportioning Crimes and Punishments, and his Bill for Establishing Religious Freedom. With the last Madison scored a stunning legislative triumph. By 1780, the Anglican establishment was doomed in Virginia. Its friends, however, aided by religionists of other sects, had come up with a new principle in Church-State relations: government support of Christianity as the religion of the commonwealth. Under this principle all citizens would be taxed for the support of all Christian ministers regardless of sect. Earlier diverted, this "general assessment" plan was revived under Henry's auspices in 1784. Madison briefed Jefferson on the issue after the fall session.

Richmond Jany. 9th. 1785.

A petition that was submitted to the Virginia General Assembly during Madison's 1785 term by Virginians west of the Alleghenies

A resolution for a legal provision for the "teachers of Christian Religion" had early in the Session been proposed by Mr. Henry, and in spite of all the opposition that could be mustered, carried by 47 against 32 votes. Many Petitions from below the blue ridge had prayed for such a law; and though several from the presbyterian laity beyond it were in a contrary Stile, the Clergy of that Sect favoured it. The other sects seemed to be passive. The Resolution lay some weeks before a bill was brought in, and the bill some weeks before it was called for; after the passage of the incorporating act it was taken up, and on the third reading, ordered by a small majority to be printed for consideration. The bill in its present dress proposes a tax of blank per Ct. on all taxable property for support of Teachers of the Christion Religion. Each person when he pays his tax is to name the society to which he dedicates it, and in case of refusal to do so, the tax is to be applied to the maintenance of a school in the county. As the bill stood for some time, the application in such cases was to be made by the Legislature to pious uses. In a committee of the whole it was determined by a majority of 7 or 8 that the word "Christian" should be exchanged for the word "Religious." On the report to the House the pathetic zeal of the late Governor Harrison gained a like majority for reinstating discrimination. Should the bill ever pass into a law in its present form it may and will be easily eluded. It is chiefly obnoxious on account of its dishonorable principle and dangerous tendency.

To the Honorable the GENERAL ASSEMBLY of the COMMON-
WEALTH of VIRGINIA.

A MEMORIAL and REMONSTRANCE.

The broadside George Mason had printed of Madison's "Memorial and Remonstrance against Religious Assessments" in June, 1785

To gain time, Madison supported an incorporation act for the Protestant Episcopal Church in exchange for postponement of decision on the general assessment bill. Baptists, Presbyterians, and Methodists rallied against it; the people voiced their opposition to this "alarming usurpation" in the spring elections of 1785; and in June Madison wrote his "Memorial and Remonstrance against Religious Assessments." Printed and circulated as a petition throughout the state, the argument was one of the strongest ever made for the twin principles of religious freedom and separation of Church and State.

[June, 1785]

We the subscribers.... remonstrate against the said Bill.

1.⁰ Because we hold it for a fundamental and undeniable truth "that Religion or the duty which we owe to our Creator and the manner of discharging it, can be directed only by reason and conviction, not by force or violence" [Virginia Declaration of Rights, Article 16]. The Religion then of every man must be left to the conviction and conscience of every man; and it is the right of every man to exercise it as these may dictate. This right is in its nature an unalienable right. It is unalienable, because the opinions of men, depending only on the evidence contemplated by their own minds cannot follow the dictates of other men: It is unalienable also, because what is here a right towards men, is a duty towards the Creator. It is the duty of every man to render to the Creator such homage and such only as he beleives to be acceptable to him. This duty is precedent, both in order of time and in degree of obligation, to the claims

The old capitol where the general assembly met from 1780 to 1788

91

Ancient Church, near Smithfield.

A Religious Encampment in a Forest.

The engravings above and opposite, from two nineteenth-century books, give a sampling of the churches in Virginia; Madison felt that some churches "instead of maintaining the purity and efficacy of Religion, have had a contrary operation."

of Civil Society. . . . We maintain therefore that in matters of Religion, no mans right is abridged by the institution of Civil Society and that Religion is wholly exempt from its cognizance. True it is, that no other rule exists, by which any question which may divide a Society, can be ultimately determined, but the will of the majority; but it is also true that the majority may trespass on the rights of the minority.

2.⁰ Because if Religion be exempt from the authority of the Society at large, still less can it be subject to that of the Legislative Body. The latter are but the creatures and vicegerents of the former. Their jurisdiction is both derivative and limited: it is limited with regard to the co-ordinate departments, more necessarily is it limited with regard to the constituents. The preservation of a free Government requires, not merely, that the metes and bounds which separate each department of power be invariably maintained: but more especially that neither of them be suffered to overleap the greater Barrier which defends the rights of the people. The Rulers who are guilty of such an encroachment, exceed the commission from which they derive their authority, and are Tyrants. The people who submit to it are governed by laws made neither by themselves nor by an authority derived from them, and are slaves.

3.⁰ Because it is proper to take alarm at the first experiment on our liberties. We hold this prudent jealousy to be the first duty of citizens, and one of the noblest characteristics of the late Revolution. . . . Who does not see that the same authority which can establish Christianity, in exclusion of all other Religions, may establish with the same ease any particular sect of Christians, in exclusion of all other Sects? that the same authority which can force a citizen to contribute three pence only of his property for the support of any one establishment, may force him to conform to any other establishment in all cases whatsoever?

4.⁰ Because the Bill violates that equality which ought to be the basis of every law, and which is more indispensable, in proportion as the validity or expediency of any law is more liable to be impeached. If "all men are by nature equally free and independent" [Virginia Declaration, Article 1], all men are to be considered as entering into Society on equal conditions; as relinquishing no more, and therefore retaining no less, one than another, of their natural rights. Above all are they to be considered as retaining an "equal title to the free exercise of Religion according to the dictates of Conscience" [Article 16]. Whilst we assert for ourselves a freedom to embrace, to profess and to observe the Religion which we believe to be of divine origin, we cannot deny an equal freedom to those whose minds have not yet yielded to the evidence which has convinced us. If this freedom be abused, it is an offence against God, not against man: To God, therefore, not to man, must an account of it be rendered....

5.⁰ Because the Bill implies either that the Civil Magistrate is a competent Judge of Religious Truth; or that he may employ Religion as an engine of Civil policy. The first is an arrogant pretension falsified by the contradictory opinions of Rulers in all ages, and throughout the world; the second an unhallowed perversion of the means of salvation.

6.⁰ Because the establishment proposed by the Bill is not requisite for the support of the Christion Religion. To say that it is, is a contradiction to the Christian Religion itself, for every page of it disavows a dependence on the powers of this world: it is a contradiction to fact; for it is known that this Religion both existed and flourished, not only without the support of human laws, but in spite of every opposition from them; and not only during the period of miraculous aid, but long after it had been left to its own evidence and the ordinary care of Providence; nay, it is a contradiction in terms, for a Religion not invented by human policy, must have pre existed and been supported, before it was established by human policy....

7.⁰ Because experience witnesseth that ecclesiastical establishments, instead of maintaining the purity and efficacy of Religion, have had a contrary operation. During almost fifteen centuries has the legal establishment of Christianity been on trial. What have been its fruits? more or less in all places, pride and indolence in the Clergy, ignorance and servility in the laity; in both, superstition, bigotry and persecution. Enquire of the Teachers of Christianity for the ages in which it appeared in its greatest lustre; those of every sect, point to the ages prior to its incorporation with Civil policy. Propose a restoration of this primitive state, in which its Teachers depended on the voluntary rewards of their flocks, many

ST. PAUL'S CHURCH, NORFOLK, VA.

ST. JOHN'S CHURCH, RICHMOND, VA.

of them predict its downfall. On which side ought their testimony to have greatest weight, when for or when against their interest?

8.⁰ Because the establishment in question is not necessary for the support of Civil Government.... If Religion be not within the cognizance of Civil Government, how can its legal establishment be necessary to Civil Government? What influence in fact have ecclesiastical establishments had on Civil Society? In some instances they have been seen to erect a spiritual tyranny on the ruins of the Civil authority: in many instances they have been seen upholding the thrones of political tyranny: in no instance have they been seen the guardians of the liberties of the people. Rulers who wished to subvert the public liberty, may have found an established Clergy convenient auxiliaries. A just Government instituted to secure & perpetuate it needs them not. Such a government will be best supported by protecting every Citizen in the enjoyment of his Religion with the same equal hand which protects his person and his property; by neither invading the equal rights of any Sect, nor suffering any Sect to invade those of another.

9.⁰ Because the proposed establishment is a departure from that generous policy, which, offering an asylum to the persecuted and oppressed of every Nation and Religion, promised a lustre to our country, and an accession to the number of its citizens. What a melancholy mark is the Bill of sudden degeneracy! Instead of holding forth an asylum to the persecuted, it is itself a signal of persecution. It degrades from the equal rank of Citizens, all those whose opinions in Religion do not bend to those of the Legislative authority. Distant as it may be in its present form from the Inquisition, it differs from it only in degree. The one is the first step, the other the last in the career of intolerance.

An ACT *for eſtabliſhing* RELIGIOUS FREEDOM, *paſſed in the aſſembly of* Virginia *in the beginning of the year* 1786.

Well aware that Almighty God hath created the mind free; that all attempts to influence it by temporal punishments or burthens, or by civil incapacitations, tend only to beget habits of hypocriſy and meannefs, and are a departure from the plan of the Holy Author of our religion, who, being Lord both of body and mind, yet choſe not to propagate it by coercions on either, as was in his Almighty power to do; that the impious preſumption of legiſlators and rulers civil, as well as ecclefiaſtical who, being themſelves but fallible and uninfpired men, have affumed dominion over the faith of others, fetting up their own opinions and modes of thinking as the only true and infaillible, and as fuch endeavouring to impofe them on others, hath eftablished and maintained falfe religions over the greateſt part of the world, and through all time: That to compel a man to furnish contributions of money for the propagation of opinions which he disbelieves, is finful and tyrannical; that even the forcing him to fupport this or that teacher of his own religious perfuafion, is depriving him of the comfortable liberty of giving his contributions to the particular paftor whofe

Printed text of Jefferson's Act for Establishing Religious Freedom

Six additional points, fifteen in all, completed Madison's argument. Meanwhile, Patrick Henry had been elected governor, thus depriving proponents of the assessment bill of their chief spokesman in the legislature. When the assembly convened in the fall, the bill died quietly. Madison capped the victory with passage of Jefferson's bill written in 1779 legalizing religious freedom. Thus was "extinguished forever the ambitious hope of making laws for the human mind," he wrote with justifiable pride to his friend in Paris. Decades later it still seemed to him, as it always did to Jefferson, one of his best achievements. "It was the Universal opinion of the Century preceding the last," he wrote in 1819, "that Civil Government could not stand without the prop of a Religious establishment, and that the Christion religion itself, would perish if not supported by a legal provision for its Clergy. The experience of Virginia conspicuously corroborates the disproof of both opinions." Jefferson was indebted to Madison for taking up the unfinished work of the revisal and, of course, shared his disappointment that more was not accomplished. After leaving the assembly in 1786, Madison reported the final outcome.

One of Madison's own horses had been stolen at Williamsburg in 1779; he put this ad in the Virginia Gazette.

New York Feby. 15th. 1787

My last was from Richmond on the 4th. of December, and contained a sketch of our legislative proceedings prior to that date. The principal proceedings of subsequent date relate as nearly as I can recollect 1st. to a rejection of the Bill on crimes and punishments, which after being altered so as to remove most of the objections as was thought, was lost by a single vote. The rage against Horse stealers had a great influence on the fate of the Bill. Our old bloody code is by this event fully restored, the prerogative of conditional pardon having been taken from the Executive by a Judgment of the Court of Appeals, and the temporary law granting it to them having expired and been left unrevived. I am not without hope that the rejected bill will find a more favorable disposition in the next Assembly. 2dly. to the bill for diffusing knowledge. It went through two readings by a small majority and was not pushed to a third one. The necessity of a systematic provision on the subject was admitted on all hands. The objections against that particular provision were   1. the expence, which was alleged to exceed the ability of the people.   2. the difficulty of executing it in the present sparse settlement of the Country.   3. the inequality of the districts as contended by the Western members. The latter objection is of little weight and might have been easily removed if it has been urged in an early stage of the discussion. The bill now rests on the same footing with the other unpassed bills in the Revisal. 3dly. to the Revisal at large. It was found impossible to get thro' the system at the late session for several reasons.   1. the changes which have taken place since its compilement, in our affairs and our laws, particularly those relating to our Courts, called for changes in some of the bills which could not be made with safety

*In New York Congress held its
sessions at the old City Hall,
which later became Federal Hall.*

by the Legislature. 2. the pressure of other business which tho' of less importance in itself, yet was more interesting for the moment. 3. the alarm excited by an approach toward the Execution Bill which subjects land to the payment of debts. This bill could not have been carried, was too important to be lost, and even too difficult to be amended without destroying its texture. 4. the danger of passing the Repealing Bill at the end of the Code before the operation of the various amendments &c. made by the Assembly could be leisurely examined by competent Judges. Under these circumstances it was thought best to hand over the residue of the work to our successors, and in order to have it made compleat, Mr. Pendleton, Mr. Wythe and Blair were appointed a Committee to amend the unpassed bills and also to prepare a supplemental revision of the laws which have been passed since the original work was executed.

Madison had meanwhile returned to Congress, then meeting in New York. Even when the laboring oar was in Virginia, his mind was on the deepening crisis of the Confederation. Nationalists like himself, anxious to stiffen the arm of Congress, had shifted their aim from the tax power to the power to regulate commerce, though the latter might encompass the former. Britain had lost an empire but she seemed determined to hold her former colonies in commercial bondage. Old markets in the West Indies were closed to the Americans; British ships took the lion's share of the carrying trade; and merchants and planters found no escape from the web of British credit. The signs of economic depression—money scarcity, falling prices, stagnation of trade—became evident in 1784. Commercial discontents produced a wave of legislation, especially in the eastern states, in retaliation against British and in favor of American trade. But thirteen separate states, each pursuing its own commercial interest, could not secure the national interest. Congress in 1784 had asked the legislatures for power to enact a uniform navigation law. It floundered, and Congress backed away from a proposed amendment vesting full power to regulate commerce in the Confederation. Madison thought such power essential. It was not only subservience to Britain that he feared but jealousies and dissensions among the states with their discordant economic interests—commercial, agricultural, manufacturing—which England would surely exploit. He expressed himself to James Monroe, then a Virginia delegate in Congress.

Orange [Virginia,] Aug: 7. 1785

Viewing in the abstract the question whether the power of regulating trade, to a certain degree at least, ought to be vested in Congress, it appears to me not to admit of a doubt, but that it should be decided in the affirmative. If it be necessary to regulate trade at all, it surely is necessary to lodge the power, where trade can be regulated with effect, and experience has confirmed what reason foresaw, that it can never be so regulated by the States acting in their separate capacities. They can no more exercise this power separately, than they could separately carry on war, or separately form treaties of alliance or Commerce. The nature of the thing therefore proves the former power, no less than the latter, to be within the reason of the fœderal Constitution. Much indeed is it to be wished, as I conceive, that no regulation of trade, that is to say, no restrictions or imposts whatever, were necessary. A perfect freedom is the System which would be my choice. But before such a system will be eligible perhaps for the U.S. they must be out of debt; before it will be attainable, all other nations must concur in it. Whilst any one of these imposes on our Vessels seamen &c in their ports, clogs from which they exempt their own, we must either retort the distinction, or renounce not merely a just profit, but our only defense against the danger which may most easily beset us. Are we not at this moment under this very alternative? The policy of G.B. (to say nothing of other nations) has shut against us the channels without which our trade with her must be a losing one; and she has consequently the triumph, as we have the chagrin, of seeing accomplished her prophetic threats, that our independence, should forfeit commercial advantages for which it would not recompence us with any new channels of trade. What is to be done? Must we remain passive victims to foreign politics; or shall we exert the lawful means which our independence has put into our hands, extorting redress? The very question would be an affront to every Citizen who loves his Country. What then are those means? Retaliating regulations of trade only. How are these to be effectuated? Only by harmony in the measures of the States. How is this harmony to be obtained? Only by an acquiescence of all the States in the opinion of a reasonable majority. If Congress as they are now constituted, can not be trusted with the power of digesting and enforcing this opinion, let them be otherwise constituted: let their numbers be encreased, let them be chosen

Madison's notes for the speech on federal regulation of commerce that he made in Congress in 1785

oftener, and let their period of service be shortned; or if any better medium than Congress can be proposed, by which the wills of the States may be concentered, let it be substituted; or lastly let no regulation of trade adopted by Congress be in force untill it shall have been ratified by a certain proportion of the States. But let us not sacrifice the end to the means: let us not rush on certain ruin in order to avoid a possible danger. I conceive it to be of great importance that the defects of the fœderal system should be amended, not only because such amendments will make it better answer the purpose for which it was instituted, but because I apprehend danger to its very existence from a continuance of defects which expose a part if not the whole of the empire to severe distress. The suffering part, even when the minor part, can not long respect a Government which is too feeble to protect their interest; But when the suffering part come to be the major part, and they despair of seeing a protecting energy given to the General Government, from what motives is their allegiance to be any longer expected. Should G.B. persist in the machinations which distress us, and seven or eight of the States be hindered by the others from obtaining relief by fœderal means, I own, I tremble at the anti-fœederal expedients into which the former may be tempted.

Lower New York from the harbor

Considerations such as these led to the movement for full-scale constitutional reform. That the initiative should have come from Virginia, a staple-producing state, was surprising. But on the invitation of the Virginia assembly in 1786, nine states agreed to send delegates to a commercial convention. Madison, who would be a delegate, explained the plan to Jefferson with more than a trace of despair for its success.

Orange [Virginia,] March 18th. 1786
A Quorum of the deputies appointed by the Assembly for a Commercial Convention had a meeting at Richmond shortly after I left it, and the Attorney [General, Edmund Randolph] tells me, it has been agreed to propose Annapolis for the place, and the first Monday in Sepr. for the time of holding the Convention. It was thought prudent to avoid the neighbourhood of Congress, and the large Commercial towns in order to disarm the adversaries to the object of insinuations of influence from either of these quarters. I have not heard what opinion is enter-

tained of this project at New York, nor what reception it has found in any of the States. It if should come to nothing, it will I fear confirm G.B. and all the world in the belief that we are not to be respected, nor apprehended as a nation in matters of Commerce. The States are every day giving proofs that separate regulations are more likely to set them by the ears, than to attain the common object. When Massts. set on foot a retaliation of the policy of G. B. Connecticut declared her ports free. N. Jersey served N. York in the same way. And Delaware I am told has lately followed the example in opposition to the commercial plans of Penna. A miscarriage of this attempt to unite the States in some effectual plan will have another effect of a serious nature. It will dissipate every prospect of drawing a steady revenue from our imports either directly into the federal treasury, or indirectly thro' the treasuries of the commercial States, and of consequence the former must depend for supplies solely on annual requisitions, and the latter on direct taxes from the property of the Country. That these dependencies are in an alarming degree fallacious is put by experience out of all question. The payments from the States under the calls of Congress have in no year borne any proportion to the public wants. . . . Another unhappy effect of a continuance of the present anarchy of our commerce will be a continuance of the unfavorable balance on it, which by draining us of our metals furnishes pretexts for the pernicious substitution of paper money, for indulgences to debtors, for postponements of taxes. In fact most of our political evils may be traced up to our commercial ones, as most of our moral may to our political. The lessons which the mercantile interests of Europe have received from late experience will probably check their propensity to credit us beyond our resources, and so far the evil of an unfavorable balance will correct itself. But the Merchants of G.B. if no others will continue to credit us at least as far as our remittances can be obtained, and that is far enough to perpetuate our difficulties unless the luxurious propensity of our own people can be otherwise checked.

This view of our situation presents the proposed Convention as a remedial experiment which ought to command every assent; but if it be a just view it is one which assuredly will not be taken by all even of those

orial Field Book of the Revolution BY BENSON J. LOSSING, 1852

The State House at Annapolis

Diego de Gardoqui

whose intentions are good. I consider the event there-fore as extremely uncertain, or rather, considering that the States must first agree to the proposition for sending deputies, that these must agree in a plan to be sent back to the States, and that these again must agree unani-mously in a ratification of it. I almost despair of success. It is necessary however that something should be tried and if this be not the best possible expedient, it is the best that could possibly be carried thro' the Legislature here. And if the present crisis cannot effect unanimity, from what future concurrence of circumstances is it to be expected?

When the convention met in September, only five states were actually represented. The delegates threw away the script and addressed Congress to call a new convention at Philadelphia in May, 1787, for the purpose of discussing all matters requisite "to render the constitu-tion of the Federal Government adequate to the exigencies of the Union." Congress complied, and although the convention was called "for the sole and express purpose of revising the Articles of Confederation," politicians of Madison's persuasion had converted the specter of commercial disaster into a glorious opportunity to create a truly national government.

Fears outran hopes in the later months of 1786, however. Almost at the time of the Annapolis Convention, Congress authorized Secretary of Foreign Affairs John Jay, then negotiating with the Spanish minister, Don Diego de Gardoqui, to suspend the American demand for navigation of the Mis-sissippi in exchange for a treaty of commerce with Spain. Madison was outraged. For years he had viewed the navigation of the Mississippi as essen-tial to the future of the West and of the Union. What faith could westerners place in a government that bargained away their most vital interest? Indeed what confidence could any state or section have in a government that so cavalierly sacrificed one part to gratify another? Madison communicated his indignation over the Jay-Gardoqui proposal to Monroe.

Orange [Virginia,] June 21st. 1786.
Your favor of the 31st. ult. did not come to hand till two days ago. As I expected to see you in a short time, I will suspend the full communication of my ideas on the sub-ject of it till I have that pleasure. I cannot however for-bear in the mean time expressing my amazement that a thought should be entertained of surrendering the Mis-sissippi and of guarantying the possessions of Spain [in] America. In the first place has not Virga., have not Con-gress themselves, and the Ministers of Congs. by their

Madison is listed as one of three delegates from Virginia to the Annapolis Convention of 1786.

orders, asserted the right of those who live on the waters of the Missisipi to use it as the high road given by nature to the sea. This being the case, have Congress any more authority to say that the western citizens of Virga. shall not pass thro the capes of Missisipi than to say that her eastern citizens shall pass thro the capes Henry and Charles. It should be remembered that the United States are not now extricating themselves from war, a crisis which often knows no law but that of necessity. The measure in question would be a voluntary barter in time of profound peace of the rights of one part of the empire to the interests of another part. What would Massachusets say to a proposition for ceding to Britain her right of fishery as the price of some stipulations in fa[vor] of to[ba]cco.

Again can there be a more shortsighted or dishonorable policy than to concur with Spain in frustrating the benevolent views of nature to sell the affections of our ultramontane brethr[en], to depreciate the richest fund we possess, to distrust an ally [France] whom we know to be able to befriend us and to have an interest in doing it against the only na[tion] whose enmity we can dread, and at the same time to court by the most precious sacrifices the alliance of a nation whose impotency is notorious, who has given no proof of regard for us and the genius of whose government religion & manners unfit them, of all the nations in Christendom for a coalition with this country. Can any thing too, as you well observe, be more unequal than a stipulation which is to open all our ports to her and some only and those the least valuable of hers to us; and which places the commercial freedom of our ports against the fettered regulations of those in Spain. I always thought the stipulation with France and Holland of the privileges of the most favoured nation as unequal, and only to be justified by the influence which the treaties could not fail to have on the event of the war. A stipulation putting Spanish subjects on the same footing with our own citizens is carrying the evil still farther without the same pretext for it; and is the more to be dreaded, as by making her the most favoured nation it would let in the other nations with whom we are now connected to the same privileges, whenever they may find it their interest to make the same compensation for them whilst we have not a reciprocal right to force them

101

James Monroe circa *1786*

into such an arrangement in case our interest should dictate it. A guaranty is if possible still more objectionable. If it be insidious we plunge ourselves into infamy. If sincere, into obligations the extent of which cannot easily be determined. In either case we get farther into the labyrinth of European politics from which we ought religiously to keep ourselves as free as possible. And what is to be gained by such a rash step? Will any man in his senses pretend that our territory needs such a safeguard, or that if it were in danger, it is the arm of Spain that is to save it. Viewing the matter in this light I cannot but flatter myself, that if the attempt you apprehend should be made, it will be rejected with becoming indignation.

Because of the Jay-Gardoqui affair, Madison hastened to return to Congress in 1787. So vehement was the sectional opposition, however, that Jay himself quietly shelved the project. Congress was in a pitiable state, much worse than when Madison had left it three years before. To his fears of congressional collapse and disunion were added dreads of social disorder. The news of Shays' Rebellion met him in New York where Congress convened. He could not pass off this insurgency in Massachusetts with the philosophical aplomb of his friend Jefferson who remarked: "I like a little rebellion now and then. It is like a storm in the atmosphere." No, Shays' Rebellion, along with the rage for paper money in states such as Rhode Island, underscored the need to recast the balance between liberty and authority. For the present, Congress could do nothing but wait the turn of events in Philadelphia. Madison summed up the uncertain prospect for Edmund Pendleton.

New York Feby. 24. 1787.
What the issue of it [the Federal Convention] will be is among the other arcana of futurity and nearly as inscrutable as any of them. In general I find men of reflection much less sanguine as to a new than despondent as to the present System. Indeed the present System neither has nor deserves advocates; and if some very strong props are not applied will quickly tumble to the ground. No money is paid into the public Treasury; no respect is paid to the federal authority. Not a single State complies with the requisitions, several pass them over in silence, and some positively reject them. The payments ever since the peace have been decreasing, and of late fall short even of the pittance necessary for the Civil list of the

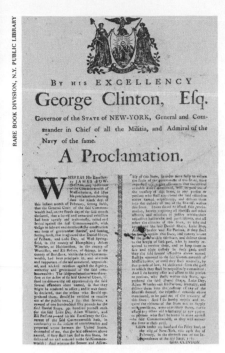

New York Governor George Clinton urged the capture of Daniel Shays.

Confederacy. It is not possible that a Government can last long under these circumstances. If the approaching Convention should not agree on some remedy, I am persuaded that some very different arrangement will ensue. The late turbulent scenes in Massts. & infamous ones in Rhode Island, have done inexpressible injury to the republican character in that part of the U. States; and a propensity towards Monarchy is said to have been produced by it in some leading minds. The bulk of the people will probably prefer the lesser evil of a partition of the Union into three more practicable and energetic governments. The latter idea I find after long confinement to individual speculations & private circles, is beginning to shew itself in the Newspapers. But tho' it is a lesser evil, it is so great a one that I hope the danger of it will rouse all the real friends to the Revolution to exert themselves in favor of such an organization of the Confederacy, as will perpetuate the Union, and redeem the honor of the Republican name.

Madison had prepared himself well for the work that lay before him in Philadelphia. Quite aside from his practical experience, he had over the last three years read widely in the history and theory of government both ancient and modern. This was not an academic exercise; it was reading with a clear political purpose in view. With knowledge and insight drawn from the whole range of human experience, he believed that government might be made a science and that man might control his political destiny. Among his contemporaries none fretted as much as he over the theoretical basis of federal government. The failures of the Confederation doubtless caused him to toss and turn when everybody else at Montpelier was sleeping soundly. Poring over the books Jefferson sent him from Paris, Madison searched the history of confederations in order to discover the solution for America. The lesson of the past was always the same: weakness at the center led to jealousies, dissensions, and disorders in and among the members. Sometime before the Federal Convention he digested what he had learned in a series of "Notes on Ancient and Modern Confederacies." Drawing on this rich fund of analogy, he then wrote a paper commonly entitled "Vices of the Political System of the United States."

[April, 1787]

1. Failure of the States to comply with the Constitutional requisitions.... This evil has been so fully experienced both during the war and since the peace, results so naturally from the number and independent authority

103

of the States and has been so uniformly exemplified in every similar Confederacy, that it may be considered as not less radically and permanently inherent in, than it is fatal to the object of, the present System.

2. Encroachments by the States on the federal authority.... Examples of this are numerous and repetitions may be foreseen in almost every case where any favorite object of a State shall present a temptation. Among these examples are the wars and Treaties of Georgia with the Indians,... the troops raised and to be kept up by Massts.

3. Violations of the law of nations and of treaties.... From the number of Legislatures, the sphere of life from which most of their members are taken, and the circumstances under which their legislative business is carried on, irregularities of this kind most frequently happen. Accordingly not a year has passed without instances of them in some one or other of the States. The Treaty of peace, the treaty with France, the treaty with Holland have each been violated....

As yet foreign powers have not been rigorous in animadverting on us. This moderation however cannot be mistaken for a permanent partiality to our faults, or a permanent security agst. those disputes with other nations, which being among the greatest of public calamitees, it ought to be least in the power of any part of the Community to bring on the whole

4. Trespasses of the States on the rights of each other.... These are alarming symptoms, and may be daily apprehended as we are admonished by daily experience. See the law of Virginia restricting foreign vessels to certain ports, of Maryland in favor of vessels belonging to her own citizens....

Paper money, instalments of debts, occlusion of Courts, making property a legal tender, may likewise be deemed aggressions on the rights of other States....

The practice of many States in restricting the commercial intercourse with other States, and putting their productions and manufactures on the same footing with those of foreign nations, though not contrary to the federal articles, is certainly adverse to the spirit of the Union, and tends to beget retaliating regulations, not less expensive & vexatious in themselves than they are destructive of the general harmony.

5. Want of concert in matters where common in-

terest requires it.... This defect is strongly illustrated in the state of our commercial affairs. How much has the national dignity, interest, and revenue suffered from this cause? Instances of inferior moment are the want of uniformity in the laws concerning naturalezation & literary property; of provision for national seminaries, for grants of incorporation for national purposes, for canals and other works of general utility, wch. may at present be defeated by the perverseness of particular states whose concurrence is necessary.

6. Want of general Guaranty to the States of their Constitutions & laws against internal violence.... The confederation is silent on this point and therefore by the second article the hands of the federal authority are tied according to Republican Theory....

7. Want of sanction to the laws, and of coercion in the government of the Confederacy.... A sanction is essential to the idea of law, as coercion is to that of Government. The federal system being destitute of both, wants the great vital principles of a Political Cons[ti]tution. Under the form of such a constitution, it is in fact nothing more than a treaty of amity and of commerce and of alliance, between so many independent and sovereign states....

8. Want of ratification by the people of the articles of Confederation.... In some of the States the Confederation is recognized by, and forms a part of the constitution. In others however it has received no other sanction than that of the Legislative authority. From this defect two evils result: 1. Whenever a law of a state happens to be repugnant to an act of Congress ... it will be at least questionable whether the former must not prevail, and as the question must be decided by the Tribunals of the State, they will be most likely to lean on the side of the State.

2. As far as the Union of the States is to be regarded as a league of sovereign powers, and not as a political Constitution by virtue of which they are become one sovereign power, so far it seems to follow from the doctrine of compacts that a breach of any of the articles of the confederation by any of the parties to it, absolves the other parties from their respective obligations, and gives them a right if they chuse to exert it, of dissolving the union altogether.

105

[Madison went on to describe still other evils: multiplicity of laws in the states, mutability of laws, injustice of laws. The fatal cause of injustice lay in the selfishness of different interests and factions in the community. Neither morality nor religion offered an adequate check. In "little republics" there was all the more danger that "a common passion or interest" would unite a majority against the rest of the people. The solution was to be found, said Madison with a flash of insight, in an "enlargement of the sphere" of government.]

If an enlargement of the sphere is found to lessen the insecurity of private rights, it is not because the impulse of a common interest or passion is less predominant in this case with the majority; but because a common interest or passion is less apt to be felt and the requisite combinations less easy to be formed by a great than by a small number. The Society becomes broken into a greater variety of interests, of pursuits, and of passions, which check each other, whilst those who may feel a common sentiment have less opportunity of communication and concert. It may be inferred that the inconveniences of popular States contrary to the prevailing Theory, are in proportion not to the extent, but to the narrowness of their limits.

The great desideratum in Government is such a modification of the Sovereignty as will render it sufficiently neutral between the different interests and factions, to controul one part of the Society from invading the rights of another, and at the same time sufficiently controuled itself, from setting up an interest adverse to that of the whole Society....

An auxiliary desideratum for the melioration of the Republican form is such a process of elections as will most certainly extract from the mass of the Society the purest and noblest characters which it contains; such as will at once feel most strongly the proper motives to pursue the end of their appointment, and be most capable to devise the proper means of attaining it.

So formidable had the vices become in Madison's eyes that he made a quantum leap from the confederate pattern of government, in which the states were the sovereign members, to a government of "national supremacy" founded on the authority of the people and armed with great powers. He sketched his ideas—a sketch of what would become the Virginia Plan—in a letter to General Washington a month before the convention met in Philadelphia. It was, as he confessed, a "radical" program. Indeed, it amounted to a repudiation of the centrifugal republicanism of the revolutionary era.

New York April 16th. 1787.

I have been honored with your letter of the 31. March, and find with much pleasure that your views of the reform which ought to be pursued by the Convention, give a sanction to those I entertained. Temporising applications will dishonor the Councils which propose them, and may foment the internal malignity of the disease, at the same time that they produce an ostensible paliation of it. Radical attempts, although unsuccessful, will at least justify the authors of them.

Having been lately led to revolve the subject which is to undergo the discussion of the Convention, and formed in my mind *some* outlines of a new system, I take the liberty of submitting them without apology, to your eye.

Conceiving that an individual independence of the States is utterly irreconcileable with their aggregate sovereignty; and that a consolidation of the whole into one simple republic would be as inexpedient as it is unattainable, I have sought for some middle ground, which may at once support a due supremacy of the national authority, and not exclude the local authorities wherever they can be subordinately useful.

I would propose as the ground-work that a change be made in the principle of representation. According to the present form of the Union in which the intervention of the States is in all great cases necessary to effectuate the measures of Congress, an equality of suffrage, does not destroy the inequality of importance, in the several members. No one will deny that Virginia and Massachusetts have more weight and influence both within and without Congress than Delaware or Rhode Island. Under a system which would operate in many essential points without the intervention of the State Legislatures, the case would be materially altered. A vote in the national Councils from Delaware, would then have the same effect and value as one from the largest State in the Union. I am ready to believe that such a change would not be attended with much difficulty. A majority of the States, and those

Mezzotint of George Washington by Charles Willson Peale, dated 1787

Madison's letter to Washington sketching his ideas for a "radical" program to present at the coming Constitutional Convention

of greatest influence, will regard it as favorable to them. To the northern States it will be recommended by their present populousness; to the Southern by their expected advantage in this respect. The lesser States must in every event yield to the predominant will. But the consideration which particularly urges a change in the representation is that it will obviate the principal objections of the larger States to the necessary concessions of power.

I would propose next that in addition to the present federal powers, the national Government should be armed with positive and compleat authority in all cases which require uniformity; such as the regulation of trade, including the right of taxing both exports and imports, the fixing the terms and forms of naturalization &c. &c.

Over and above this positive power, a negative *in all cases whatsoever* on the legislative acts of the States, as heretofore exercised by the Kingly prerogative, appears to me to be absolutely necessary, and to be the least possible encroachment on the State jurisdictions. Without this defensive power every positive power that can be given on paper will be evaded or defeated. The States will continue to invade the national jurisdiction, to violate treaties and the law of Nations and to harass each other with rival and spiteful measures dictated by mistaken views of interest. Another happy effect of this prerogative would be its controul on the internal vicissitudes of State policy, and the aggressions of interested majorities on the rights of minorities and of individuals. The great desideratum which has not yet been found for Republican Governments, seems to be some disinterested and dispassionate umpire in disputes between different passions and interests in the State. The majority who alone have the right of decision, have frequently an interest real or supposed in abusing it. . . . Might not the national prerogative here suggested be found sufficiently disinterested for the decision of local questions of policy, whilst it would itself be sufficiently restrained from the pursuit of interests adverse to those of the whole Society? There has not been any moment since the peace at which the representatives of the Union would have given an assent to paper money or any other measure of a kindred nature.

The national supremacy ought also to be extended as I conceive to the Judiciary departments. If those who are to expound and apply the laws, are connected by their interests and their oaths with the particular States wholly, and not with the Union, the participation of the Union in the making of the laws may be possibly rendered unavailing. It seems at least necessary that the oaths of the Judges should include a fidelity to the general as well as local Constitution, and that an appeal should be to some national tribunals in all cases to which foreigners or inhabitants of other States may be parties. The admiralty jurisdiction seems to fall entirely within the purview of the national Government.

The national supremacy in the Executive departments is liable to some difficulty, unless the officers administering them could be made appointable by the supreme Government. The Militia ought certainly to be placed in some form or other under the authority which is entrusted with the general protection and defence.

A Government composed of such extensive powers should be well organized and balanced. The Legislative department might be divided into two branches; one of them chosen every ___ years by the people at large, or by the Legislatures; the other to consist of fewer members, and to go out in such a rotation as always to leave in office a large majority of old members. Perhaps the negative on the laws might be most conveniently exercised by this branch. As a further check, a council of revision including the great ministerial officers might be superadded.

A national Executive must also be provided. I have scarcely ventured as yet to form my own opinion either of the manner in which it ought to be constituted or of the authorities with which it ought to be cloathed.

An article should be inserted expressly guarantying the tranquility of the States against internal as well as external dangers.

In like manner the right of coercion should be expressly declared. With the resources of commerce in hand, the national administration might always find means of exerting it either by sea or land; But the difficulty & awkwardness of operating by force on the collective will of a State, render it particularly desirable that the necessity of it might be precluded. Perhaps the negative on the laws might create such a mutuality of dependence between the general and particular authorities, as to answer this purpose. Or perhaps some defined objects of taxation might be submitted along with commerce, to the general authority.

To give a new system its proper validity and energy, a ratification must be obtained from the people, and not merely from the ordinary authority of the Legislatures. This will be the more essential as inroads on the *existing Constitutions* of the States will be unavoidable.

In sum, this man so often portrayed as mild, timid, and the soul of prudence struck out for Independence Hall with boldness in his eyes and a prescription for radical reform in his pocket.

A Picture Portfolio

Man from Montpelier

A New and Accurate
MAP OF
VIRGINIA
Wherein most of the
COUNTIES
are laid down from
ACTUAL SURVEYS.
With
A Concise Account of the
Number of
Inhabitants, the Trade, Soil, and Produce
of that
PROVINCE.
By JOHN HENRY.

Engraved by Thomas Jefferys Geographer to the KING.

HOME OF A LIFETIME

For most of his eighty-five full and productive years, James Madison called home a plantation in the beautiful hill country of Orange County, Virginia. Over the years his father had built it into a splendid estate, which Madison, as the eldest son, inherited in 1801. In the detail of the 1770 map at left, drawn by John Henry—the father of another of Virginia's most famous sons, Patrick Henry—Orange County can be seen just to the southeast of the magnificent Blue Ridge Mountains which cut diagonally across the top left corner. The Madison house, perched on the side of a mountain of its own, had a fine view of the Blue Ridge some thirty miles away across broad meadows and sweeping forests. When Madison was about ten, the family moved from a simple wooden house to the handsome brick mansion below that they were building nearby. Madison made many improvements to the house over the years and first called it Montpelier in the late 1790s. When the Baroness Hyde de Neuville, wife of the French Minister to the United States, painted this charming watercolor in 1818, the classic portico designed by Thomas Jefferson, Madison's closest friend and Virginia neighbor, had long since been added and the two flanking wings completed.

EARLY INFLUENCES

Madison's mother, Nelly Conway Madison, and his father, James Madison, Sr., both came from families who had decided early to leave Virginia's Tidewater region and settle in the sparsely inhabited area to the west known as the Piedmont. The two families prospered there and James Madison, Sr., became as prominent locally as his son was to become nationally. Of the Madisons' twelve children, eleven are indicated on the bottom line of the family tree James Madison, Jr., drew sometime between 1813 and 1819 (right); another son lived for only one day. Young "Jemmy" was exceptionally fortunate in his schooling. In 1762, and for five years thereafter, he was sent away to a school run by Donald Robertson, of whom Madison has been quoted as saying: "All that I have been in my life I owe largely to that man." Surviving among Madison's papers is a copybook kept during those school years. Two of its 102 pages are reproduced at far right, showing Madison's youthful doodle of a human face in the center of Copernicus's solar system and a page of sophisms copied in a careful hand. For two more years he was tutored at home, along with his brothers and sisters, by the Reverend Thomas Martin, the new rector of the local church and a graduate of the College of New Jersey.

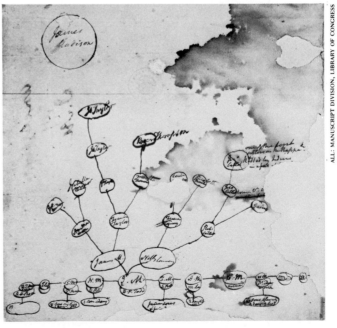

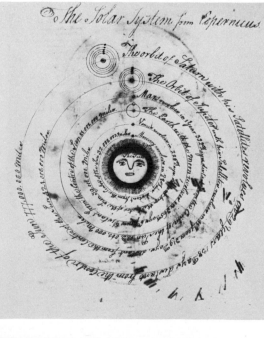

A North West Prospect of Nassau Hall with a Fron

NORTH TO COLLEGE

Unlike many young Virginians of his day, Madison did not go to the College of William and Mary in Williamsburg but instead headed north to the College of New Jersey in Princeton, where the moral and religious tone was more to the liking of his father and his recent tutor. There he found an imposing building, Nassau Hall (below), where more than a hundred students slept, dined, studied, and went to church under one roof. The president, whose house is at right in this old print, was an impressive Scottish Presbyterian minister, Dr. John Witherspoon (left). His advice to his students for conduct in public life was succinct: "Lads, ne'er do ye speak unless ye ha' something to say, and when ye are done, be sure and leave off." Madison worked extremely hard, to the great detriment of his health, and completed the four-year course in two. He received his diploma (far left) in the fall of 1771 but stayed another six months for further study with Dr. Witherspoon.

VIRGINIA LEGISLATOR

For several years following his graduation from Princeton, Madison remained at Montpelier regaining his health and reading voraciously. Politics soon became his main interest, fanned by the events leading to the Revolution. In 1776 when he was first elected to the Virginia Convention, he visited Williamsburg, the small but elegant capital seen at right in a French map of the period. Madison lived with his second cousin, the Reverend James Madison, president of William and Mary, in the charming house to the right of the college buildings in the view at top. In 1780 the capital was moved to Richmond. When Madison served there as an Orange County delegate to the Virginia General Assembly for four sessions beginning in 1784, Mayo Bridge, shown in the 1822 watercolor above, had not yet been built and the James River was crossed by ferryboat.

39. Camp à Williamsburg le 26. Septembre, 7. miles de Archés hupe.

le 27. Sejour.

YOUNGEST DELEGATE

When Madison was appointed to the Continental Congress at Philadelphia in 1779, he was, at age twenty-nine, the youngest delegate. As the miniature below shows, however, he looked considerably younger, "no bigger than half a piece of soap," and was described by a delegate's wife as "a gloomy stiff creature...nothing engaging or even bearable in his manners." He took lodgings with Mrs. Mary House at Fifth and Market streets, three blocks west of the junction of Market and Second pictured in the Birch engraving at left and only a block from the Pennsylvania State House (left, below) where Congress held its sessions. The year after Madison arrived, the steeple on the State House decayed so badly that it had to be dismantled and replaced by the low roof seen here. As was characteristic of him, Madison kept at his post for nearly four years with only two short breaks—a remarkable and unmatched record. But his life was briefly brightened by a charming young lady (below right), not yet sixteen, who also lived at Mrs. House's with her father William Floyd, a delegate from New York. When Charles Willson Peale painted these miniatures in 1783, Madison and Kitty Floyd planned to be married. But Miss Floyd changed her mind, and Madison wrote sorrowfully to Jefferson of her "profession of indifference at what has happened."

FATHER OF THE CONSTITUTION

In 1787 Madison returned to Philadelphia to take part in the Federal Convention that would draft the Constitution of the United States. No man was better prepared for the task. In addition to his practical legislative experience, he had pored over countless volumes on the history and theory of government, and he took his seat in the handsome east chamber of the State House (depicted in the nineteenth-century painting above during the signing ceremony) with a well-thought-out program. He chose a seat in the front row where he could hear everything and take copious notes; his first page is at left. For the major role he played in the Convention, he has been called the Father of the Constitution. A fellow delegate wrote that "he always comes forward the best informed man of any point in debate. The affairs of the United States, he perhaps has the most correct knowledge of, of any man in the union."

Jas. W. Smith

THE FEDERALIST:

A COLLECTION OF

E S S A Y S,

WRITTEN IN FAVOUR OF THE

NEW CONSTITUTION,

AS AGREED UPON BY THE

FEDERAL CONVENTION,

SEPTEMBER 17, 1787.

[*With Mr. Madison's corrections.*]

IN TWO VOLUMES.
VOL. I.

NEW-YORK:
PRINTED AND SOLD BY JOHN TIEBOUT,
No. 358 PEARL-STREET.
1 7 9 9.

POLITICAL STRATEGISTS

Drafting the Constitution was one thing; getting the states to ratify it was quite another. Brilliant, thirty-year-old Alexander Hamilton of New York (right) chose to fight for adoption with a series of newspaper articles designed to convince the doubters. As his collaborators he picked John Jay, an experienced diplomat (above), and James Madison. Under the collective pen name of Publius, these three young men produced seventy-seven essays in six months. With eight more they were published in book form as *The Federalist* (above, left), which is generally considered to be the outstanding work on the basic theory of American government. When the states debated ratification, some pressed for amendments, including a bill of rights. In order to assure widespread support after ratification, Madison condensed their demands and shepherded twelve of them (above, far right) through the new Congress as it met in New York's Federal Hall (above, right). The first two were never ratified, but the ten that remained became those amendments to the Constitution known as the Bill of Rights.

"THE GREAT LITTLE MADISON"

"Thou must come to me," Dolley Payne Todd wrote her best friend in May, 1794. "Aaron Burr says that the great little Madison has asked to be brought to see me this evening." Dolley, an effervescent and attractive young woman (right, in Gilbert Stuart's portrait now on loan to the White House), had lost her husband and one of her two sons in the yellow fever epidemic of the previous year and was one of Philadelphia's most eligible widows. Madison, now forty-three, had been back in that city ever since Congress returned there in 1790 and inevitably became aware of the twenty-six-year-old charmer whose home was only a block from the State House. Few letters exist between them; they were seldom separated after their marriage that September, only four months after being introduced. The fragment below is of a letter Madison wrote in August after receiving Dolley's acceptance of his proposal. When Jefferson became President in 1801, he appointed his old and close friend Secretary of State. A description of him made at this time closely parallels the Madison seen in the fine portrait by Thomas Sully at left: "I never knew him to wear any other color than black . . . his breeches short, with buckles at the knees, black silk stockings, and shoes with strings. . . ."

BY GILBERT STUART, 1804; PENNSYLVANIA ACADEMY OF THE FINE ARTS, COURTESY WHITE HOUSE HISTORICAL ASSOCIATION

UNDER ☆ MY ☆ ☆ WINGS ☆ ☆ EVERY ☆ ☆THING☆ ☆ PROSPERS

SECRETARY OF STATE

When the Madisons moved to Washington in May, 1801, they lived for a short time in the President's House (above), and Dolley was able to exercise her talents as a hostess for the widower Jefferson (above, left). Her husband, in his office a few blocks away, was demonstrating his own skills as the President's indispensable first minister. For eight years Jefferson had many occasions to appreciate fully "the rich and ready resources" of the "luminous and discriminating mind" of his Secretary of State. One of the high points of their administration was the skillful negotiation with France leading to the Louisiana Purchase in 1803. Not only did this include the strategic port of New Orleans (painted at left in the year of the transfer), which both Jefferson and Madison considered crucial, but also 828,000 square miles of land that doubled the size of the United States overnight. When his term was ended, Jefferson wrote in tribute: "Mr. Madison is justly entitled to his full share of the measures of my administration. Our principles were the same, and we never differed sensibly in our application of them."

129

Chapter 4

Father of the Constitution

I n his own lifetime James Madison would be venerated as the Father of the Constitution. He thought this more praise than belonged to him. The Constitution was not "like the fabled Goddess of Wisdom, the off-spring of a single brain," but rather "the work of many heads and many hands." Fifty-five heads to be exact. They came from twelve states (Rhode Island was not represented); they were lawyers, merchants, planters, and physicians and ranged in age from twenty-six to eighty-one; thirty-nine of them had served in Congress, hence were schooled in the frustrations of the Confederation. At thirty-six years of age, one of seven elected Virginia delegates, Madison was in his prime. He had studied politics as a science and practiced it as his profession. One delegate, William Pierce of Georgia, wrote of him: "Every person seems to acknowledge his greatness. He blends together the profound politician, with the scholar.... The affairs of the United States, he perhaps has the most correct knowledge of, of any man in the Union."

Arriving on May 3, one of the first delegates on the scene, Madison took his usual lodgings at Mrs. House's boardinghouse. The convention was scheduled to open on May 14, but it was not until the twenty-fifth that a quorum of seven states could be mustered. Meanwhile, Madison enjoyed the pleasures of Philadelphia. He met and dined with the celebrated Franklin, himself a delegate; he joined with Washington and others in an outing along the Schuylkill. For the most part, however, he laid his plans for the convention and pressed his views on the delegates tumbling into Philadelphia. When the Virginia corps was completed on May 17, Madison brought them together to hammer out the Virginia Plan. It was Madison's plan, essentially, and it became the basis for the deliberations of the convention. Most of what is known about the debates in the convention derives from Madison. The delegates met behind closed doors; although a secretary was appointed, he kept only a journal of proceedings. But Madison, realizing the importance of the event for the nation's history and for the science of government, kept extensive notes on the debates. They would not be published until Congress bought them and authorized their publication in 1840, four years after his death. In a preface written in the 1830s, Madison explained his role as unofficial chronicler of the convention.

Debates in the Federal Convention
[*c.* 1830–36]

The curiosity I had felt during my researches into the History of the most distinguished Confederacies, particularly those of antiquity, and the deficiency I found in the means of satisfying it more especially in what related to the process, the principles, the reasons, & the anticipations, which prevailed in the formation of them, determined me to preserve as far as I could an exact account of what might pass in the Convention whilst executing its trust, with the magnitude of which I was duly impressed, as I was with the gratification promised to future curiosity by an authentic exhibition of the objects, the opinions, & the reasonings from which the new System of Govt was to receive its peculiar structure & organization. Nor was I unaware of the value of such a contribution to the fund of materials for the History of a Constitution on which would be staked the happiness of a people great even in its infancy, and possibly the cause of Liberty throughout the world.

In pursuance of the task I had assumed I chose a seat in front of the presiding member, with the other members on my right & left hands. In this favorable position for hearing all that passed, I noted in terms legible & in abbreviations & marks intelligible to myself what was read from the Chair or spoken by the members; and losing not a moment unnecessarily between the adjournment & reassembling of the Convention I was enabled to write out my daily notes during the session or within a few finishing days after its close in the extent and form preserved in my own hand on my files.

In the labour & correctness of doing this, I was not a little aided by practice & by a familiarity with the style and the train of conversation & reasoning which characterized the principal speakers. It happened, also that I was not absent a single day, nor more than a casual fraction of an hour in any day, so that I could not have lost a single speech, unless a very short one.

A view of the Falls of Schuylkill, five miles above Philadelphia

The convention met daily, six days a week, from late morning to early evening for almost four months. When not in his seat at the State House (Independence Hall), Madison spent countless hours over his notes in his quarters at Mrs. House's. He wrote few letters and, under the injunction of secrecy, had virtually nothing to communicate. After the business began, he wrote to Jefferson about the delegates, explained the restraint on his pen, and passed typically unflattering comments on Patrick Henry, who had disdained the convention because he "smelt a rat," and on John Adams, whose *A Defence of the Constitutions of Government of the United States of America* had just appeared.

Philada. June 6th. 1787.

In furnishing you with this list of names, I have exhausted all the means which I can make use of for gratifying your curiosity. It was thought expedient in order to secure unbiased discussion within doors, and to prevent misconceptions and misconstructions without, to establish some rules of caution which will for no short time restrain even a confidential communication of our proceedings. The names of the members will satisfy you that the States have been serious in this business. The attendance of Genl. Washington is a proof of the light in which he regards it. The whole Community is big with expectation. And there can be no doubt but that the result will in some way or other have a powerful effect on our destiny.

Mr. Adams' Book which has been in your hands of course, has excited a good deal of attention. An edition has come out here and another is on the press at N. York. It will probably be much read, particularly in the Eastern States, and contribute with other circumstances to revive the predilections of this Country for the British Constitution. Men of learning find nothing new in it, Men of taste many things to criticize. And men without either, not a few things, which they will not understand. It will nevertheless be read, and praised, and become a powerful engine in forming the public opinion. The name and character of the Author, with the critical situation of our affairs, naturally account for such an effect. The book also has merit, and I wish many of the remarks in it, which are unfriendly to republicanism, may not receive fresh weight from the operations of our Government.

I learn from Virginia that the appetite for paper money grows stronger every day. Mr. H-n-y is an avowed

BOSTON ATHENAEUM

John Adams by Mather Brown

*The city and port of Philadelphia
as it was in the eighteenth century*

patron of the scheme, and will not fail I think to carry it through unless the County which he is to represent shall bind him hand and foot by instructions. I am told that this is in contemplation. He is also said to be unfriendly to an acceleration of Justice. There is good reason to believe too that he is hostile to the object of the convention and that he wishes either a partition or total dissolution of the confederacy.

The Virginia Plan, presented by Governor Edmund Randolph and adopted as the working model on May 29, called for a vigorous national government founded in the authority of the people and acting directly on them. A national legislature in two branches, the first elected by the people, the second by the first branch; a body empowered "to legislate in all cases to which the separate states are incompetent," to negate all state laws contravening the articles of the Union, and to coerce the states where necessary; a separate national executive and national judiciary — these were the principal features of the "supreme national government" proposed by Virginia. A big step toward its realization was taken on June 6 when the committee of the whole voted for popular election of the lower house. On this matter Madison spoke as follows.

Debates in the Federal Convention
June 6, 1787

Mr. Madison considered an election of one branch at least of the Legislature by the people immediately, as a clear principle of free Govt. and that this mode under proper regulations had the additional advantage of securing better representatives, as well as of avoiding too great an agency of the State Governments in the General one.—He differed from the member from Connecticut [Mr. Sharman] in thinking the objects mentioned to be all the principal ones that required a National Govt. Those were certainly important and necessary objects; but he combined with them the necessity of providing more effectually for the security of private rights, and the steady dispensation of Justice. Interferences with these were evils which had more perhaps than any thing else, produced this convention. Was it to be supposed that republican liberty could long exist under the abuse of it practised in some of the States. The gentleman [Mr. Sharman] had admitted that in a very small State, faction & oppression wd. prevail. It was to be inferred then that wherever these prevailed the State was too small. Had they not prevailed in the largest as well as the smallest tho' less than in the smallest; and were we not thence admonished to enlarge the sphere as far as the nature of the Govt. would admit. This was the only defence agst. the inconveniences of democracy consistent with the democratic form of Govt. All civilized Societies would be divided into different Sects, Factions, & interests, as they happened to consist of rich & poor, debtors & creditors, the landed, the manufacturing, the commercial interests, the inhabitants of this district or that district, the followers of this political leader or that political leader, the disciples of this religious Sect or that religious Sect. In all cases where a majority are united by a common interest or passion, the rights of the minority are in danger. What motives are to restrain them? A prudent regard to the maxim that honesty is the best policy is found by experience to be as little regarded by bodies of men as by individuals. Respect for character is always diminished in proportion to the number among whom the blame or praise is to be divided. Conscience, the only remaining tie, is known to be inadequate in individuals: In large numbers, little is to be expected from

Edmund Randolph's notes of May 29 on discussion of the Virginia Plan

Delegates passing through the State House garden (above) were besieged by prisoners begging through the windows of Walnut Street Prison (below) and forced to endure their "foul and horrid imprecations."

it. Besides, Religion itself may become a motive to persecution & oppression.—These observations are verified by the Histories of every Country antient & modern. In Greece & Rome the rich & poor, the creditors & debtors, as well as the patricians & plebians alternately oppressed each other with equal unmercifulness. What a source of oppression was the relation between the parent cities of Rome, Athens & Carthage, & their respective provinces: the former possessing the power, & the latter being sufficiently distinguished to be separate objects of it? Why was America so justly apprehensive of Parliamentary injustice? Because G. Britain had a separate interest real or supposed, & if her authority had been admitted, could have pursued that interest at our expence. We have seen the mere distinction of colour made in the most enlightened period of time, a ground of the most oppressive dominion ever exercised by man over man. What has been the source of those unjust laws complained of among ourselves? Has it not been the real or supposed interest of the major numbers? Debtors have defrauded their creditors. The landed interest has borne hard on the mercantile interest. The Holders of one species of property have thrown a disproportion of taxes on the holders of another species. The lesson we are to draw from the whole is that where a majority are united by common sentiment, and have an opportunity, the rights of the minor party become insecure. In a Republican Govt. the Majority if united have always an opportunity. The only remedy is to enlarge the sphere, & thereby divide the community into so great a number of interests & parties, that in the 1st. place a majority will not be likely at the same moment to have a common interest separate from that of the whole or of the minority; and in the 2d. place, that in case they shd. have such an interest, they may not be apt to unite in the pursuit of it. It was incumbent on us then to try this remedy, and with that view to frame a republican system on such a scale & in such a form as will controul all the evils wch. have been experienced.

This speech, of course, had its basis in Madison's studies prior to the convention and also anticipated the fully developed "theory of factions" in the most famous of *The Federalist* papers. In reaction against the abuses of majoritarian democracy as practiced by the lower houses of the state legislatures, Madison had come to believe that the salvation of the Republic lay in enlarging the sphere of government so as to embrace a greater number of interests and factions. The theory turned the conventional wisdom from Aristotle to Montesquieu on its head. The idea that a republican government could not exist in a large territory, such as the United States, was wrong; in truth, said Madison, it could exist in no other. He had come to see this clearly after reading David Hume's "Idea of a Perfect Commonwealth," an explicit rebuttal of the equation of republicanism with smallness; but experience, too, had been his guide. Interests founded on property were the moving forces of government, he had learned. And because these interests cut across state lines, the great conflict that had broken out in the convention between large and small states was, in fact, a figment of the imagination, as he pointed out to his colleagues.

George Washington presiding over the Constitutional Convention

Debates in the Federal Convention
June 30, 1787

He [Mr. Madison] admitted that every peculiar interest whether in any case of citizens, or any description of States, ought to be secured as far as possible. Wherever there is danger of attack there ought be given a constitutional power of defence. But he contended that the States were divided into different interests not by their difference of size, but by other circumstances; the most material of which results partly from climate, but principally from the effects of their having or not having slaves. These two causes concurred in forming the great division of interests in the U. States. It did not lie between the large & small States: It lay between the Northern & Southern.

Madison's experience in the struggle for religious freedom in Virginia had also been important, for he had discovered that the principle could be best secured in a pluralistic environment of competing sects, no one of which could tyrannize over the others. The theory of factions applied to the political sphere a truth drawn from the religious sphere.

For six weeks the small-state bloc, fearing their powerlessness in the proposed government, fought to secure the representation of the states in the legislative branch. On June 7 it was agreed that the members of the upper house should be appointed by the state legislatures. Only the most strident nationalists, like Madison and James Wilson of Pennsylvania, opposed this concession to federalism. By itself it offered no protection to the small states, for the Virginia Plan still called for proportional representation in both branches. The committee of the whole went on record in favor of this rule on June 11. At this point the small-state leaders brought forth the so-called New Jersey Plan as a substitute for the Virginia Plan. Presented by William Paterson of New Jersey, the plan looked to amendment rather than overturn of the Articles of Confederation. A national executive and national judiciary would be created, but Congress would receive, sparingly, only additional enumerated powers, and equal representation of the states would remain the rule. "You see the consequence of pushing things too far," John Dickinson of Delaware said to Madison. "Some of the members from the small States wish for two branches in the General Legislature and are friends to a good National Government; but we would sooner submit to a foreign power than submit to be deprived of an equality of suffrage in both branches of the Legislature, and thereby be thrown under the domination of the large States." But on this issue Madison was immovable.

The New Jersey Plan was soon set aside, and the convention, unable to resolve the great question of representation, went on to less contentious matters. One of these was the duration of the term of members of the upper house. Already some men were conceiving of this body (the Senate) as the representation of the states with the lower house the representation of the people in the government. This was not Madison's conception. He viewed the Senate as a necessary check on the democracy—"the fickleness and passion"—of the lower house.

Debates in the Federal Convention
June 26, 1787

John Dickinson of Delaware

Mr. Madison. In order to judge of the form to be given to this institution, it will be proper to take a view of the ends to be served by it. These were first to protect the people agst. their rulers: secondly to protect the people agst. the transient impressions into which they themselves might be led. A people deliberating in a temperate moment, and with the experience of other nations before them, on the plan of Govt. most likely to secure their happiness, would first be aware, that those chargd. with the public happiness, might betray their trust. An obvious precaution agst. this danger wd. be to divide the trust between different bodies of men, who might watch & check each other.... It wd. next occur to such a people, that they themselves were liable to temporary errors, thro' want of information as to their true interest, and that men chosen for a short term, & employed but a small portion of that in public affairs, might err from the same cause. This reflection wd. naturally suggest that the Govt. be so constituted, as that one of its branches might have an oppy. of acquiring a competent knowledge of the public interests. Another reflection equally becoming

On July 17 a group of delegates, including Madison, rode out to visit William Bartram's gardens.

a people on such an occasion, wd. be that they themselves, as well as a numerous body of Representatives, were liable to err also, from fickleness and passion. A necessary fence agst. this danger would be to select a portion of enlightened citizens, whose limited number, and firmness might seasonably interpose agst. impetuous councils. It ought finally to occur to a people deliberating on a Govt. for themselves, that as different interests necessarily result from the liberty meant to be secured, the major interest might under sudden impulses be tempted to commit injustice on the minority. In all civilized Countries the people fall into different classes havg a real or supposed difference of interests. There will be creditors & debtors, farmer, merchts. & manufacturers. There will be particularly the distinction of rich & poor. It was true as had been observd. [by Mr. Pinkney] we had not among us those hereditary distinctions, of rank which were a great source of the contests in the ancient Govts. as well as the modern States of Europe, nor those extremes of wealth or poverty which characterize the latter. We cannot however be regarded even at this time, as one homogeneous mass, in which every thing that affects a part will affect in the same manner the whole. In framing a system which we wish to last for ages, we shd. not lose sight of the changes which ages will produce. An increase of population will of necessity increase the proportion of those who will labour under all the hardships of life, & secretly sigh for a more equal distribution of its blessings. These may in time outnumber those who are placed above the feelings of indigence. According to the equal laws of suffrage, the power will slide into the hands of the former. No agrarian attempts have yet been made in this Country, but symtoms, of a leveling spirit, as we have understood, have sufficiently appeared in a certain quarters to give notice of the future danger. How is this danger to be guarded agst. on republican principles? How is the danger in all cases of interested coalitions to oppress the minority to be guarded agst? Among other means by the establishment of a body in the Govt. sufficiently respectable for its wisdom & virtue to aid on such emergencies, the preponderance of justice by throwing its weight into that scale. Such being the objects of the second branch in the proposed Govt. he [Mr. Madison] thought a considerable duration ought to be given to it.

He did not conceive that the term of nine years could threaten any real danger; but in pursuing his particular ideas on the subject, he should require that the long term allowed to the 2d. branch should not commence till such a period of life, as would render a perpetual disqualification to be re-elected little inconvenient either in a public or private view. He observed that as it was more than probable we were now digesting a plan which in its operation wd. decide for ever the fate of Republican Govt. we ought not only to provide every guard to liberty that its preservation cd. require, but be equally careful to supply the defects which our own experience had particularly pointed out.

James Wilson of Pennsylvania

Whatever the theoretical merits of Madison's position on representation, more and more delegates were becoming convinced it was impractical. The country, after all, was composed of corporate political units—states—and they could not be left out of the general government. On July 2 Connecticut moved for state equality in the upper house. A tie vote resulted; stalemate was complete. When a motion was made to send the issue to a committee for decision, Madison smelled a compromise and opposed it. But the committee was appointed, and the next day it reported the "great compromise": equal representation of the states in the upper house, proportional representation in the lower, provided that all money bills originate in the latter. Madison and the hardcore nationalists fought the compromise until July 16, when it was narrowly adopted. The ultranationalists had lost control of the convention. From this point the strongly "consolidated" union envisioned by the Virginia Plan was replaced by the moderate conception of a government with a "mixed constitution," partly national, partly federal, of which, ironically, James Madison himself would become the great expounder in *The Federalist.*

Without compromise there would have been no new government, but the price of compromise was a garbled and mutilated constitution. Certainly this was Madison's belief as he watched other parts of the Virginia Plan cut away and discarded. Instead of a congressional negative over state laws, the convention relied upon the expedient of the New Jersey Plan declaring the constitution and the laws made under it "the supreme law of the land" in the several states. Instead of a plenary grant of legislative power, the convention chose to enumerate specific powers granted to Congress. Madison fought for the negative without success. He tried to expand the list of enumerated powers—powers to establish a national university, to promote useful knowledge, to grant corporate charters, to tax exports— again without success. When it came to the executive, Madison himself took leave of the Virginia Plan. Wishing a strong and independent executive, one that would express the will of the nation and not be answerable to partial interests or congressional cabals, he saw the importance of founding the appointment directly on the popular suffrage. His speech arguing this position is spiced with his pessimistic opinion of human nature when arrayed in the garments of power.

Debates in the Federal Convention
July 25, 1787

Mr. Madison. There are objections agst. every mode that has been, or perhaps can be proposed. The election must be made either by some existing authority under the Natil. or State Constitutions—or by some special authority derived from the people—or by the people themselves.—The two Existing authorities under the Natl. Constitution wd. be the Legislative & Judiciary. The latter he presumed was out of the question. The former was in his Judgment liable to insuperable objections. Besides the general influence of that mode on the independence of the Executive,   1. the election of the Chief Magistrate would agitate & divide the legislature so much that the public interest would materially suffer by it. Public bodies are always apt to be thrown into contentions, but into more violent ones by such occasions than by any others.   2. the candidate would intrigue with the Legislature, would derive his appointment from the predominant faction, and be apt to render his administration subservient to its views.   3. The Ministers of foreign powers would have and make use of, the opportunity to mix their intrigues & influence with the Election. Limited as the powers of the Executive are, it will be an object of great moment with the great rival powers of Europe who have American possessions, to have at the head of our Governmt. a man attached to their respective politics & interests. No pains, nor perhaps expence, will be spared, to gain from the Legislature an appointmt. favorable to their wishes.... The existing authorities in the States are the Legislative, Executive & Judiciary. The appointment of the Natl. Executive by the first, was objectionable in many points of view, some of which had been already mentioned. He would mention one which of itself would decide his opinion. The Legislatures of the States had betrayed a strong propensity to a variety of pernicious measures. One object

Washington was a guest in Robert Morris's home during the summer of 1787. As President, he and Martha lived in the same house.

Robert Morris of Pennsylvania

of the Natl. Legislr. was to controul this propensity. One object of the Natl. Executive, so far as it would have a negative on the laws, was to controul the Natl. Legislature, so far as it might be infected with a similar propensity. Refer the appointmt. of the Natl. Executive to the State Legislatures, and this controuling purpose may be defeated. The Legislatures can & will act with some kind of regular plan, and will promote the appointmt. of a man who will not oppose himself to a favorite client. Should a majority of the Legislatures at the time of election have the same object, or different objects of the same kind, The Natl. Executive would be rendered subservient to them....The option before us then lay between an appointment by Electors chosen by the people—and an immediate appointment by the people. He thought the former mode free from many of the objections which had been urged agst. it, and greatly preferable to an appointment by the Natl. Legislature. As the electors would be chosen for the occasion, would meet at once, & proceed immediately to an appointment, there would be very little opportunity for cabal, or corruption....The remaining mode was an election by the people or rather by the qualified part of them, at large. With all its imperfections he liked this best. He would not repeat either the general argumts. for or the objections agst. this mode. He would only take notice of two difficulties which he admitted to have weight. The first arose from the disposition in the people to prefer a Citizen of their own State, and the disadvantages this wd. throw on the smaller States. Great as this objection might be he did not think it equal to such as lay agst. every other mode which had been proposed. He thought too that some expedient might be hit upon that would obviate it. The second difficulty arose from the disproportion of qualified voters in the N. & S. States and the disadvantages which this mode would throw on the latter. The answer to this objection was 1. that this disproportion would be continually decreasing under the influence of the Republican laws introduced in the S. States, and the more rapid increase of their population. 2. That local considerations must give way to the general interest. As an individual from the S. States he was willing to make the sacrifice.

Indirect election of the President through the medium of an electoral college was, of course, the mode finally chosen. It was quite acceptable to Madison. The convention finished its work on September 17. Only thirty-eight of the original fifty-five delegates were still in attendance. The summer's heat had taken its toll; some delegates had been called home, others had walked out in protest. After the final reading of the engrossed Constitution, the aged Franklin rose to plead for unanimous approval. "I consent, Sir, to this Constitution, because I expect no better, and because I am not sure, that it is not the best." Madison could subscribe to this philosophy. More ardent centralists than he—Alexander Hamilton, James Wilson, Gouverneur Morris—signed the document. The three who did not, Elbridge Gerry of Massachusetts and the Virginians George Mason and Edmund Randolph, feared the strength, not the weakness, of the new government.

The delegates had provided for ratification of the Constitution by popularly elected conventions in the several states, the approval of nine states only being sufficient to establish the government. Some men had balked at this "new set of ideas," strangely democratic and unknown to the Articles of Confederation, but the majority had readily assented to Madison's argument that the legitimacy of the government must be founded in the sovereignty of the people.

Debates in the Federal Convention
July 23, 1787

Mr. Madison thought it clear that the Legislatures were incompetent to the proposed changes. These changes would make essential inroads on the State Constitutions,

Resolution (left) submitting the Constitution to Congress with the signature of George Washington, president; aged Benjamin Franklin (above) pleaded for its approval.

and it would be a novel & dangerous doctrine that a Legislature could change the constitution under which it held its existence. There might indeed be some Constitutions within the Union, which had given a power to the Legislature to concur in alterations of the federal Compact. But there were certainly some which had not; and in the case of these, a ratification must of necessity be obtained from the people. He considered the difference between a system founded on the Legislatures only, and one founded on the people, to be the true difference between a *league* or *treaty*, and a *Constitution*. The former in point of *moral obligation* might be as inviolable as the latter. In point of *political operation*, there were two important distinctions in favor of the latter. 1. A law violating a treaty ratified by a pre-existing law, might be respected by the Judges as a law, though an unwise or perfidious one. A law violating a constitution established by the people themselves, would be considered by the Judges as null & void. 2. The doctrine laid down by the law of Nations in the case of treaties is that a breach of any one article by any of the parties, frees the other parties from their engagements. In the case of a union of people under one Constitution, the nature of the pact has always been understood to exclude such an interpretation. Comparing the two modes in point of expediency he thought all the considerations which recommended this Convention in preference to Congress for proposing the reform were in favor of State Conventions in preference to the Legislatures for examining and adopting it.

Madison returned to Congress to plan the strategy of the ratification campaign. The Constitution was well below his expectations, but he embraced it in the confidence it was the strongest medicine the public would swallow. In the wider controversy now beginning he would bury his doubts and scruples, though he did not disguise them in a lengthy report sent to Jefferson in France on the convention and its work.

New York Octr. 24. 1787

You will herewith receive the result of the Convention, which continued its session till the 17th of September. I take the liberty of making some observations on the subject which will help to make up a letter, if they should answer no other purpose.

*Gouverneur Morris of Pennsylvania
was known as "an eternal speaker."*

It appeared to be the sincere and unanimous wish of the Convention to cherish and preserve the Union of the States. No proposition was made, no suggestion was thrown out in favor of a partition of the Empire into two or more Confederacies.

It was generally agreed that the objects of the Union could not be secured by any system founded on the principle of a confederation of sovereign States. A voluntary observance of the federal law by all the members could never be hoped for. A compulsive one could evidently never be reduced to practice, and if it could, involved equal calamities to the innocent and the guilty, the necessity of a military force both obnoxious and dangerous, and in general, a scene resembling much more a civil war, than the administration of a regular Government.

Hence was embraced the alternative of a government which instead of operating, on the States, should operate without their intervention on the individuals composing them: and hence the change in the principle and proportion of representation.

This ground-work being laid, the great objects which presented themselves were 1. to unite a proper energy in the Executive and a proper stability in the Legislative departments, with the essential characters of Republican Government. 2. To draw a line of demarkation which would give to the Central Government every power requisite for general purposes, and leave to the States every power which might be most beneficially administered by them. 3. To provide for the different interests of different parts of the Union. 4. To adjust the clashing pretensions of the large and small States. Each of these objects was pregnant with difficulties. The whole of them together formed a task more difficult than can be well conceived by those who were not concerned in the execution of it. Adding to these considerations the natural diversity of human opinions on all new and complicated subjects, it is impossible to consider the degree of concord which ultimately prevailed as less than a miracle.

The first of these objects as it respects the Executive, was peculiarly embarrassing. On the question whether it should consist of a single person, or a plurality of coordinate members, on the mode of appointment, on the duration in office, on the degree of power, on the re-eligibility, tedious and reiterated discussions took place. The plurality of co-ordinate members had finally but few advocates. Governour Randolph was at the head of them. The modes of appointment proposed were various, as by the people at large—by electors chosen by the people—by the Executives of the States—by the Congress, some preferring a joint ballot of the two Houses—some a separate concurrent ballot allowing to each a negative on the other house—some a nomination of several candidates by one House, out of whom a choice should be made by the other.... The expedient at length adopted seemed to give pretty general satisfaction to the members. As to the duration in office, a few would have preferred a tenure during good behaviour—a considerable number would have done so in case an easy and effectual removal by impeachment could be settled. It was much agitated whether a long term, seven years for example, with a subsequent and perpetual ineligibility, or a short term with a capacity to be re-elected, should be fixed.... The questions concerning the degree of power turned chiefly on the appointment to offices and the controul on the Legislature. An absolute appointment to all offices—to some offices—to no offices, formed the scale of opinions of the first point. On the second, some contended for an absolute negative, as the only possible mean of reducing to practice, the theory of a free government which forbids a mixture of the Legislative and Executive powers. Others would be content with a revisionary power to be overruled by three fourths of both Houses. It was warmly urged that the judiciary department should be associated in the revision. The idea of some was that a separate revision should be given to the two departments—that if either objected two thirds; if both three fourths, should be necessary to overrule.

In forming the Senate, the great anchor of the Government, the questions as they came within the first object turned mostly on the mode of appointment, and the duration of it. The different modes proposed were, 1. by the House of Representatives, 2. by the Executive, 3. by electors chosen by the people for the purpose, 4. by the State Legislatures. On the point of duration, the propositions descended from good behavior to four years, through the intermediate terms of nine, seven, six and five years. The election of the other branch was first determined to

Jared Ingersoll of Pennsylvania did not speak during the entire summer.

be triennial, and afterwards reduced to biennial.

The second object, the due partition of power, between the General and local Governments, was perhaps of all, the most nice and difficult. A few contended for an entire abolition of the States: Some for indefinite power of Legislation in the Congress, with a negative on the laws of the States: some for such a power without a negative: some for a limited power of legislation, with such a negative: the majority finally for a limited power without the negative. The question with regard to the Negative underwent repeated discussions, and was finally rejected by a bare majority. As I formerly intimated to you my opinion in favor of this ingredient, I will take this occasion of explaining myself on the subject....

1. Without such a check in the whole over the parts, our system involves the evil of imperia in imperio [a government within a government]. If a compleat supremacy some where is not necessary in every Society, a controuling power at least is so, by which the general authority may be defended against encroachments of the subordinate authorities, and by which the latter may be restrained from encroachments on each other. If the supremacy of the British Parliament is not necessary as has been contended, for the harmony of that Empire, it is evident I think that without the royal negative or some equivalent controul the unity of the system would be destroyed. The want of some such provision seems to have been mortal to the antient Confederacies and to be the disease of the modern.... Still more to the purpose is our own experience both during the war and since the peace. Encroachments of the States on the general authority, sacrifices of national to local interests, interferences of the measures of different States, form a great part of the history of our political system. It may be said that the new Constitution is founded on different principles, and will have a different operation. I admit the difference to be material. It presents the aspect rather of a feudal system of republics, if such a phrase may be used, than of a Confederacy of independent States. And what has been the progress and event of the feudal Constitutions? In all of them a continual struggle between the head and the inferior members, until a final victory has been gained in some instances by one, in others, by the other of them.... It may be said that the Judicial

authority under our new system will keep the States within their proper limits, and supply the place of a negative on their laws. The answer is that it is more convenient to prevent the passage of a law, than to declare it void after it is passed; that this will be particularly the case where the law aggrieves individuals, who may be unable to support an appeal against a State to the supreme Judiciary, that a State which would violate the Legislative rights of the Union, would not be very ready to obey a Judicial decree in support of them, and that a recurrence to force, which in the event of disobedience would be necessary, is an evil which the new Constitution meant to exclude as far as possible.

2. A Constitutional negative on the laws of the States seems equally necessary to secure individuals against encroachments on their rights. The mutability of the laws of the States is found to be a serious evil. The injustice of them has been so frequent and so flagrant as to alarm the most stedfast friends of Republicanism. I am persuaded I do not err in saying that the evils issuing from these sources contributed more to that uneasiness which produced the Convention, and prepared the public mind for a general reform, than those which accrued to our national character and interest from the inadequacy of the Confederation to its immediate objects. A reform therefore which does not make provision for private rights, must be materially defective. . . . It may be asked how private rights will be more secure under the Guardianship of the General Government than under the State Governments, since they are both founded on the republican principle which refers the ultimate decision to the will of the majority, and are distinguished rather by the extent within which they will operate, than by any material difference in their structure. . . . I will state some of the ideas which have occurred to me on this subject. Those who contend for a simple Democracy, or a pure republic, actuated by the sense of the majority, and operating within narrow limits, assume or suppose a case which is altogether fictitious. They found their reasoning on the idea, that the people composing the Society enjoy not only an equality of political rights; but that they have all precisely the same interests and the same feelings in every respect. Were this in reality the case, their reasoning would be conclusive. The interest

Three delegates refused to sign the Constitution: George Mason (top left) and Edmund Randolph (bottom left), Virginia; Elbridge Gerry, Massachusetts (top). Luther Martin, Maryland (above), had left early.

147

of the majority would be that of the minority also; the decisions could only turn on mere opinion concerning the good of the whole of which the major voice would be the safest criterion; and within a small sphere, this voice could be most easily collected and the public affairs most accurately managed. We know however that no Society ever did or can consist of so homogeneous a mass of Citizens. In the savage State indeed, an approach is made towards it; but in that state little or no Government is necessary. In all civilized Societies, distinctions are various and unavoidable. A distinction of property results from that very protection which a free Government gives to unequal faculties of acquiring it. There will be rich and poor; creditors and debtors; a landed interest, a monied interest, a mercantile interest, a manufacturing interest.... If then there must be different interests and parties in Society; and a majority when united by a common interest or passion can not be restrained from oppressing the minority, what remedy can be found in a republican Government, where the majority must ultimately decide, but that of giving such an extent to its sphere, that no common interest or passion will be likely to unite a majority of the whole number in an unjust pursuit. In a large Society, the people are broken into so many interests and parties, that a common sentiment is less likely to be felt, and the requisite concert less likely to be formed, by a majority of the whole. The same security seems requisite for the civil as for the religious rights of individuals. If the same sect form a majority and have the power, other sects will be sure to be depressed. Divide et impera [divide and rule], the reprobated axiom of tyranny, is under certain qualifications, the only policy, by which a republic can be administered on just principles. It must by observed however that this doctrine can only hold within a sphere of a mean extent. As in too small a sphere oppressive combinations may be too easily formed against the weaker party; so in too extensive a one a defensive concert may be rendered too difficult against the oppression of those entrusted with the administration. The great desideratum in Government is, so to modify the sovereignty as that it may be sufficiently neutral between different parts of the Society to controul one part from invading the rights of another, and at the same time sufficiently controuled itself, from setting up an interest adverse to that of the entire Society.... In the extended Republic of the United States, the General Government would hold a pretty even balance between the parties of particular States, and be at the same time sufficiently restrained by its dependence on the community, from betraying its general interests.

Begging pardon for this immoderate digression, I return to the third object abovementioned, the adjustment of the different interests of different parts of the Continent. Some contended for an unlimited power over trade including exports as well as imports, and over slaves as well as other imports; some for such a power, provided the concurrence of two thirds of both Houses were required; some for such a qualification of the power, with an exemption of exports and slaves, others for an exemption of exports only. The result is seen in the Constitution. [The importation of slaves could not be prohibited prior to 1808; trade could be regulated by vote of a simple majority.] S. Carolina and Georgia were inflexible on the point of the slaves.

The remaining object, created more embarrassment, and a greater alarm for the issue of the Convention than all the rest put together. The little States insisted on retaining their equality in both branches, unless a compleat abolition of the State Governments should take place; and made an equality in the Senate a sine qua non. The

Scenes familiar to convention delegates included Chestnut Street, where Congress Hall was being built that summer (opposite), and the markets along High Street.

large States on the other hand urged that as the new Government was to be drawn principally from the people immediately and was to operate directly on them, not on the States; and consequently as the States would lose that importance which is now proportioned to the importance of their voluntary compliances with the requisitions of Congress, it was necessary that the representation in both Houses should be in proportion to their size. It ended in the compromise which you will see, but very much to the dissatisfaction of several members from the large States.

The advocates of the new system took the name of Federalists. Those in opposition were perforce Antifederalists, though they professed to be the true friends of both federalism and republicanism. "Since the world began," a Pennsylvanian remarked, "I believe no question has ever been more repeatedly and strictly scrutinized or more fairly and freely argued, than the proposed Constitution." The most distinguished product of this debate was the series of seventy-seven letters of "Publius" contributed to the New York press and later published collectively with eight more as *The Federalist.* Publius was the composite creation of two New Yorkers, John Jay and Alexander Hamilton, and Madison. Hastily written in the heat of campaign, *The Federalist* nevertheless became the classic commentary on the Constitution. Twenty-nine of the papers may be credited to Madison. Most important at the time were those in which Madison, with statesmanlike ingenuity, gave theoretical form and coherence to the disjointed work of the convention. Suppressing his own disappointments, allaying the fears of his opponents, Madison fabricated a working model of the new system such as had scarcely been imagined before, and so compelling was it that it could never be escaped thereafter. In Number 39, for example, he set forth the idea of a "compound republic," partly national and partly federal, which overcame the polarity of these terms and laid the basis for political accommodation.

[January 16, 1788]

In order to ascertain the real character of the government it may be considered in relation to the foundation on which it is to be established; to the sources from which its ordinary powers are to be drawn; to the operation of those powers; to the extent of them; and to the authority by which future changes in the government are to be introduced.

On examining the first relation, it appears on one hand that the Constitution is to be founded on the assent and ratification of the people of America, given by deputies elected for the special purpose; but on the other, that this assent and ratification is to be given by the people, not as individuals composing one entire nation; but as composing the distinct and independent States to which they respectively belong. It is to be the assent and ratification of the several States, derived from the supreme authority in each State, the authority of the people themselves. The act therefore establishing the Constitution, will not be a *national* but a *federal* act.

That it will be a federal and not a national act, as these terms are understood by the objectors, the act of the people as forming so many independent States, not as forming one aggregate nation, is obvious from this single consideration that it is to result neither from the decision of a *majority* of the people of the Union, nor from that of a *majority* of the States. It must result from the *unanimous* assent of the several States that are parties to it, differing no other wise from their ordinary assent than in its being expressed, not by the legislative authority, but by that of the people themselves. Were the people regarded in this transaction as forming one nation, the will of the majority of the whole people of the United States, would bind the minority; in the same manner as the majority in each State must bind the minority; and the will of the majority must be determined either by a comparison of the individual votes; or by considering the will of a majority of the States, as evidence of the will of a majority of the people of the United States. Neither of these rules has been adopted. Each State in ratifying the Constitution, is considered as a sovereign body independent of all others, and only to be bound by its own voluntary act. In this relation then the new Constitution will, if established, be a *federal* and not a *national* Constitution.

The next relation is to the sources from which the ordinary powers of government are to be derived. The house of representatives will derive its powers from the people of America, and the people will be represented in the same proportion, and on the same principle, as they are in the Legislature of a particular State. So far the Government is *national* not *federal*. The Senate on the other hand will derive its powers from the States, as political and co-equal societies; and these will be represented on the principle of equality in the Senate, as

John Jay (above, by John Trumbull) and Alexander Hamilton (below, by James Sharples) collaborated with Madison on The Federalist.

52   THE FEDERALIST.

long as it exifts by a conftitutional neceffity for local purpofes, though it fhould be in perfect fubordination to the general authority of the union, it would ftill be, in fact and in theory, an affociation of ftates, or a confederacy. The propofed conftitution, fo far from implying an abolition of the ftate governments, makes them conftituent parts of the national fovereignty by allowing them a direct reprefentation in the fenate, and leaves in their poffeffion certain exclufive and very important portions of fovereign power.—This fully correfponds, in every rational import of the terms, with the idea of a federal government.

In the Lycian confederacy, which confifted of twenty-three CITIES, or republics, the largeft were intitled to *three* votes in the COMMON COUNCIL, thofe of the middle clafs to *two*, and the fmalleft to *one*. The COMMON COUNCIL had the appointment of all the judges and magiftrates of the refpective CITIES. This was certainly the moft delicate fpecies of interference in their internal adminiftration; for if there be any thing that feems exclufively appropriated to the local jurifdictions, it is the appointment of their own officers. Yet Montefquieu, fpeaking of this affo-ciation, fays, " Were I to give a model of an excellent " confederate republic, it would be that of Lycia." Thus we perceive that the diftinctions infifted upon were not within the contemplation of this enlightened civilian, and we fhall be led to conclude, that they are the novel refinements of an erroneous theory.

PUBLIUS.

NUMBER X.
The fame Subject continued.

AMONG the numerous advantages promifed by a well conftructed union, none deferves to be more accurately developed than its tendency to break and control the violence of faction. The friend of popular governments,

Number 10 of The Federalist *was the most celebrated of the twenty-nine essays credited to Madison.*

they now are in the existing Congress. So far the government is federal, not national. The executive power will be derived from a very compound source. The immediate election of the President is to be made by the States in their political characters. The votes alloted to them, are in a compound ratio, which considers them partly as distinct and co-equal societies; partly as unequal members of the same society. The eventual election, again is to be made by that branch of the Legislature which consists of the national representatives; but in this particular act, they are to be thrown into the form of individual delegations from so many distinct and co-equal bodies politic. From this aspect of the Government, it appears to be of a mixed character presenting at least as many *federal* as *national* features.

The difference between a federal and national Government as it relates to the *operation of the Government* is supposed to consist in this, that in the former, the powers operate on the political bodies composing the confederacy, in their political capacities: In the latter, on the individual citizens, composing the nation, in their individual capacities. On trying the Constitution by this criterion, it falls under the *national*, not the *federal* character; though perhaps not so compleatly, as has been understood. . . .

But if the Government be national with regard to the *operation* of its powers, it changes its aspect again when we contemplate it in relation to the *extent* of its powers. The idea of a national Government involves in it, not only an authority over the individual citizens; but an indefinite supremacy over all persons and things, so far as they are objects of lawful Government. Among a people consolidated into one nation, this supremacy is compleatly vested in the national Legislature. Among communities united for particular purposes, it is vested partly in the general, and partly in the municipal Legislatures. In the former cases, all local authorities are subordinate to the supreme; and may be controuled, directed or abolished by it at pleasure. In the latter the local or municipal authorities form distinct and independent portions of the supremacy, no more subject within their respective spheres to the general authority, than the general authority is subject to them, within its own sphere. In this relation then the proposed Government cannot be deemed a *national* one; since its jurisdiction extends to certain enumerated objects only, and leaves to the several States a residuary and inviolable sovereignty over all other objects. It is true that in controversies relating to the boundary between the two jurisdictions, the tribunal which is ultimately to decide, is to be established under the general Government. But this does not change the principle of the case. The decision is to be impartially made, according to the rules of the Constitution; and all the usual and most effectual precautions are taken to secure this impartiality. Some such tribunal is clearly essential to prevent an appeal to the sword, and a dissolution of the compact; and that it ought to be established under the general, rather than under the local Governments; or to speak more properly, that it could be safely established under the first alone, is a position not likely to be combated.

If we try the Constitution by its last relation, to the authority by which amendments are to be made, we find it neither wholly *national*, nor wholly *federal*. Were it wholly national, the supreme and ultimate authority would reside in the *majority* of the people of the Union; and this authority would be competent at all times, like that of a majority of every national society, to alter or abolish its established Government. Were it wholly federal on the other hand, the concurrence of each State in the Union would be essential to every alteration that would be binding on all. The mode provided by the plan of the Convention is not founded on either of these principles. In requiring more than a majority, and particularly, in computing the proportion by *States*, not by *citizens*, it departs from the *national*, and advances towards the *federal* character: In rendering the concurrence of less than the whole number of States sufficient, it loses again the *federal*, and partakes of the *national* character.

The proposed Constitution therefore is in strictness neither a national nor a federal constitution; but a composition of both. In its foundation, it is federal, not national; in the sources from which the ordinary powers of the Government are drawn, it is partly federal, and partly national: in the operation of these powers, it is national, not federal: In the extent of them again, it is federal, not national: And finally, in the authoritative

By the United States in Congress assembled,

SEPTEMBER 13, 1788.

WHEREAS the Convention assembled in Philadelphia, pursuant to the Resolution of Congress of the 21st February, 1787, did, on the 17th of September in the same year, report to the United States in Congress assembled, a Constitution for the People of the United States; whereupon Congress, on the 28th of the same September, did resolve unanimously, " That the said report, with the Resolutions and Letter accompanying the same, be transmitted to the several Legislatures, in order to be submitted to a Convention of Delegates chosen in each State by the people thereof, in conformity to the Resolves of the Convention made and provided in that case:" And whereas the Constitution so reported by the Convention, and by Congress transmitted to the several Legislatures, has been ratified in the manner therein declared to be sufficient for the establishment of the same, and such Ratifications duly authenticated have been received by Congress, and are filed in the Office of the Secretary—therefore,

RESOLVED, That the first Wednesday in January next, be the day for appointing Electors in the several States, which before the said day shall have ratified the said Constitution; that the first Wednesday in February next, be the day for the Electors to assemble in their respective States, and vote for a President; and that the first Wednesday in March next, be the time, and the present Seat of Congress the place for commencing Proceedings under the said Constitution.

Chas Thomson Secy

Madison's essay Number 39 stated: "The immediate election of the President is to be made by the States...." A broadside issued a year later announced the date for the electors to vote for President.

153

mode of introducing amendments, it is neither wholly federal, nor wholly national.

In December, as the first state conventions assembled, Madison sent another report to Jefferson.

New York. Decr. 9th. 1787

The Constitution proposed by the late Convention engrosses almost the whole political attention of America. All the Legislatures except that of R. Island, which have been assembled, have agreed in submitting it to State Conventions. Virginia has set the example of opening a door for amendments, if the Convention there should chuse to propose them. Maryland has copied it. The States which preceded, referred the Constitution as recommended by the General Convention, to be ratified or rejected as it stands. The Convention of Pennsylvania, is now sitting. There are about 44 or 45, on the affirmative and about half that number on the opposite side. ... The returns of deputies for the Convention of Connecticut are known, and prove, as is said by those who know the men that a very great majority will adopt it in that State. The event in Massachusetts lies in greater uncertainty. The friends of the New Government continue to be sanguine. N. Hampshire from every account, as well as from some general inducements felt there, will pretty certainly be on the affirmative side. So will New Jersey and Delaware. N. York is much divided. She will hardly dissent from N. England, particularly if the conduct of the latter should coincide with that of N. Jersey and Pennsylva. A more formidable opposition is likely to be made in Maryland than was at first conjectured.... The body of the people in Virgina. particularly in the upper and lower Country, and in the Northern Neck, are as far as I can gather, much disposed to adopt the new Constitution. The middle Country, and the South side of James River are principally in the opposition to it. As yet a large majority of the people are under the first description. As yet also are a majority of the Assembly. What change may be produced by the united influence of exertions of Mr. Henry, Mr. [George] Mason, and the Governor with some pretty able auxiliaries, is uncertain. My information leads me to suppose there must be three parties in Virginia. The first for adopting without

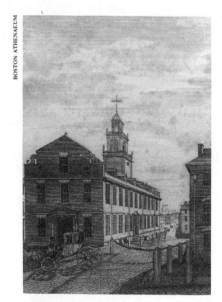

The State House in Boston where the Massachusetts convention for ratification of the Constitution met

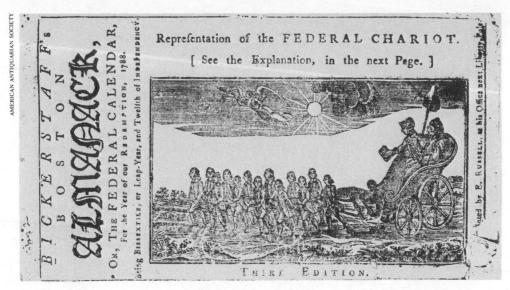

The cover of this 1788 Almanac crudely depicts George Washington and Benjamin Franklin escorting the new Constitution to its ratification by the states.

attempting amendments. This includes Genl. W and the other deputies who signed the Constitution, Mr. Pendleton (Mr. Marshal I believe), Mr. Nicholas, Mr. Corbin, Mr. Zachy. Johnson, Col. Innis, (Mr. B. Randolph as I understand) Mr. Harvey, Mr. Gabl. Jones, Docr. Jones, &c. &c. At the head of the 2d. party which urges amendments are the Govr. & Mr. Mason. These do not object to the substance of the Governt. but contend for a few additional guards in favor of the Rights of the States and of the people. I am not able to enumerate the characters which fall in with their ideas, as distinguished from those of a third Class, at the head of which is Mr. Henry. This class concurs at present with the patrons of amendments, but will probably contend for such as strike at the essence of the System, and must lead to an adherence to the principle of the existing Confederation, which most thinking men are convinced is a visionary one, or to a partition of the Union into several Confederacies....Mr. Henry is the great adversary who will render the event precarious. He is I find with his usual address, working up every possible interest, into a spirit of opposition. It is worthy of remark that whilst in Virga. and some of the other States in the middle & Southern Districts of the Union, the men of intelligence, patriotism, property, and independent circumstances, are thus divided: all of this description, with a few exceptions, in the Eastern States, and most of the middle States, are zealously attached to the proposed Constitution. In N. England, the men of letters, the principal officers of Government, the Judges and Lawyers, the Clergy, and men of property, furnish only here and there an adversary. It is not less worthy of remark that in Virginia where the mass of the people have been so much accustomed to be guided by their rulers on all new and intricate questions, they should on the present which certainly surpasses the judgment of the greater part of them, not only go before, but contrary to their most popular leaders. And the phenomenon is the more wonderful as a popular ground is taken by all the adversaries to the new Constitution. Perhaps the solution in both these cases, would not be very difficult; but it would lead to observations too diffusive; and to you unnecessary. I will barely observe that the case in Virga. seems to prove that the body of sober and steady people, even of the lower order, are tired of the vicisitudes, injustice and follies which have so much characterised public measures, and are impatient for some change which promises stability and repose.

Madison was rightly apprehensive about Virginia. Six states were under the new roof when he left New York for home in March, 1788, to seek election to the Virginia convention. He was successful, and it was generally thought the Federalists had won a slight edge in the delegate count. Eight states had ratified (Rhode Island had rejected the Constitution and the New Hampshire convention had adjourned without decision) when the delegates assembled in Richmond on June 2. All eyes were on Virginia, not simply because she would make the ninth state but because without Virginia the Union would be impoverished, cut in two, deprived of Washington's leadership, probably rebuffed by New York, and left to waste away. Madison did not underestimate his opposition. Patrick Henry, bespectacled, bewigged, slightly stooped now, still flashed the oratorical brilliance that had electrified the colonists in 1765. Ably assisted though he was, Henry was the colossus of the Antifederalists. Conjuring up the specter of "one great consolidated empire," he mocked and scorned the Constitution. Federal tax gatherers would suck the blood of the people; a standing army would oppress them; the states would be annihilated; and a northern sectional majority in Congress would ride roughshod over the farmers of the South, abandon the Mississippi, and even strike at slavery.

"What can avail your specious, imaginary balances, your rope-dancing, chain-rattling ridiculous ideal checks and contrivances?" The Constitution had "an awful squinting," said Henry, touching on the executive; "it squints at monarchy, and does not this raise indignation in the breast of every true American?"

To Henry's frightful rhetoric, Madison opposed dispassionate reason. He had no other eloquence: frail in body, frail in voice, he was not a commanding figure; but he spoke to the point with calmness and composure, and he addressed the intelligence, not the fears, of the delegates. "In fine," it was later said, "the good genius of the country was in him personified." The following is taken from Madison's first reply to Henry.

Debates of the Convention of Virginia
June 6, 1788

Patrick Henry

We ought sir, to examine the Constitution on its own merits solely: we are to inquire whether it will promote the public happiness: its aptitude to produce this desirable object ought to be the exclusive subject of our present researches. In this pursuit, we ought not to address our arguments to the feelings and passions, but to those understandings and judgments which were selected by the people of this country, to decide this great question by a calm and rational investigation. I hope that gentlemen, in displaying their abilities on this occasion, instead of giving opinions and making assertions, will condescend to prove and demonstrate, by a fair and regular discussion. It gives me pain to hear gentlemen continually distorting the natural construction of language, for it is sufficient if any human production can stand a fair discussion....I must take the liberty to make some observations on what was said by another gentleman, (Mr. Henry.) He told us that this Constitution ought to be rejected because it endangered the public liberty, in his opinion, in many instances. Give me leave to make one answer to that observation: Let the dangers which this system is supposed to be replete with be clearly pointed out: if any dangerous and unnecessary powers be given to the general legislature, let them be plainly demonstrated, and let us not rest satisfied with general assertions of danger, without examination. If powers be necessary, apparent danger is not a sufficient reason against conceding them. He has suggested that licentiousness has seldom produced the loss of liberty; but that the tyranny of rulers has almost always effected it. Since the general civilization of mankind, I believe there are more instances of the abridgment of the freedom of the people by gradual and silent encroachments of those in power, than by violent and sudden usurpations; but, on a candid examination of history, we shall find that turbulence, violence, and abuse of power, by the majority trampling on the rights of the minority, have produced factions and commotions, which, in republics, have, more frequently than any other cause, produced despotism. If we go over the whole history of ancient and modern republics, we shall find their destruction to have generally resulted from those causes. If we consider the peculiar situation of the United States, and what are the sources of that diversity of sentiment which pervades its inhabitants, we shall find great danger to fear that the same causes may terminate here in the same fatal effects which they produced in those republics. This danger ought to be wisely guarded against....

I must confess I have not been able to find his usual consistency in the gentleman's argument on this occasion. He informs us that the people of the country are at perfect repose,—that is, every man enjoys the fruits of his labor peaceably and securely, and that every thing is in perfect tranquility and safety. I wish sincerely, sir, this were true. If this be their happy situation, why has every state acknowledged the contrary? Why were deputies from all the states sent to the general Convention? Why have complaints of national and individual distresses been echoed and re-echoed throughout the continent? Why has our general government been so shamefully disgraced, and our Constitution violated? Wherefore have laws been made to authorize a change, and wherefore are we now assembled here? A federal government is formed for the protection of its individual members. Ours has attacked itself with impunity. Its authority has been disobeyed and despised. I think I perceive a glaring inconsistency in another of his arguments. He complains of this Constitution, because it requires the consent of at least three fourths of the states to introduce amendments which shall be necessary for the happiness of the people. The assent of so many he urges as too great an obstacle to the admission of salutary amendments, which, he strongly insists, ought to be at the will of a bare majority. We hear this argument, at the very moment we are called

Virginia, HOWE

*Red Hill in Charlotte County,
Virginia, Patrick Henry's home*

upon to assign reasons for proposing a constitution which puts it in the power of nine states to abolish the present inadequate, unsafe, and pernicious Confederation! In the first case, he asserts that a majority ought to have the power of altering the government, when found to be inadequate to the security of public happiness. In the last case, he affirms that even three fourths of the community have not a right to alter a government which experience has proved to be subversive of national felicity! nay, that the most necessary and urgent alterations cannot be made without the absolute unanimity of all the states! Does not the thirteenth article of the Confederation expressly require that no alteration shall be made without the unanimous consent of all the states? Could any thing in theory be more perniciously improvident and injudicious than this submission of the will of the majority to the most trifling minority? Have not experience and practice actually manifested this theoretical inconvenience to be extremely impolitic? Let me mention one fact, which I conceive must carry conviction to the mind of any one: the smallest state in the Union has obstructed every attempt to reform the government; that little member has repeatedly disobeyed and counteracted the general authority; nay, has even supplied the enemies of its country with provisions. Twelve states had agreed to certain improvements which were proposed, being thought absolutely necessary to preserve the existence of the general government; but as these improvements, though really indispensable, could not, by the Confederation, be introduced into it without the consent of every state, the refractory dissent of that little state prevented their adoption. The inconveniences resulting from this requisition, of unanimous concurrence in alterations in the Confederation, must be known to every member in this Convention; it is therefore needless to remind them of them. Is it not self-evident that a trifling minority ought not to bind the majority? Would not foreign influence be exerted with facility over a small minority? Would the honorable gentlemen agree to continue the most radical defects in the old system, because the petty state of Rhode Island would not agree to remove them? ...

But the honorable member has satirized, with peculiar acrimony, the powers given to the general government by this Constitution. I conceive that the first question on this subject is, whether these powers be necessary; if they be, we are reduced to the dilemma of either submitting to the inconvenience or losing the Union. Let us consider the most important of these reprobated powers; that of direct taxation is most generally objected to. With respect to the exigencies of government, there is no question but the most easy mode of providing for them will be adopted. When, therefore, direct taxes are not necessary, they will not be recurred to. It can be of little advantage of those in power to raise money in a manner oppressive to the people. To consult the conveniences of the people will cost them nothing, and in many respects, will be advantageous to them. Direct taxes will only be recurred to for great purposes. What has brought on other nations those immense debts, under the pressure of which many of them labor? Not the expenses of their governments, but war. If this country should be engaged in war, —and I conceive we ought to provide for the possibility of such a case, —how would it be carried on? By the usual means provided from year to year. As our imports will be necessary for the expenses of government and other common exigencies, how are we to carry on the means of defence? How is it possible a war could be supported without money or credit? And would it be possible for a government to have credit without having the power of raising money? No; it would be impossible for any government, in such a case, to defend itself. Then I say, sir, that it is necessary to establish funds for extraordinary exigencies, and to give this power to the general government; for the utter inutility of previous requisitions on the states is too well known....

But it is urged that its consolidated nature, joined to the power of direct taxation, will give it a tendency to destroy all subordinate authority; that its increasing influence will speedily enable it to absorb the state governments. I cannot think this will be the case. If the general government were wholly independent of the governments of the particular states, then, indeed, usurpation might be expected to the fullest extent. But, sir, on whom does this general government depend? It derives its authority from these governments, and from the same sources from which their authority is derived. The members of the federal government are taken from the same men from whom those of the state legislatures are taken.

A November, 1788, resolution from
the Virginia assembly calling for
a second constitutional convention

If we consider the mode in which the federal representatives will be chosen, we shall be convinced that the general will never destroy the individual governments; and this conviction must be strengthened by an attention to the construction of the Senate. The representatives will be chosen probably under the influence of the members of the state legislatures; but there is not the least probability that the election of the latter will be influenced by the former. One hundred and sixty members represent this commonwealth in one branch of the legislature, are drawn from the people at large, and must ever possess more influence than the few men who will be elected to the general legislature.

In the end the Virginia debate came down to the question of whether amendments should be sought before or after the ratification of the Constitution. Some of the amendments proposed by the Antifederalists were plainly designed to cripple the new government; others, however, were intended to meet the widespread demand for a bill of rights. Madison and his associates firmly opposed amendments of the first class, and Federalists everywhere had taken high ground against a bill of rights. But in a bid to reconcile moderate Antifederalists to the Constitution, the Virginia advocates pledged to seek subsequent amendments that would secure the fundamental liberties of the citizens without crippling the government. Henry spurned the pledge. "Do you enter into a compact first, and afterwards settle the terms of the government?" he asked scornfully. But Henry was defeated on the resolution for prior amendments, and on June 25 the convention approved the Constitution, 89 for, 79 against. Unknown to the delegates, New Hampshire already had become the ninth state to ratify; nevertheless, it was the Virginia verdict that set the wheels of the new system in motion and exerted a powerful influence on the outcome in the main Antifederalist stronghold, New York.

Madison at once set out for New York. The changeover to the new government must go smoothly under the ministrations of the old; New York must ratify; Antifederalist demands for a "second convention" must be put down. A visiting Frenchman in New York described Madison as tired, worn out by the labors of the past year, and still burdened with cares. "His expression was that of a stern censor; his conversation disclosed a man of learning; and his countenance was that of a person conscious of his talents and of his duties." From all sides, pressures mounted for a federal declaration or bill of rights. Without conceding the merits of the case, Madison came to see the political prudence of the measure. It would be a gesture of conciliation. Quieting apprehensions of the new system, it would at one and the same time steal the Antifederalists' thunder and allow them to save face while yielding to the Constitution. Even so, the project had no charms for him, as he explained in a letter to Jefferson.

New York Ocr. 17. 1788

The little pamphlet herewith inclosed will give you a collective view of the alterations which have been proposed for the new Constitution. Various and numerous as they appear they certainly omit many of the true grounds of opposition. The articles relating to Treaties, to paper money, and to contracts, created more enemies than all the errors in the System positive and negative put together. It is true nevertheless that not a few, particularly in Virginia have contended for the proposed alterations from the most honorable and patriotic motives; and that among the advocates for the Constitution there are some who wish for further guards to public liberty and individual rights. As far as these may consist of a constitutional declaration of the most essential rights, it is probable they will be added; though there are many who think such addition unnecessary, and not a few who think it misplaced in such a Constitution. There is scarce any point on which the party in opposition is so much divided as to its importance and its propriety. My own opinion has always been in favor of a bill of rights; provided it be so framed as not to imply powers not meant to be included in the enumeration. At the same time I

In October, 1788, Madison wrote these observations on the "Draught of a Constitution for Virginia."

Notes made of a speech Hamilton gave in defense of the Constitution

have never thought the omission a material defect, nor been anxious to supply it even by subsequent amendment, for any other reason than that it is anxiously desired by others. I have favored it because I supposed it might be of use, and if properly executed could not be of disservice. I have not viewed it in an important light 1. because I conceive that in a certain degree, though not in the extent argued by Mr. Wilson, the rights in question are reserved by the manner in which the federal powers are granted. 2 because there is great reason to fear that positive declaration of some of the most essential rights could not be obtained in the requisite latitude. I am sure that the rights of conscience in particular, if submitted to public definition would be narrowed much more than they are likely ever to be by an assumed power. One of the objections in New England was that the Constitution by prohibiting religious tests opened a door for Jews Turks and infidels. 3. because the limited powers of the federal Government and the jealousy of the subordinate Governments, afford a security which has not existed in the case of the State Governments, and exists in no other. 4. because experience proves the inefficacy of a bill of rights on those occasions when its controul is most needed. Repeated violations of these parchment barriers have been commited by overbearing majorities in every State. In Virginia I have seen the bill of rights violated in every instance where it has been opposed to a popular current. Notwithstanding the explicit provision contained in that instrument for the rights of Conscience it is well known that a religious establishment would have taken place in that State, if the legislative majority had found as they expected, a majority of the people in favor of the measure; and I am persuaded that if a majority of the people were now of one sect, the measure would still take place and on narrower ground than was then proposed, notwithstanding the additional obstacle which the law has since created. Wherever the real power in a Government lies, there is the danger of oppression. In our Governments the real power lies in the majority of the Community, and the invasion of private rights is chiefly to be apprehended, not from acts of Government contrary to the sense of its constituents, but from acts in which the Government is the mere instrument of the major number of the constituents. This is a truth of great

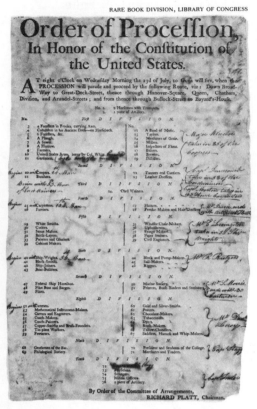

Triumphal "Order of Procession"
for a parade held in New York
City in honor of the Constitution

importance, but not yet sufficiently attended to: and is probably more strongly impressed on my mind by facts, and reflections suggested by them, than on yours which has contemplated abuses of power issuing from a very different quarter [that is, from the despotism of European princes]. Wherever there is an interest and power to do wrong, wrong will generally be done, and not less readily by a powerful and interested party than by a powerful and interested prince.... What use then it may be asked can a bill of rights serve in popular Governments? I answer the two following which though less essential than in other Governments, sufficiently recommend the precaution. 1. The political truths declared in that solemn manner acquire by degrees the character of fundamental maxims of free Government, and as they become incorporated with the national sentiment, counteract the impulses of interest and passion. 2. Altho' it be generally true as above stated that the danger of oppression lies in the interested majorities of the people rather than in usurped acts of the Government, yet there may be occasions on which the evil may spring from the latter sources; and on such, a bill of rights will be a good ground for an appeal to the sense of the community. Perhaps too there may be a certain degree of danger, that a succession of artful and ambitious rulers, may by gradual & well-timed advances, finally erect an independent Government on the subversion of liberty. Should this danger exist at all, it is prudent to guard against it, especially when the precaution can do no injury. At the same time I must own that I see no tendency in our governments to danger on that side. It has been remarked that there is a tendency in all Governments to an augmentation of power at the expense of liberty. But the remark as usually understood does not appear to me well founded. Power when it has attained a certain degree of energy and independence goes on generally to further degrees. But when below that degree, the direct tendency is to further degrees of relaxation, until the abuses of liberty beget a sudden transition to an undue degree of power. With this explanation the remark may be true; and in the latter sense only is it in my opinion applicable to the Governments in America. It is a melancholy reflection that liberty should be equally exposed to danger whether the Government have too much or too little power; and that the line which divides these extremes should be so inaccurately defined by experience.

Supposing a bill of rights to be proper the articles which ought to compose it, admit of much discussion. I am inclined to think that absolute restrictions in cases that are doubtful, or where emergencies may overrule them, ought to be avoided. The restrictions however strongly marked on paper will never be regarded when opposed to the decided sense of the public; and after repeated violations in extraordinary cases, they will lose even their ordinary efficacy. Should a Rebellion or insurrection alarm the people as well as the Government, and a suspension of the Hab. Corp. [habeas corpus] be dictated by the alarm, no written prohibitions on earth would prevent the measure. Should an army in time of peace be gradually established in our neighbourhood by Britn: or Spain, declarations on paper would have as little effect in preventing a standing force for the public safety. The best security agst these evils is to remove the pretext for them.

If Madison saw the problem in America as the creation of a government strong enough to preserve liberty, Jefferson, on the scene of Europe at the dawn of the French Revolution, naturally saw the problem in a different light. The people were always entitled to the most sovereign guarantees of their personal liberties. Whatever the deficiency of "parchment barriers," they were better than no barriers. "The inconveniences of the Declaration [of Rights] are that it may cramp government in its useful exertions. But the evil of this is shortlived, moderate, and reparable. The inconveniences of the want of a Declaration are permanent, afflicting and irreparable: they are in constant progression from bad to worse." Jefferson's cool but shattering argument did not convert Madison to the cause; political necessity had accomplished that in Richmond, in his own congressional district, and in his calculus of the national interest. But Jefferson's letter, aided by his own reflection, led Madison to champion the cause of a bill of rights with the ardor of a true believer. In the face of formidable apathy, even of those who had paraded in this cause, Madison almost singlehandedly framed and pushed through the First Congress those amendments to the Constitution that compose the Bill of Rights. Ironically, the Bill of Rights, like the Constitution of which he would become the legendary father, was in some sense a political afterthought of Madison's original conception. If this is a sobering reflection, it does not reduce one whit—indeed it magnifies—the creative genius that infused the work.

Chapter 5

First Man in Congress

In what capacity Madison would be permitted to serve the new government was quite uncertain as the year 1788 came to a close. The Antifederalist complexion of Virginia politics embarrassed his prospects in that quarter. His name was put in candidacy for the United States Senate, but Henry and company elected two of their own and then, in carving out the congressional districts, joined Madison's Orange constituency with neighboring counties disposed to Antifederalism. To counteract these "machinations," Madison's friends begged him to return home and declare for Congress. His own preference, clearly, was for a seat in the House of Representatives, but he was not eager to take to the hustings. An executive appointment was in reach; Washington, whose political confidant Madison had become, would surely use him in some high office. After pondering his course for several weeks and observing the strength of Federalism in the elections of members to the First Congress from other states, Madison decided to go home and make the race. He explained himself to Jefferson.

> Philadelphia Decr. 8. 1788.
>
> Notwithstanding the formidable opposition made to the new federal Government, first in order to prevent its adoption, and since in order to place its administration in the hands of disaffected men, there is now both a certainty of its peaceable commencement in March next, and a flattering prospect that it will be administred by men who will give it a fair trial. General Washington will certainly be called to the Executive department. Mr. Adams who is *pledged to support him* will probably be the vice president. The enemies to the Government, at the head the most inveterate of whom, is Mr. Henry are laying a train for the election of Governour [George] Clinton [of New York], but it cannot succeed unless the

federal votes be more dispersed than can well happen. Of the seven States which have appointed their Senators, Virginia alone will have antifederal members in that branch.... In the House of Representatives the proportion of antifederal members will of course be greater, but can not, if present appearances are to be trusted, amount to a majority, or even a very formidable minority. The election for this branch has taken place as yet no where except in Penna. and here the returns are not yet come in from all the Counties. It is certain however that seven out of the eight, and probable that the whole eight representatives will bear the federal stamp. Even in Virginia where the enemies to the Government form 2/3 of the *legislature* it is computed that more than half the number of Representatives, who will be elected by the *people*, formed into districts for the purpose, will be of the same stamp. By some it is computed that 7 out of the 10, allotted to that State, will be opposed to the politics of the present Legislature....

...I shall leave this place in a day or two for Virga. where my friends who wish me to cooperate in putting our political machine into activity as a member of the House of Representatives, press me to attend. They made me a candidate for the Senate, for which I had not allotted my pretensions. The attempt was defeated by Mr. Henry who is omnipotent in the present legislature and who added to the expedients common on such occasions, a public philippic agst. my federal principles. He has taken equal pains in forming the Counties into districts for the election of Reps. to associate with Orange such as are most devoted to his politics, and most likely to be swayed by the prejudices excited agst. me. From the best information I have of the prevailing temper of the district, I conclude that my going to Virga. will answer no other purpose than to satisfy the Opinions and intreaties of my friends. The trip is in itself very disagreeable both on account of its electioneering appearance, and the sacrifice of the winter for which I had assigned a task with the intermission of Congressional business would have made convenient at New York.

James Monroe, Madison's friendly rival in first congressional race

Madison's low-keyed electioneering proved successful. Against a friendly opponent, James Monroe, he won with ease. In the process, however, he discovered firsthand the popularity of Antifederalism and trimmed his political sails accordingly. He went to Congress not only pledged to a bill of rights but also convinced that only under a course of moderation could the perils of Antifederalism be avoided and the Constitution make its way into the affections of the people. En route to New York he stopped at Mount Vernon, as had become his habit, and wrote the draft of the brief inaugural address that Washington would deliver from the portico of Federal Hall (formerly the City Hall of New York) on April 30, 1789. In the new Congress Madison at once resumed the leadership he had had in the old. Everyone saw him as "our first man." The First Congress, though covered with confusion and perplexity, must have an extraordinary influence on the future of the government. Rising to this responsibility, Madison coped with measures creating the executive departments, forming the judiciary, establishing the revenue system, framing the Bill of Rights, and so on. In the third month of the session he reported to Jefferson.

New York June 30. 1789.

The federal business has proceeded with a mortifying tardiness, chargeable in part on the incorrect draughts of Committees, and the prolixity of discussion incident to a public body, every member of which almost takes a positive agency, but principally resulting from the novelty and complexity of the subjects of Legislation. We are in a wilderness without a single footstep to guide us. Our successors will have an easier task, and by degrees the way will become smooth short and certain.

My last informed you of some of the difficulties attending a regulation of the duties. The bill on that subject has at length received the fiat of both Houses and will be forthwith made a law by the concurrence of the President. The rates are not precisely on the scale first settled by the House of Reps....

The Senate has prevailed on another point in the bill which had undergone more discussion and produced more difficulty. It had been proposed by the H. of Reps. that, besides a discrimination in the tonnage, a small reduction should be made in the duty on distilled spirits imported from countries in treaty with the U. States. The Senate were opposed to any discrimination whatsoever, contending that even G. Britain should stand on the same footing with the most favored nations. The arguments on that side of the question were that the U.S. were not bound by treaty to give any commercial preferences to particular nations—that they were not bound by gratitude, since our allies had been actuated by their own interest and had obtained their compensation in the dismemberment of a rival empire—that in national and particularly in commercial measures, gratitude was moreover, no proper motive, interest alone being the Statesman's guide—that G.B. made no discrimination against the U.S. compared with other nations; but on the contrary distinguished them by a number of advantages—that if G.B. possessed almost the whole of our trade it proceeded from causes which proved that she could carry it on for us on better terms than the other nations of Europe—that we were too dependent on her trade to risk her displeasure by irritating measures which might induce her to put us on a worse footing than at present—that a small discrimination could only irritate without operating on her interests or fears—that if any thing were done it would be best to make a bolder stroke at once, and that in fact the Senate had appointed a committee to consider the subject in that point of view.—On the other side it was contended that it would be absurd to *give* away every thing that could *purchase* the stipulations wanted by us, that the motives in which the new Government originated, the known sentiments of the people at large, and the laws of most of the States subsequent to the peace shewed clearly that a distinction between nations in Treaty and nations not in Treaty would coincide with the public opinion, and that it would be offensive to a great number of citizens to see G.B. in particular put on the footing of the most favored nations, by the first act of a Government instituted for the purpose of uniting the States in the vindication of their commercial interests against her monopolizing regulations—that this respect to the sentiments of the people was the more necessary in the present critical state of the Government—that our trade at present entirely contradicted the advantages expected from the Revolution, no new channels being opened with other European nations, and the British channels being narrowed by a refusal of the most natural and valuable one to the U.S.—that this evil proceeded from the deep hold the British monopoly had taken of our Country, and the difficulty experienced by France Holland, &c. in entering into competition with her—that in order to break this monopoly, those nations ought to be aided till they could contend on equal terms—that the market of France was particu-

MOUNT VERNON LADIES' ASSOCIATION OF THE UNION

Madison often stopped at Mount Vernon en route from Montpelier to meetings of Congress.

169

Madison went to Washington's house on Cherry Street to escort him to Federal Hall for the inauguration.

larly desirable to us—that her disposition to open it would depend on the disposition manifested on our part &c. &c....—that it would be sufficient to begin with a moderate discrimination, exhibiting a readiness to invigorate our measures as circumstances might require—that we had no reason to apprehend a disposition in G.B. to resort to a commercial contest, or the consequences of such an experiment, her dependence on us being greater than ours on her. The supplies of the United States are necessary to the existence, and their markets to the value, of her islands. The returns are either superfluities or poisons. In time of famine, the cry of which is heard every three or four years, the bread of the United States is essential. In time of war, which is generally decided in the West Indies, friendly offices, not violating the duties of neutrality, might effectually turn the scale in favor of an adversary. In the direct trade with Great Britain, the consequences ought to be equally dreaded by her. The raw and bulky exports of the United States employ her shipping, contribute to her revenue, enter into her manufactures, and enrich her merchants who stand between the United States and the consuming nations of Europe. A suspension of the intercourse would suspend all these advantages, force the trade into rival channels from which it might not return, and besides a temporary loss of a market for 1/4 of her exports, hasten the establishment of manufactures here, which would so far cut off the market forever. On the other side, the United States would suffer but little. The manufactures of Great Britain, as far as desirable, would find their way through other channels, and if the price were a little augmented it would only diminish an excessive consumption. They could do almost wholly without such supplies, and better without than with many of them.... The event of the tonnage bill, in which the discrimination was meant to be most insisted on by the House of Representatives, is not yet finally decided. But here, also, the Senate will prevail. It was determined yesterday in that House to *adhere* to their amendment for striking out the clause, and there is no reason to suppose that the other House will let the Bill be lost....

The other bills depending relate to the collection of the Impost, and the establishment of a war, foreign, and Treasury Department. The bills on the two first of these departments have passed the House of Representatives, and are before the Senate. They gave birth to a very interesting constitutional question — by what authority removals from office were to be made. The Constitution being silent on the point, it was left to construction. Four opinions were advanced: 1. That no removal could be made but by way of impeachment. To this it was objected that it gave to every officer, down to tide waiters and tax gatherers, the tenure of good behavior. 2. That it devolved on the Legislature, to be disposed of as might be proper. To this it was objected that the Legislature might then dispose of it to be exercised by themselves, or even by the House of Representatives. 3. That it was incident to the power of appointment, and therefore belonged to the President and Senate. To this it was said that the Senate, being a *Legislative* body, could not be considered in an *Executive* light farther than was expressly declared; that such a construction would transfer the trust of seeing the laws duly executed from the President, the most responsible, to the Senate, the least responsible branch of the Government; that officers would intrench themselves behind a party in the Senate, bid defiance to the President, and introduce anarchy and discord into the Executive Department; that the Senate were to be Judges in case of impeachment, and ought not, therefore, to be previously called on for a summary opinion on questions of removal; that in their Legislative character they ought to be kept as cool and unbiased as possible, as the constitutional check on the passions and parties of the other House, and should, for that reason also, be as little concerned as possible in those *personal* matters, which are the great source of factious animosities. 4. That the Executive power being generally vested in the President, and the Executive function of removal not expressly taken away, it remained with the President. To this was objected the rule of construction on which the third opinion rested, and the danger of creating too much weight in the Executive scale. After very long debates the 4th opinion prevailed, as most consonant to the text of the Constitution, to the policy of mixing the Legislative and Executive Departments as little as possible, and to the requisite responsibility and harmony in the Executive Department. What the decision of the Senate will be cannot yet be even conjectured.

As one might surmise from this letter, it was Madison's opinion that prevailed on the question of executive removal power — a constitutional decision of great import for the office of the Presidency — while his opinion was defeated on the question of commercial discrimination. It proved a costly defeat, one that he and Jefferson would try repeatedly to reverse but without success. The commercial aspirations that had brought the Constitution into being could not be fulfilled, Madison thought, if Congress began by discarding the weapon of commercial discrimination. To combat British monopoly and British influence, to encourage American shipping and navigation, to open new markets in a widening system of free trade pivoted on the French alliance — these were Madison's objectives, and he argued that the national government was morally committed to their realization. But interests as different as those of southern planters and eastern merchants, each in its own way tied into the British system, combined to defeat Madison's project. The division on this issue presaged the great conflict still to come.

Early in 1790, Alexander Hamilton, who had been appointed Secretary of the Treasury, gave Congress his *Report on the Public Credit.* Hamilton had been Madison's choice for the Treasury post; they were political allies and expected to remain so. With much of Hamilton's plan for paying the debt and establishing the public credit Madison was in complete accord. Under this plan the national debt of some fifty-two million dollars, of which twelve million was owed abroad, would be funded by the government, interest paid, and provision made for discharge. But justice was revolted, Madison said, by the Secretary's proposition to put original and present holders of the domestic debt on the same footing and to fund the whole at face value in specie. In the course of depreciation over the years, the debt had become an article of speculation. The needs of the original creditors — soldiers, farmers, tradesmen — had led them to sell their securities at a fraction of their nominal value. Probably not more than one-fifth of the debt remained in the hands of the wartime creditors. Hamilton's plan rewarded the speculative greed of the few to the exclusion of justice for the many. Madison, although he had earlier rejected the idea, proposed a discrimination between the two classes of creditors. Original holders would be paid in full; holders by transfer would be paid at the market value, with the difference between the face value and the market value going to the primary creditors. Whatever the justice of the arrangement, it was full of difficulties and met defeat in the House.

Madison was more successful in opposing Hamilton's plan for the assumption of the state debts, estimated at about twenty-five million dollars. The issue for Madison was not "state rights" or excessive taxation or fear of the power to be erected on this mass of debt. Again, the issue was justice. Since the war the states had moved to pay their debts at a very uneven pace. For the general government simply to assume these debts as they stood in

1790 would be to penalize the fiscally responsible states to the benefit of the delinquents. So Madison argued that the debts should be assumed as they stood in 1783 and, in addition, that more generous provision be made for allocating "common charges" among the states. Obviously, this plan would have increased the national debt substantially above the level set by Hamilton. Others opposed assumption on other grounds, though equity was always a consideration. Madison discussed both discrimination and assumption in a letter to Edmund Pendleton, a district judge in Virginia.

N. York March 4. 1790.

The only act of much consequence which the present Session has yet produced, is one for enumerating the Inhabitants as the basis of a reapportionment of the Representation. The House of Reps. has been cheifly employed of late on the Report of the Secy. of the Treasury. As it has been printed in all the Newspapers I take for granted that it must have fallen under your eye. The plan which it proposes is in general well digested, and illustrated &c supported by very able reasoning. It has not however met with universal concurrence in every heart. I have myself been of the number who could not suppress objections. I have not been able to persuade myself that the transactions between the U. S. and those whose services were most instrumental in saving their country, did in fact extinguish the claims of the latter on the justice of the former; or that there must not be something radically wrong in suffering those who rendered a bona fide consideration to lose 7/8 of their dues, and those who have no particular merit towards their Country, to gain 7 or 8 times as much as they advanced. In pursuance of this view of the subject, a proposition was made for redressing in some degree the inequality. After much discussion, a large majority was in the negative. The subject at present before a Committee of the whole, is the proposed assumption of the State debts. On this, opinions seem to be pretty equally divided. Virga. is endeavoring to incorporate with the measure some effectual provision for a final settlement and payment of balances among the States. Even with this ingredient, the project will neither be just nor palatable, if the assumption be referred to the present epoch, and by that means deprives the States who have done most, of the benefit of their exertions. We have accordingly made an effort but without success to refer the assumption to the State of the

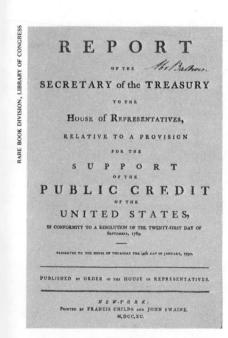

REPORT

OF THE

SECRETARY of the TREASURY

TO THE

HOUSE of REPRESENTATIVES,

RELATIVE TO A PROVISION

FOR THE

SUPPORT

OF THE

PUBLIC CREDIT

OF THE

UNITED STATES,

IN CONFORMITY TO A RESOLUTION OF THE TWENTY-FIRST DAY OF
SEPTEMBER, 1789.

PRESENTED TO THE HOUSE ON THURSDAY THE 14th DAY OF JANUARY, 1790.

PUBLISHED BY ORDER OF THE HOUSE OF REPRESENTATIVES.

NEW-YORK:
PRINTED BY FRANCIS CHILDS AND JOHN SWAINE.
M,DCC,XC.

Title page of Alexander Hamilton's Report on the Public Credit, *1790*

Edmund Pendleton

debts at the close of the war. This would probably add 1/3 more to the amount of the Debts, but would more than compensate for this by rendering the measure more just & satisfactory. A simple unequalified assumption of the existing debts would bear peculiarly hard on Virginia. She has paid I believe a greater part of her quotas since the peace than Massts. She suffered far more during the war. It is agreed that she will not be less a Creditor on the final settlement, yet if such an assumption were to take place she would pay towards the discharge of the debts, in the proportion of 1/5 and receive back to her Creditor Citizens 1/7 or 1/8, whilst Massts. would pay not more than 1/7 or 1/8, and receive back not less than 1/5. The case of S. Carola. is a still stronger contrast. In answer to this inequality we are referred to the final liquidation for which provision may be made. But this may *possibly* never take place. It will *probably* be at some distance. The payment of the balances among the States will be a fresh source of delay & difficulties. The merits of the plan independently of the question of equity, are also controvertible, tho' on the other side there are advantages which have considerable weight.

The House balked at assumption and sent the funding bill, *sans* assumption, to the Senate in June. But the advocates of assumption promised "no assumption, no funding." In short they would block any plan for establishing the national credit, thus jeopardizing the Union in its infancy, unless the state debts were included. As it happened, however, the Senate was at this time also entangled on the old nettle of a permanent seat of government. Madison and the Virginians, with most southerners, favored the location of the capital on the Potomac, while the rival claims of New York and Philadelphia divided the northerners. Thus the stage was set for the first sectional compromise under the Constitution. It would be a mistake to say that everything was settled between the principals, Madison and Hamilton, around Thomas Jefferson's dinner table. That famous dinner, arranged by the newly appointed Secretary of State, may have had more symbolic than actual importance. The result, at any rate, was a modified plan of assumption, which was quite acceptable to Madison, and the location of the capital on the Potomac after a temporary residence of ten years in Philadelphia. Votes were pledged and the two measures squeaked through Congress in July. Three hurried dispatches from Madison to Monroe chart the tortuous course of compromise.

New York, June 1, 1790.

The assumption has been revived, and is still depending. I do not believe it will take place, but the event may possibly be governed by circumstances not at present fully in view. The funding bill for the proper debt of the United States is engrossed for the last reading. It conforms in substance to the plan of the Secretary of the Treas. You will have seen by late papers that an experiment for navigation and commercial purposes has been introduced. It has powerful friends, and from the present aspect of the House of Representatives will succeed there by a great majority. In the Senate its success is not improbable, if I am rightly informed. You will see by the inclosed paper that a removal from this place has been voted by a large majority of our House. The other is pretty nearly balanced. The Senators of the 3 Southern States are disposed to couple the permanent with the temporary question. If they do, I think it will end in either an abortion of both, or in a decision of the former in favour of the Delaware. I have good reason to believe that there is no serious purpose in the Northern States to prefer the Potowmac, and that, if supplied with a pretext for a very hasty

This cartoon of the "Constitution" going to the devil with Congress on board and Robert Morris at the helm indicated public dissatisfaction with the assumption-residence compromise. Dissenters are being towed along by the majority on the way to Philadelphia.

HISTORICAL SOCIETY OF PENNSYLVANIA

decision, they will indulge their secret wishes for a permanent establishment on the Delaware. As Rhode Island is again in the Union, and will probably be in the Senate in a day or two, the Potowmac has the less to hope and the more to fear from this quarter.

New York, July 4, 1790

You will find by one of the Gazettes herewith sent, that the bill fixing the permanent seat of Government on the Potowmac, and the temporary at Philadelphia, has got through the Senate. It passed by a single voice only, Izzard and Few having both voted against it. Its passage through the House of Representatives is probable, but attended with great difficulties. If the Potowmac succeeds, even on these terms, it will have resulted from a fortuitous coincidence of circumstances which might never happen again.

The provision for the public debt has been suspended for some time in the Senate by the question relating to the seat of Government. It is now resumed in that House, and it is to be hoped will soon be brought to an issue. The assumption sleeps, but I am persuaded will be awakened on the first dawn of a favorable opportunity. It seems, indeed, as if the friends of the measure were determined to risk everything rather than suffer that finally to fail.

First page of an act concerning duties on distilled spirits in 1790

This house on Ninth Street in Philadelphia was intended for the President, but he never lived there.

New York, July 24, 1790.

After all the vicissitudes through which the assumption has passed, it seems at present in a fair way to succeed as part of the general plan for the public debt. The Senate have included it among their amendments to the funding bill, and a vote of yesterday in the House of Representatives indicates a small majority in favor of the measure. In its present form it will very little affect the interest of Virginia in either way. I have not been able to overcome my other objections, or even to forbear urging them. At the same time, I cannot deny that the crisis demands a spirit of accommodation to a certain extent. If the measure should be adopted, I shall wish it to be considered as an unavoidable evil, and *possibly* not the worst side of the dilemma.

In an end-of-session letter to his father, Madison described the final outcome of the vote on assumption.

N. Y. July 31. 1790.

The funding bill has at length passed the two Houses with a qualified assumption of the state debts.... The assumption was carried by a small majority in both Houses. Many who voted for it did so on a supposition that it was a lesser evil than to risk the effect of a rejection on the states which insisted on the measure. I could not bring myself to concur with them, but am sensible that there was serious danger of a very unfavorable issue to the Session from a contrary decision, and consider it as now incumbent on us all to make the best of what is done. The truth is that in a pecuniary light, the assumption is no longer of much consequence to Virginia, the sum allotted to her being about her proportion of the whole, & rather exceeding her present debt. She will consequently pay no more to the general Treasury than she now pays to the State Treasy. and perhaps in a mode which will be less disagreeable to the people, tho not more favorable to their true interests.

The Ways & means are now under consideration. The impost will be made equal to the federal debt. The provision for the State debts will be put off till the next session. It will be likely to consist chiefly of duties on rum distilled in the U.S. and on a few imported articles that will best bear a further augmentation.

We expect that an adjournment will take place in about a week. I shall set out for Virginia as soon thereafter as I can pack up my books papers &c. which will detain me here some days. Mr. Jefferson wishes me to wait for his setting out and as his company will be particularly grateful & also convenient I am not sure that I shall resist the invitation, if he finds that he can be ready for the Journey within a reasonable time. I shd. not hesitate, if I did not wish to be in Orange by the election, tho' as an attendance cannot be given at more than one of the 8 Counties, it does not seem worth while to sacrifice much to that consideration.

Madison and Jefferson often traveled to and from Virginia together now that Jefferson had been persuaded to become part of the government at home rather than Minister to France. Congress convened at the old stand, in Philadelphia, in the fall. Before long Hamilton submitted to the House his report on a national bank. The proposed bank, like the century-old Bank of England, would harness private interest and profit to public convenience. It would act as the financial arm of the government and also mount a large paper circulation in the form of bank notes, thereby multiplying the active capital of the country and stimulating enterprise. Of the capital of ten million dollars the government would furnish only one-fifth, the rest being subscribed by private investors, primarily in the form of public securities. In effect, the holders of the funded debt would be privileged to incorporate as a bank, empowered to engage in commercial business, and blessed with the largest account in the economy, that of the federal government. Leading the fight against the bill in the House, Madison dwelled less on the character of the bank as a financial institution or on its features of capitalist privilege than on its unconstitutionality. His principal speech was reported, in part, as follows.

Annals of Congress [February 2, 1791]

Is the power of establishing an incorporated Bank among the powers vested by the Constitution in the Legislature of the United States? This is the question to be examined.

After some general remarks on the limitations of all political power, he [Madison] took notice of the peculiar manner in which the Federal Government is limited. It is not a general grant, out of which particular powers are excepted; it is a grant of particular powers only, leaving the general mass in other hands. So it had been understood by its friends and its foes, and so it was to be interpreted....

Reviewing the Constitution...it was not possible to discover in it the power to incorporate a Bank. The only clauses under which such a power could be pretended are either:

1. The power to lay and collect taxes to pay the debts, and provide for the common defence and general welfare: or,

2. The power to borrow money on the credit of the United States: or,

3. The power to pass all laws necessary and proper to carry into execution those powers.

The bill did not come within the first power. It laid no tax to pay the debts, or provide for the general welfare. It laid no tax whatever. It was altogether foreign to the subject.

No argument could be drawn from the terms "common defence and general welfare." The power as to these general purposes was limited to acts laying taxes for them; and the general purposes themselves were limited and explained by the particular enumeration subjoined. To understand these terms in any sense, that would justify the power in question, would give to Congress an unlimited power; and would render nugatory the enumeration of particular powers; would supersede all the powers reserved to the State Governments. These terms are copied from the articles of Confederation; had it ever been pretended that they were to be understood otherwise than as here explained?

It has been said, that "general welfare" meant cases in which a general power might be exercised by Congress, without interfering with the powers of the States; and that the establishment of a National Bank was of this sort. There were, he said, several answers to this novel doctrine.

1. The proposed Bank would interfere, so as indirectly to defeat a State Bank at the same place.

2. It would directly interfere with the rights of the States to prohibit as well as to establish Banks, and the circulation of Bank notes. He mentioned a law in Virginia actually prohibiting the circulation of notes payable to bearer.

3. Interference with the power of the States was no

Madison led the fight in the House against Alexander Hamilton (above) and his report on a national bank.

REPORT.

THE Charter of incorporation granted to the Bank of the United States, amongst other rights, privileges and abilities therein conveyed, having impowered the President, Directors and Company of the said Bank, to make, ordain, establish and put in execution, such bye-laws, ordinances and regulations, as shall seem necessary and convenient for the Government of the said Corporation: Be it ordained by the President, Directors and Company of the Bank of the United States,

SECT. 1. That the Bank shall be open for the transaction of business, every day in the year (Sundays, Christmas-day and the Fourth of July excepted) during such hours as the Board of Directors shall deem adviseable.

SECT. 2. That the Books and Accounts of the Bank shall be kept in Dollars and Cents, and shall be regularly balanced on the first Mondays in January and July, in each year; when the half-yearly dividends shall be declared and published in at least four of the public news-papers.

SECT. 3. That the Bank shall take charge of the Cash of all those who chuse to place it there (free of expence) and shall keep it subject to their order, payable at sight; and shall receive deposits of Ingots of Gold, Bars of Silver, Wrought Plate, or other valuable articles of small bulk, in the same manner, and return them on demand of the depositor.

SECT. 4. That the Bank shall receive and pay all specie coins, according to the rates and value that have been or shall hereafter be established by Congress.

SECT. 5. That until offices of Discount and Deposit are established, there shall be at least two discount days in every week, when meetings of the Board of Directors shall be assembled. — Discounts shall be made at such rate (not less than 5 per cent, nor more than 6 per cent. per annum) as the Board of Directors shall deem proper, on Notes or Bills of Exchange that have not more than 60 days to run, and with such securities, and under such modifications, as the Board of Directors in their discretion shall deem satisfactory and expedient.

SECT. 6. That the President shall have power to convene the Directors on special occasions, and with the approbation of the Board of Directors, to affix the seal of the Corporation to all Conveyances or other instruments, and sign the same in behalf of the Corporation. — The said seal shall always remain in the custody and safe-keeping of the President.

SECT. 7. That a Committee of the Board, consisting of at least three Members to be elected monthly by ballot, shall visit the vaults, in which the cash and other effects shall be deposited, at least once in every month, and make an inventory of the same, to be compared with the books, in order to ascertain whether they perfectly agree therewith.

SECT

constitutional criterion of the power of Congress. If the power was not given, Congress could not exercise it; if given, they might exercise it, although it should interfere with the laws, or even the Constitution of the States.

4. If Congress could incorporate a Bank merely because the act would leave the States free to establish Banks also, any other incorporations might be made by Congress. They could incorporate companies of manufacturers, or companies for cutting canals, or even religious societies, leaving similar incorporations by the States, like State Banks, to themselves. Congress might even establish religious teachers in every parish, and pay them out of the Treasury of the United States, leaving other teachers unmolested in their functions. These inadmissible consequences condemned the controverted principle.

The case of the Bank established by the former Congress had been cited as a precedent. This was known, he said, to have been the child of necessity. It never could be justified by the regular powers of the articles of Confederation. . . .

The second clause to be examined is that which empowers Congress to borrow money.

Is this bill to borrow money? It does not borrow a shilling. Is there any fair construction by which the bill can be deemed an exercise of the power to borrow money? The obvious meaning of the power to borrow money, is that of accepting it from, and stipulating payment to those who are able and willing to lend.

To say that the power to borrow involves a power of creating the ability, where there may be the will, to lend, is not only establishing a dangerous principle, as will be immediately shown, but is as forced a construction as to say that it involves the power of compelling the will, where there may be the ability to lend.

The third clause is that which gives the power to pass all laws necessary and proper to execute the specified powers.

Whatever meaning this clause may have, none can be admitted, that would give an unlimited discretion to Congress.

Its meaning must, according to the natural and obvious force of the terms and the context, be limited to means

An invoice listing seeds, including beets, turnips, peas, and flowers, Madison purchased in March, 1791

When Hamilton's bank bill passed, plans were made to erect this building to house the Bank in Philadelphia, then the capital.

necessary to the end, and incident to the nature of the specified powers....

The essential characteristics of the Government, as composed of limited and enumerated powers, would be destroyed, if, instead of direct and incidental means, any means could be used, which, in the language of the preamble to the bill, "might be conceived to be conducive to the successful conducting of the finances, or might be conceived to tend to give facility to the obtaining of loans." He urged an attention to the diffuse and ductile terms which had been found requisite to cover the stretch of power contained in the bill. He compared them with the terms necessary and proper, used in the Constitution, and asked whether it was possible to view the two descriptions as synonymous, or the one as a fair and safe commentary on the other.

If, proceeded he, Congress, by virtue of the power to borrow, can create the means of lending, and, in pursuance of these means, can incorporate a Bank, they may do any thing whatever creative of like means....

With all this evidence of the sense in which the Constitution was understood and adopted, will it not be said, if the bill should pass, that its adoption was brought about by one set of arguments, and that it is now administered under the influence of another set? and this reproach will have the keener sting, because it is applicable to so many individuals concerned in both the adoption and administration.

In fine, if the power were in the Constitution, the immediate exercise of it cannot be essential; if not there, the exercise of it involves the guilt of usurpation, and establishes a precedent of interpretation levelling all the barriers which limit the powers of the General Government, and protect those of the State Governments. If the point be doubtful only, respect for ourselves, who ought to shun the appearance of precipitancy and ambition; respect for our successors, who ought not lightly to be deprived of the opportunity of exercising the rights of legislation; respect for our constitutents who have had no opportunity of making known their sentiments, and who are themselves to be bound down to the measure for so long a period; all these considerations require that the irrevocable decision should at least be suspended until another session.

Thomas Paine

It appeared on the whole, he concluded, that the power exercised by the bill was condemned by the silence of the Constitution; was condemned by the rule of interpretation arising out of the Constitution; was condemned by its tendency to destroy the main characteristic of the Constitution; was condemned by the expositions of the friends of the Constitution, whilst depending before the public; was condemned by the apparent intention of the parties which ratified the Constitution; was condemned by the explanatory amendments proposed by Congress themselves to the Constitution; and he hoped it would receive its final condemnation by the vote of this House.

But the bill passed and became law on February 25 after President Washington rejected the counsels of strict construction in favor of Hamilton's doctrine of implied powers. The split between Madison and Hamilton—between Jefferson and Hamilton, too—defined the fundamental constitutional issue in an emerging division of parties. Why Madison chose to take such a strict view of federal powers is not easily explained. Doubtless he was influenced by the remonstrance of the Virginia assembly against the assumption of state debts. Not only was that measure unconstitutional, it was, said the assembly, antirepublican and designed to prostrate agriculture at the feet of "a large monied interest." While he did not agree with this opinion of assumption, Madison recognized the widespread fears aroused by Hamilton's measures, especially to the southward, and he began to see these measures as forming a system of privilege that threatened the precarious balance of the republican experiment. The people in their conventions had adopted a strictly limited constitution, and it was to this constitution, not to the one he had advocated at Philadelphia or even in *The Federalist*, that Madison was bound. If its restraints were broken, there was no limit to which men like Hamilton, whose republican commitment was frail at best, might go. Madison once remarked that the Constitution had two enemies, "one that would stretch it to death, and one that would squeeze it to death." Death by stretching, he felt, was the danger in 1791.

Madison's hostility to Hamiltonian policy increased in the coming months. The speculative scramble for the Bank stocks implicated the government in the mean arts of jobbery and chicanery and helped to identify the "paper and stock" interest behind the Treasury program. Ideological affinity between this faction and the Burkian assault on the French Revolution was suggested by the controversy whipped up around the publication of Thomas Paine's *The Rights of Man*. The volume included an unintended preface by

Jefferson—actually a private letter printed without his permission—in which the Secretary of State recommended the book as a republican antidote to the "political heresies" lately abroad in the press—an unmistakable allusion to Vice President Adams's atrabilious "Discourses on Davila." British partisans loudly disapproved of Jefferson's remarks, fearing the Secretary's support of Paine would offend the British court. Madison feared that Adams's writings would be equally offensive to the French. Madison considered the French Revolution an emanation from the American—the awakening of the Old World to "the voice of liberty"—and felt that every true republican must wish for its success. In May, just as this affair was breaking, Madison and Jefferson set out on a leisurely excursion to Lake Champlain. On their return Madison lingered in New York and continued writing to Jefferson, who had gone on to Philadelphia, on the progress of speculation and ideological encounter.

N. York May 12, 1791.

I had seen Payne's pamphlet with the preface of the Philada. Editor. It immediately occurred that you were brought into the Frontispiece in the manner you explain[ed]. But I had not foreseen the particular use made of it by the British partizans. Mr. Adams can least of all complain; under a mock defence of the Republican Constitutions of his Country, he attacked them with all the force he possessed, and this in a book with his name to it whilst he was the Representative of his Country at a foreign Court [A *Defence of the Constitutions*, written while Adams was the first American Minister to Great Britain, 1785–88]. Since he has been the 2d. magistrate in the new Republic, his pen has constantly been at work in the same cause; and tho' his name has not been prefixed to his antirepublican discourses, the author has been as well known as if that formality had been observed. Surely if it be innocent & decent in one servant of the public thus to write attacks agst its Government, it can not be very criminal or indecent in another to patronize a written defense of the principles on which that govt. is founded. The sensibility of H. & B. [George Hammond and Phineas Bond, British Minister and Consul, respectively, to the United States] to the indignity to the Brit: Court is truly ridiculous. If offence cd. be justly taken in that quarter, what would France have a right to say to Burke's pamphlet [*Reflections on the French Revolution*] and the Countenance given to it & its author, particularly by the King himself? What in fact might not the U.S. say, whose revolution & demo-

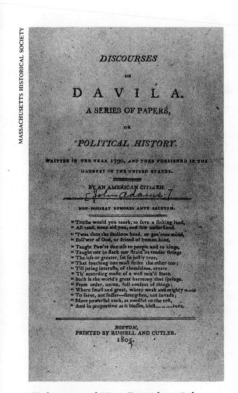

Title page of Vice President John Adams's Discourses on Davila

cratic governments come in for a large share of the scurrility lavished on those of France.

N. York July 10. 1791

The Bank-Shares have risen as much in the Market here as at Philadelphia. It seems admitted on all hands now that the plan of the institution gives a moral certainty of gain to the subscribers with scarce a physical possibility of loss. The subscriptions are consequently a mere scramble for so much public plunder which will be engrossed by those already loaded with the spoils of indi-[vi]duals. The event shews what would have been the operation of the plan, if, *as originally proposed*, subscriptions had been limited to the 1st. of April and to the favorite species of stock which the Bank-Jobbers had monopolized. It pretty clearly appears also in what proportions the public debt lies in the Country—what sort of hands hold it; and by whom the people of the U.S. are to be governed. Of all the shameful circumstances of this business, it is among the greatest to see the members of the Legislature who were most active in pushing this Job, openly grasping its emoluments. [Philip] Schuyler [Senator from New York and Hamilton's father-in-law] is to be put at the Head of the Directors, if the weight of the N. Y. subscribers can effect it. Nothing new is talked of here. In fact stock-jobbing drowns every other subject. The Coffee House is in an eternal buzz with the gamblers.

New York, July 13, 1791.

Beckely [John Beckley, Clerk of the House of Representatives] has just got back from his Eastern trip. He says that the partizans of Mr. Adams's heresies in that quarter are perfectly insignificant in point of number; that particularly in Boston he is become distinguished for his unpopularity; that Publicola [author of a series of anti-Paine, pro-Adams letters] is probably the manufacture of his son [John Quincy] out of materials furnished by himself, and that the publication is generally as obnoxious in New England as it appears to be in Pennsylvania. If young Adams be capable of giving the dress in which Publicola presents himself, it is very probable he may have been made Editor of his father's doctrines.

...I mentioned to you some time ago an extract from a piece in the Poughkeepsie paper as a sensible comment on Mr. Adams's doctrines. The whole has since been republished here, and is evidently from a better pen than any of the Anti-Publicolas I have seen.

N. York Aug:8. 1791.

I take the liberty of putting the inclosed into your hands....You will find an allusion to some mysterious cause for a phoenomenon in the Stocks. It is surmized that the deferred [state] debt is to be taken up at the next session, and some anticipated provision made for it. This may either be an invention of those who wish to sell: or it may be a reality imparted in confidence to the purchasers or smelt out by their sagacity. I have had a hint that something is intended and had dropt from —— —— which has led to this speculation. I am unwilling to credit the fact, untill I have further evidence, which I am in a train of getting if it exists. It is said that packet boats & expresses are again sent from this place to the Southern States, to buy up the paper of all sorts which has risen in the market here. These & other abuses make it a problem whether the system of the old paper under a bad Government, or of the new under a good one, be chargeable with the greater substantial injustice. The true difference seems to be that by the former the few were the victims to the many; by the latter the many to the few. It seems agreed on all hands now that the bank is a certain & gratuitous augmentation of the capitals sub[s]cribed, on a proportion of not less than 40 or 50 PerCt. and if the deferred debt should be immediately provided for in favor of the purchasers of it in the deferred shape, & since the unanimous vote that no change shd. be made in the funding system, my imagination will not attempt to set bounds to the daring depravity of the times. The stockjobbers will become the pretorian band of the Government—at once its tool & its tyrant; bribed by its largesses, & overaweing it, by clamours & combinations.

John Quincy Adams by Copley

One of Madison's errands in New York was to persuade his old college friend Philip Freneau to go to Philadelphia and edit a national newspaper devoted to the republican cause. Such a vehicle of intelligence was necessary to combat the Federalist newspaper, John Fenno's *Gazette of the United States,* "a paper of pure Toryism" in Jefferson's opinion. Freneau finally consented and the *National Gazette* began publication in the fall. Madison was soon writing for it. His little essays on a variety of subjects in political economy and statecraft, several of which are excerpted here, became increasingly partisan as the political temperature soared in Philadelphia. Taken together, they form a kind of primer of the emerging Republican party.

Madison's college friend Philip Freneau (above) started publishing a newspaper (below) to which Madison contributed short political essays.

"Consolidation" [December 3, 1791]

Much has been said, and not without reason, against a consolidation of the States into one government. Omitting lesser objections, two consequences would probably flow from such a change in our political system, which justify the cautions used against it. First, it would be impossible to avoid the dilemma, of either relinquishing the present energy and responsibility of a *single* executive magistrate, for some *plural* substitute, which by dividing so great a trust might lessen the danger of it; or suffering so great an accumulation of powers in the hands of that officer, as might by degrees transform him into a monarch. The incompetency of one Legislature to regulate all the various objects belonging to the local governments, would evidently force a transfer of many of them to the executive department; whilst the encreasing splendour and number of its prerogatives supplied by this source, might prove excitements to ambition too powerful for a sober execution of the elective plan, and consequently strengthen the pretexts for an hereditary designation of the Magistrate. Second, were the State governments abolished, the same space of country that would produce an undue growth of the executive power, would prevent that controul on the Legislative body, which is essential to a faithful discharge of its trust....

But if a consolidation of the States into one government be an event so justly to be avoided, it is not less to be desired, on the other hand, that a consolidation should prevail in their interests and affections; and this too, as it fortunately happens, for the very reasons, among others, which lie against a governmental consolidation. For, in the first place, in proportion as uniformity is found to prevail in the interests and sentiments of the different states, will be the practicability of accommodating *Legislative* regulations to them, and thereby of withholding new and dangerous prerogatives from the executive.

Again, the greater the mutual confidence and affection of all parts of the Union, the more likely they will be to concur amicably, or to differ with moderation, in the elective designation of the Chief Magistrate; and by such examples, to guard and adorn the vital principle of our republican constitution. Lastly, the less the supposed difference of interests, and the greater the concord and confidence throughout the great body of the people, the more readily must they sympathize with each other, the more seasonably can they interpose a common manifestation of their sentiments, the more certainly will they take the alarm at usurpation or oppression, and the more certainly will they *consolidate* their defence of the public liberty.

In December, 1791, Judge George Turner of the Northwest Territory gave this report of the Indians on the Ohio to Madison and Congress.

"Public opinion" [December 19, 1791]
Public opinion sets bounds to every government, and is the real sovereign in every free one.

As there are cases where the public opinion must be obeyed by the government; so there are cases, where not being fixed, it may be influenced by the government. This distinction, if kept in view, would prevent or decide many debates on the respect due from the government to the sentiments of the people.

In proportion as government is influenced by opinion, it must be so, by whatever influences opinion. This decides the question concerning a *Constitutional Declaration of Rights*, which requires an influence on government, by becoming a part of the public opinion.

The larger a country, the less easy for its real opinion to be ascertained, and the less difficult to be counterfeited; when ascertained or presumed, the more respectable it is in the eyes of individuals. This is favorable to the authority of government. For the same reason, the more extensive a country, the more insignificant is each individual in his own eyes. This may be unfavorable to liberty.

Whatever facilitates a general intercourse of sentiments, as good roads, domestic commerce, a free press, and particularly *a circulation of newspapers through the entire body of the people*, and *Representatives going from, and returning among every part of them*, is equivalent to a contraction of territorial limits, and is favorable to liberty, where these may be too extensive.

"Spirit of Governments" [February 20, 1792]
No Government is perhaps reducible to a sole principle of operation. Where the theory approaches nearest to this character, different and often heterogeneous principles mingle their influence in the administration. It is useful nevertheless to analyse the several kinds of government, and to characterize them by the spirit which predominates in each.

Montesquieu has resolved the great operative principles of government into fear, honor, and virtue, applying the first to pure despotisms, the second to regular monarchies, and the third to republics. The portion of truth blended with the ingenuity of this system, sufficiently justifies the admiration bestowed on its author. Its accuracy however can never be defended against the criticisms which it has encountered. Montesquieu was in politics not a Newton or a Locke, who established immortal systems, the one in matter, the other in mind. He was in his particular science what Bacon was in universal science: He lifted the veil from the venerable errors which enslaved opinion, and pointed the way to those luminous truths of which he had but a glimpse himself.

May not governments be properly divided, according to their predominant spirit and principles into three species of which the following are examples?

First. A government operating by a permanent military force, which at once maintains the government, and is maintained by it; which is at once the cause of burdens on the people, and of submission in the people to their burdens. Such have been the governments under which human nature has groaned through every age. Such are the governments which still oppress it in almost every country of Europe, the quarter of the globe which calls itself the pattern of civilization, and the pride of humanity.

Secondly. A government operating by corrupt influence; substituting the motive of private interest in place of public duty; converting its pecuniary dispensations into bounties to favorites, or bribes to opponents; accommodating its measures to the avidity of a part of the nation instead of the benefit of the whole: in a word, enlisting an army of interested partizans, whose tongues, whose pens, whose intrigues, and whose active combinations, by supplying the terror of the sword, may support a real domination of the few, under an apparent liberty

Washington (standing at right) and his first Cabinet: Henry Knox, seated; Thomas Jefferson, Edmund Randolph (back to artist), and Alexander Hamilton, standing

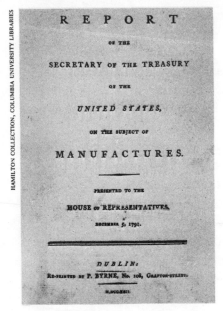

REPORT

ON THE

SECRETARY OF THE TREASURY

OF THE

UNITED STATES,

ON THE SUBJECT OF

MANUFACTURES.

PRESENTED TO THE

HOUSE OF REPRESENTATIVES,

DECEMBER 5, 1791.

DUBLIN:

Re-printed by P. BYRNE, No. 108, Grafton-street.

M.DCC.XCII.

Madison and Jefferson both opposed Hamilton's Report on Manufactures.

of the many. Such a government, wherever to be found, is an imposter. It is happy for the new world that it is not on the west side of the Atlantic. It will be both happy and honorable for the United States, if they never descend to mimic the costly pageantry of its form, nor betray themselves into the venal spirit of its administration.

Thirdly. A government, deriving its energy from the will of the society, and operating by the reason of its measures, on the understanding and interest of the society. Such is the government for which philosophy has been searching, and humanity been sighing, from the most remote ages. Such are the republican governments which it is the glory of America to have invented, and her unrivalled happiness to possess. May her glory be compleated by every improvement on the theory which experience may teach; and her happiness be perpetuated by a system of administration corresponding with the purity of the theory.

Political alignments took definite form in 1792. Congressmen spoke of "Mr. Madison's party." Leading Federalists said he had become "a desperate party leader." If this seemed a strange role for one who disliked parties, it was because he now realized that the natural countervailing action of competing interests, on which he had relied, was not working and that it was necessary to build a broad republican consensus to overcome the powerful combination—speculative, mercantile, manufacturing, Anglican—that Treasury influence had formed around the administration. Hamilton's *Report on Manufactures,* proposing a centralized system of economic development for the sprawling young agricultural country, not only bid defiance of the Constitution but disclosed the whole consolidating tendency of the administration. In Madison's view the choice was between two alternatives: consolidate power and divide the people or divide power and consolidate the people. The latter offered the only sure foundation of republican union.

The growing division in Congress was duplicated in Washington's Cabinet. Hamilton and Jefferson were increasingly at odds on issues of foreign policy, the former soft on Britain and hard on France, the latter just the reverse. By May, 1792, Hamilton was claiming that the two Virginians spearheaded a faction seeking to subvert the government. About Madison he was frankly puzzled. Whether his apostasy was the result of Jefferson's wily influence or the seductions of Virginia politics, he did not know; but it was Jefferson, more than Madison, whom he feared. In July, Hamilton himself took up the attack in Fenno's *Gazette,* charging Jefferson—and, to a lesser extent,

Madison—with hostility to the Constitution, to funding and credit, and to the administration he pretended to serve. He accused Jefferson of employing Freneau, a part-time clerk in his own department, in vicious newspaper warfare on the administration. Shocked by this development, Madison rode over to Monticello from Orange to talk strategy with Jefferson. In the public mind at least, Hamilton had built Jefferson into *the* Republican leader. While Jefferson held aloof from the turmoil, Madison and Monroe put their pens to work in his defense. Of Hamilton's charge regarding the *National Gazette,* Madison wrote to Attorney General Edmund Randolph.

Orange [Virginia,] Sepr. 13—1792

Your favor of the 12 Ult. having arrived during an excurtion into Albemarle [County], I did not receive it till my return on yesterday. I lose not a moment in thanking you for it; particularly for the very friendly paragraph in the publication in Fenno's paper. As I do not get his paper here, it was by accident I first saw this extraordinary maneuvre of Calumny; the quarter, the motive, and the object of which speak for themselves. As it respects Mr. Jefferson, I have no doubt that it will be of service both to him & to the public, if it should lead to such an investigation of his political opinions and character as may be expected. With respect to myself the consequence in a public view is of little account. In any view, there could not have been a charge founded on a grosser perversion of facts, & consequently against which I could feel myself more invulnerable.

That I wished & recomme[n]ded Mr. Freneau to be appd to his present Clerkship is certain. But the Department of State was not the only, nor as I recollect the first one to which I mentioned his name & character. I was governed in these recommendations by an acquaintance of long standing, by a respect for his talents, & by a knowledge of his merit & sufferings in the course of the revolution. Had I been less abstemious in my practice from Solicitations in behalf of my friends, I should probably have been more early in thinking of Mr. F. The truth is, that my application when made did not originate with myself. It was suggested by another Gentleman [Henry Lee] who could feel no motive but a disposition to patronize merit, & who wish'd me to cooperate with him. That with others of Mr. Freneau's particular acquaintances I wish'd & advis'd him to establish a press at Philada. instead of one meditated by him in N Jersey, is also certain. I advised the change because I thought his interest would

For the NATIONAL GAZETTE.

A candid State of PARTIES.

AS it is the business of the contemplative statesman to trace the history of parties in a free country, so it is the duty of the citizen at all times to understand the actual state of them. Whenever this duty is omitted, an opportunity is given to designing men, by the use of artificial or nominal distinctions, to oppose and balance against each other those who never differed as to the end to be pursued, and may no longer differ as to the means of attaining it. The most interesting state of parties in the United States may be referred to three periods: Those who espoused the cause of independence and those who adhered to the British claims, formed the parties of the first period; if, indeed, the disaffected class were considerable enough to deserve the name of a party. This state of things was superseded by the treaty of peace in 1783. From 1783 to 1787 there were parties in abundance, but being rather local than general, they are not within the present review.

The Federal Constitution, proposed in the latter year, gave birth to a second and most interesting division of the people. Every one remembers it, because every one was involved in it.

Among those who embraced the constitution, the great body were unquestionably friends to republican liberty; tho' there were, no doubt, some who were openly or secretly attached to monarchy and aristocracy; and hoped to make the constitution a cradle for these hereditary establishments.

Among those who opposed the constitu-

Madison's essay "A candid State of Parties" as it appeared in the National Gazette *September 26, 1792*

be advanced by it, & because as a friend I was desirous that his interest should be advanced. This was my primary & governing motive. That as a consequential one, I entertain'd hopes that a *free* paper meant for general circulation and edited by a man of genius, of republican principles, & a friend to the Constitution, would be some antidote to the doctrines & discourses circulated in favour of Monarchy and Aristocracy, & would be an acceptable vehicle of public information in many places not sufficiently supplied with it; this also is a certain truth; but it is a truth which I never could be tempted to conceal, or to wish to be concealed. If there be a temptation in the case it would be to make a merit of it.

But that the establishment of Mr. Fs. press was wished in order to sap the Constitution, and that I forwarded the measure; or that my agency negociated it, by an illicit or improper connection between the functions of a translating Clerk in a public office, & those of an Editor of a Gazette, these are charges which ought to be as impotent as they are malicious. The first is surely incredible, if any charge could be so: & the second is I hope at least improbable, & not to be credited, until unequivocal proof shall be subtituted for anonymous & virulent assertion.

The political temperature in Philadelphia soared with the approach of the fall elections. Washington—the only man capable of holding the government together—happily consented to another term at the urging of all concerned; but party spirit ran high in congressional contests. Seeking to advance the Republican cause, Madison contributed "A candid State of Parties" to the *National Gazette*.

[September 26, 1792]

The most interesting state of parties in the United States may be referred to three periods: Those who espoused the cause of independence and those who adhered to the British claims, formed the parties of the first period; if, indeed, the disaffected class were considerable enough to deserve the name of a party. This state of things was superseded by the treaty of peace in 1783. From 1783 to 1787 there were parties in abundance, but being rather local than general, they are not within the present review.

The Federal Constitution, proposed in the latter year,

191

MEMBERS OF CONGRESS.

SENATORS.

New-Hampshire.
John Langdon, No. 223, Market ft.
Paine Wingate, No. 155, n. Second ft.

Massachusetts.
George Cabot, No. 96, Union ft.
Caleb Strong, No. 56, n. Third ft.

Rhode-Island.
Theodore Foster, No. 29, Callow Hill ft.
Joseph Stanton, 285, f. Second ft.

Connecticut.
Oliver Ellsworth, No. 221, f. Third ft.
Roger Sherman, No. 155, n. Second ft.

Vermont.
Stephen R. Bradley, No. 153, Market ft.]
Moses Robinson, No. 20, n. Third ft.

New-York.
Aaron Burr, No. 147, n. Second ft.
Rufus King, No. 104, Spruce ft.

New-Jersey.
Philemon Dickinson, Chesnut ft. upper end.
John Rutherford, No. 56, n. Fourth ft.

Pennsylvania.
Robert Morris, corner of Market and Sixth ft.

Delaware.
Richard Bassett.
George Read, No. 33, Dock ft.

Maryland.
Charles Carroll.
John Henry, No. 170, Market ft.

Virginia.
James Monroe, No. 179, Arch ft.
John Taylor.

Kentucky.
John Brown, corner of Third and Vine ft.
John Edwards, No. 28, Arch ft.

North Carolina.
Benjamin Hawkins, No. 170, Market ft.
Samuel Johnston, No. 189, f. Third ft.

South Carolina.
Pierce Butler, Market between Seventh and Eighth ft.
Ralph Izard, No. 169, Chesnut ft.

Georgia.
William Few, 14, Cherry Alley.
James Gunn.

REPRESENTATIVES.

New-Hampshire.
Nicholas Gilman, No. 9, n. Fourth ft.
Samuel Livermore, No. 235, Market ft.
Jeremiah Smith, No. 9, n. Fourth ft.

Massachusetts.
Fisher Ames, No. 235, Market ft.
Shearjashub Bourne, No. 65, Walnut ft.
Eldridge Gerry, No. 105, n. Front ft.
Benjamin Goodhue, No. 72, n. Third ft.
George Leonard, No. 65, Walnut ft.
Theodore Sedgwick, No. 104, Spruce ft.
George Thatcher, No. 235, Market ft.
Artemas Ward, No. 155, n. Second ft.

Rhode-Island.
Benjamin Bourne, No. 235, Market ft.

Connecticut.
James Hillhouse, No. 72, n. Third ft.
Amasa Learned, No. 67, Pine ft.
Jonathan Sturges, No. 72, n. Third ft.
Jonathan Trumbull, (Speaker) No. 67, Pine ft.
Jeremiah Wadsworth.

Vermont.
Nathaniel Niles, No. 155, n. Second ft.
Israel Smith, No. 20, n. Third ft.

New-York.
Egbert Benson, No. 104, Spruce ft.
James Gordon, No. 184, f. Front ft.
John Laurance, No. 155, Chesnut ft.
Cornelius C. Schoonmaker, No. 98, n. Third ft.
Peter Silvester, No. 128, Second ft.
Thomas Tredwell, No. 98, n. Third ft.

New-Jersey.
Elias Boudinot, N. 229, Market ft.
Abraham Clark, No. 66, Market ft.
Jonathan Dayton, No. 47, n. Third ft.
Aaron Kitchell, No. 66, Market ft.

Pennsylvania.
William Findley, No. 67, Vine ft.
Thomas Fitzsimons, corner of Spruce & 4th ft.
Andrew Gregg.
Thomas Hartley, No. 105 n. Front ft.
Daniel Heister, No. 67 Vine ft.
Israel Jacobs, 42, f. Second ft.
John Wilkes Kittera, 81, Market ft.
Frederick Augustus Muhlenberg, 84, n. Second ft.

Delaware.
Jone Vining.

Maryland.
Philip Key, 214, Market ft.
John Francis Mercer, City Tavern.
William Vans Murray, 81, f. Third ft.
Joshua Seney.
Upton Sheridine.
Samuel Sterret.

Virginia.
William B. Giles, 170, Market ft.
Samuel Griffin, 43, Spruce ft.
Richard Bland Lee, 53, Race ft.
James Madison, 170, Market ft.
Andrew Moore, 184, f. Front ft.
John Page, 214, Market ft.
Josiah Parker, 56 n. Fourth ft.
Abraham Venable, 170, Market ft.
Alexander White, 18 Chesnut ft.

Kentucky.
Christopher Greenup, 28, Arch ft.
Alexander D. Orr, Corner Vine and Third ft.

North-Carolina.
John Baptist Ashe, 132, Vine ft.
William Barry Grove, Corner Vine & Third ft.
Nathaniel Macon, do. do.
John Steele, 96, n. Third ft.
Hugh Williamson, Corner Vine and Third ft.

South Carolina.
Robert Barnwell, 104, Spruce ft.
Daniel Huger, 9, n. Fourth ft.
William Smith, 165, Chesnut ft.
Thomas Sumpter, 110, n. Second ft.
Thomas Tudor Tucker, 9, n. Fourth ft.

Georgia.
Abraham Baldwin, 97, Vine ft.
John Milledge, do.
Francis Willis, 69, n. Sixth ft.

☞ The gentlemen to whose names no place of abode is annexed, have not arrived.

List of members of Congress in 1792 and their addresses in Philadelphia; Madison lived at Mrs. House's, 170 Market Street, as did a number of other senators and congressmen.

gave birth to a second and most interesting division of the people. Every one remembers it, because every one was involved in it.

Among those who embraced the constitution, the great body were unquestionably friends to republican liberty; tho' there were, no doubt, some who were openly or secretly attached to monarchy and aristocracy; and hoped to make the constitution a cradle for these hereditary establishments.

Among those who opposed the constitution, the great body were certainly well affected to the union and to good government, tho' there might be a few who had a leaning unfavourable to both. This state of parties was terminated by the regular and effectual establishment of the federal government in 1788; out of the administration of which, however, has arisen a third division, which being natural to most political societies, is likely to be of some duration in ours.

One of the divisions consists of those who from particular interest, from natural temper, or from the habits of life, are more partial to the opulent than to the other classes of society; and having debauched themselves into a persuasion that mankind are incapable of governing themselves, it follows with them, of course, that government can be carried on only by the pageantry of rank, the influence of money and emoluments, and the terror of military force. Men of those sentiments must naturally wish to point the measures of government less to the interest of the many than of a few, and less to the reason of the many than to their weaknesses; hoping perhaps in proportion to the ardor of their zeal, that by giving such a turn to the administration, the government itself may by degrees be narrowed into fewer hands, and approximated to an hereditary form.

The other division consists of those who believing in the doctrine that mankind are capable of governing themselves, and hating hereditary power as an insult to the reason and an outrage to the rights of man, are naturally offended at every public measure that does not appeal to the understanding and to the general interest of the community, or that is not strictly conformable to the principles, and conducive to the preservation of republican government.

This being the real state of parties among us, an experienced and dispassionate observer will be at no loss to decide on the probable conduct of each.

The antirepublican party, as it may be called, being the weaker in point of numbers, will be induced by the most obvious motives to strengthen themselves with the men of influence, particularly of moneyed, which is the most active and insinuating influence. It will be equally their true policy to weaken their opponents by reviving exploded parties, and taking advantage of all prejudices, local, political, and occupational, that may prevent or disturb a general coalition of sentiments.

The Republican party, as it may be termed, conscious that the mass of people in every part of the union, in every state, and of every occupation must at bottom be with them, both in interest and sentiment, will naturally find their account in burying all antecedent questions, in banishing every other distinction than that between enemies and friends to republican government, and in promoting a general harmony among the latter, wherever residing, or however employed.

Whether the republican, or the rival party will ultimately establish its ascendance, is a problem which may be contemplated now; but which time alone can solve. On one hand experience shows that in politics as in war, stratagem is often an overmatch for numbers: and among more happy characteristics of our political situation, it is now well understood that there are peculiarities, some temporary, others more durable, which may favour that side in the contest. On the republican side, again, the superiority of numbers is so great, their sentiments are so decided, and the practice of making a common cause, where there is a common sentiment and common interest, in spight of circumstancial and artificial distinctions, is so well understood, that no temperate observer of human affairs will be surprised if the issue in the present instance should be reversed, and the government be administered in the spirit and form approved by the great body of the people.

The Republicans scored impressive gains in the 1792 elections. Then, early in the new year, events abroad gave a fresh turn to American affairs. Against the invading armies of the "conspiracy of kings" (Great Britain, Spain, and Holland), France, now a republic, waged war to preserve and extend her revolution. Enthusiasm for France ran high in the United States. Republicans coupled her cause with the American and worried lest the failure of liberty abroad tip the political scales disastrously at home. Madison's opinion was unequivocal, as he made clear in a letter to George Nicholas, a political ally and the Attorney General of Kentucky.

Edmond Charles Genêt

> Philada. Mar: 15 1793.
>
> Our accounts from abroad are not of very late date nor of a very decisive cast. It is still a problem whether war will take place between England & France. The war in which the latter is at present engaged seems likely to be pushed by her enemies during the ensuing campaign. As yet her conduct has been great both as free and as martial nation. We hope it will continue so, and finally baffle all her enemies, who are in fact the enemies of human nature. We have every motive in America to pray for her success, not only from a general attachment to the liberties of mankind, but from a peculiar regard to our own. The symtoms of disaffection to Republi-[can gov]ernment have risen, & subsided among us in such visible [cor]respondence with the prosperous and adverse accounts from the French Revolution, that a miscarriage of it would threaten us with the most serious dangers to our present forms & principles of our governments.

War between Britain and France had, in fact, already begun. Not only was the United States an ally of France, pledged to defend her West Indian possessions, but the war inevitably threatened American peace on the high seas. Moreover, contrary dispositions toward these two great powers were woven into the texture of American politics. Federalists despised the infection of Jacobinical democracy, which they detected in their opponents, and wished trade and friendship with Britain. The Republican commitment to France involved matters of principle, of gratitude, and of hostility to Britain, as well as the shrewd political calculation that popular frenzy for France could be converted into party capital.

Madison was at home when the new French minister, Edmond Charles Genêt, arrived to a tumultuous welcome in the spring. Except for Jefferson, however, the administration received him coldly. (Hamilton had been opposed to receiving him at all.) On April 22, 1793, the President issued the Proclamation of Neutrality. It put the belligerents on the same level and enjoined "conduct friendly and impartial" toward both. Jefferson, although he disliked the proclamation, acquiesced in it and called upon his friends to do the same. Madison was at first puzzled and then revolted by the proclamation. The subsequent administration of the policy, he felt, gave an appallingly "anglified complexion" to the government. He expressed his views in three letters to Jefferson.

Orange [Virginia,] May 8th. 1793.
I anxiously wish that the reception of Genet may testify what I believe to be the real affections of the people. It is the more desireable as a seasonable plum after the bitter pills which it seems must be administered. Having neither the Treaty nor Law of Nations at hand I form no opinion as to the stipulations of the former or the precise neutrality defined by the latter. I had always supposed that the terms of the Treaty made some sort of difference, at least as far as would consist with the Law of Nations, between France & Nations not in Treaty, particularly G. Britain. I should still doubt whether the term *impartial* in the Proclamation is not stronger than was necessary, if not than was proper. Peace is no doubt to be preserved at any price that honor and good faith will permit. But it is no less to be considered that the least departure from these will not only be most likely to end in the loss of peace, but is pregnant with every other evil that could happen to us. In explaining our engagements under the Treaty with France, it would be honorable as well as just to adhere to the sense that would at the time have been put on them. The attempt [by

A view of the harbor of New York with the frigate Ambuscade, *which had brought Genèt to America*

Hamilton] to shuffle off the Treaty altogether by quibbling on Vattel [the author of *Law of Nations*] is equally contemptible for the meanness & folly of it. If a change of Govt. is an absolution from public engagements, why not from those of a domestic as well as of a foreign nature; and what then becomes of public debts &c &c. In fact, the doctrine would perpetuate every existing Despotism, by involving in a reform of the Govt. a destruction of the social pact, an annihilation of property, and a compleat establishment of the State of Nature. What most surprises me is that such a proposition shd. have been discussed.

Orange [Virginia,] June 13. 93.

I observe that the Newspapers continue to criticize the President's proclamations; and I find that some of the criticisms excite the attention of dispassionate & judicious individuals here. I have heard it remarked by such with some surprise that the P. should have declared the U.S. to be neutral in the unqualified terms used, when we were so notoriously & unequivally under *eventual engagements* to defend the American possessions of F. I have heard it remarked also that the impartiality enjoined on the people was as little reconciliable with their moral obligations, as the unconditional neutrality proclaimed by the Government with the express articles of the Treaty. It has been asked also whether the authority of the Executive extended by any part of the Constitution to a declaration of the *Disposition* of the U.S. on the subject of war & peace? I have been mortified that on these points I could offer no bona fide explanations that ought to be satisfactory. On the last point I must own my surprise that such a prerogative should have been exercised. Perhaps I may have not attended to some part of the Constitution with sufficient care, or may have misapprehended its meaning: But, as I have always supposed & still conceive, a proclamation on the subject could not properly go beyond a declaration of the fact that the U.S. were at war or peace and an injunction of a suitable conduct on the Citizen [Genêt]. The right to decide the question whether the duty & interest of the U.S. require war or peace under any given circumstances, and whether their disposition be towards the one or the other seems to be

One of the areas of friction between France and Great Britain was the West Indies. This print shows the capture of the disputed island of Tobago by the British in April, 1793.

essentially & exclusively involved in the right vested in the Legislature, of declaring war in time of peace; and in the P. & S. [Senate] of making peace in time of war. Did no such view of the subject present itself in the discussions of the Cabinet? I am extremely afraid that the P. may not be sufficiently aware of the snares that may be laid for his good intentions by men whose politics at bottom are very different from his own. An assumption of prerogatives not clearly found in the Constitution & having the appearance of being copied from a Monarchical model, will beget animadversion equally mortifying to him, & disadvantageous to the Government.

Orange [Virginia,] June 19, 1793. Every Gazette I see (except that of the U.S.) [Fenno's] exhibits spirit of criticism on the anglified complexion charged in the Executive politics. I regret extremely the position into which the P. has been thrown. The unpopular cause of Anglomany is openly laying claim to him. His enemies masking themselves, under the popular cause of France, are playing off the most tremendous batteries on him. The proclamation was in truth a most unfortunate error. It wounds the National honor, by seeming to disregard the stipulated duties to France. It wounds the popular feelings by a seeming indifference to the cause of liberty. And it seems to violate the forms & spirit of the Constitution, by making the executive Magistrate the organ of the disposition the duty & the interest of the Nation in relation to war & peace, subjects appropriated to other departments of the Government. It is mortifying to the real friends of the P. that his fame & his influence should have been unnecessarily made to depend in any degree on political events in a foreign quarter of the Globe: and particularly so that he should have any thing to apprehend from the success of liberty in another country, since he owes his pre-eminence to the success of it in his own. If France triumphs the ill-fated proclamation will be a millstone which would sink any other character, and will force a struggle even on his.

Madison's confidence in the President was shaken, but he continued to defend him as a man misled and misused by the Fed-

A paper on the liquidation of the American debt to France from Citizen Genêt to Jefferson, printed in a collection of 1793

eralists, with Hamilton the chief culprit. In June, as "Pacificus," Hamilton commenced a series of articles in Fenno's *Gazette* on the Proclamation of Neutrality. He upheld its constitutionality, declared the French alliance in abeyance, and denounced her revolution. "For God's sake, my dear sir," Jefferson implored Madison, "take up your pen, select the most striking heresies and cut him to pieces in the face of the public." Madison, as "Helvidius," complied, but found it the "most grating" task he had ever undertaken and broke off after scoring the narrow constitutional point earlier stated to Jefferson. "Citizen" Genêt, meanwhile, hoping to capitalize on popular support for the French cause, commissioned American privateers to attack British shipping, armed French prizes in American ports, and enlisted American adventurers in grandiose expeditions against Spanish and British territories in North America. By his intemperate — and illegal — actions, however, Genêt jeopardized his own cause and turned even Jefferson against him. No more calamitous appointment was ever made, Jefferson told Madison, and unless the Republicans abandoned Genêt they would sink with him. Still at Montpelier, Madison had some difficultly understanding the sudden metamorphosis of Genêt from hero into villain. But he toned down resolutions intended for Republican assemblages in the counties to counteract the anti-French blast of the Federalists. He explained the change of tactics to his coadjutor, Monroe.

LETTERS

OF

HELVIDIUS:

WRITTEN IN REPLY TO

PACIFICUS,

ON THE

PRESIDENT's PROCLAMATION OF NEUTRALITY.

Published originally in the Year 1793.

PHILADELPHIA:
PRINTED BY SAMUEL H. SMITH, No. 118, CHESNUT STREET.
M.DCC.XCVI.

Title page of Madison's Letters of Helvidius, *written in reply to those of Hamilton as "Pacificus" supporting the Proclamation of Neutrality*

[Orange, Virginia,] Sepr. 15. 93.

Since I parted from you I have had several letters from Mr. J. in which all the *facts* involving Genet are detailed. His conduct has been that of a mad man. He is abandoned even by his votaries in Philada. Hutcheson [Dr. James Hutchinson, Republican leader] declares that he has ruined the Republican interest in that place. I wish I could forward the details I have recd. but they are too confidential to be hazarded by the casual conveyance to which this is destined. They ought however to have no other effect on the steps to be pursued, than to caution agst. founding any of them on the presumed inculpability of Genet. As he has put himself on such unjustifiable ground, perhaps it is fortunate that he has done it in so flagrant a manner. It will be the more easily believed now that he has acted agst. the sense of his Constituents, and the latter will be the less likely to support him in his errors. I find that the Anglicans & Monocrats from Boston to Philada. are betrayed by the occasion into the most palpable discovery of their real views. They already lose sight of the Agent; and direct their hostilities *immediately agst. France*. This will do good, if proper use be made of it. You will see by the late papers that G. B. has made war on our commerce, by interrupting uncontraband articles bound to unblockaded ports, and taking them to herself at her own price. This must bring on a crisis with us, unless the order be revoked on our demand, of which there is not the least probability.

What Madison described as the British "war on our commerce" helped to save Republicans from Genêt's ineptitude and enabled Jefferson, before he went into retirement at the year's end, to divert attention from French to British violations of American neutrality. In one of his last acts Jefferson dropped a bombshell into Congress: his *Report on Commerce* calling for retaliation against British restrictions on American trade and navigation. On January 3, 1794, Madison presented a series of resolutions in the House to implement this policy. France lurked behind the Republican plan, Federalists charged. On the contrary, Madison retorted, the policy was as old as the American Revolution and only looked to the national system of commerce that had been a paramount aim of the Constitution. The majority rallied to Madison's resolutions. He reported to Jefferson on the prospects in March.

Philada. March 2d. 1794.

I was in hopes every week to be able to furnish you with the proceedings on the subject grounded on your Commercial Report; and particularly with such of them as related to yourself. It has so happened that I never could find leisure to make out for the press, the share I had in them till very lately. The earlier part of my observations were sent to the Printer several weeks ago, but never made their appearance till Thursday evening last. The latter part is following, as you will find, as fast I can write it out, which from the extreme length of it, the brevity of my notes, and the time that has run since the observations were delivered, is a task equally tedious & laborious. The sequel will be forwarded to you as soon as it gets into print. As you are so little supplied with the current information it may be necessary to apprize you that after the general discussions on the measure proposed by me, had been closed, and the first general resolution agreed to by a majority of 5 or 6, several of the Eastern members friendly to the object insisted on a postponement till the first monday in March. It was necessary to gratify them, and the postponement was carried by a small majority against the

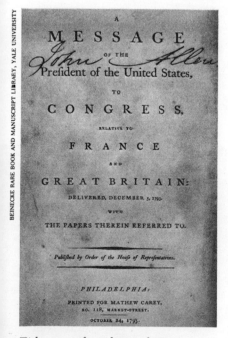

Title page of a volume of state papers concerning the relations of the United States with France and Great Britain at the end of 1793

The SECRETARY *of* STATE, *to whom was referred by the* HOUSE *of* REPRESENTATIVES, *the* REPORT *of a* COMMITTEE *on the written* MESSAGE *of the* PRESIDENT *of the* UNITED STATES, *of the 14th of February, 1791, with instruction to report to Congress the nature and extent of the* PRIVILEGES *and* RESTRICTIONS *of the* COMMERCIAL INTERCOURSE *of the United States with Foreign Nations, and the measures which he should think proper to be adopted, for the improvement of the Commerce and Navigation of the same, has had the same under consideration, and thereupon makes the following*

REPORT:

THE countries with which the UNITED STATES have their chief commercial intercourse, are, SPAIN, PORTUGAL, FRANCE, GREAT-BRITAIN, the UNITED NETHERLANDS, DENMARK, and SWEDEN, and their American possessions: and the articles of export which constitute the basis of that commerce, with their respective amounts, are—

	Dollars.
Bread-stuff, that is to say, bread-grains, meals, and bread, to the annual amount of	7,649,887
Tobacco	4,349,567
Rice	1,753,796
Wood	1,263,534
Salted fish	941,696
Pot and pearl-ash	839,093
Salted meats	599,130
Indigo	537,379
Horses and mules	339,753
Whale oil	252,591
Flax-seed	236,072
Tar, pitch and turpentine	217,177
Live provisions	137,743
Ships	
Foreign goods	620,274

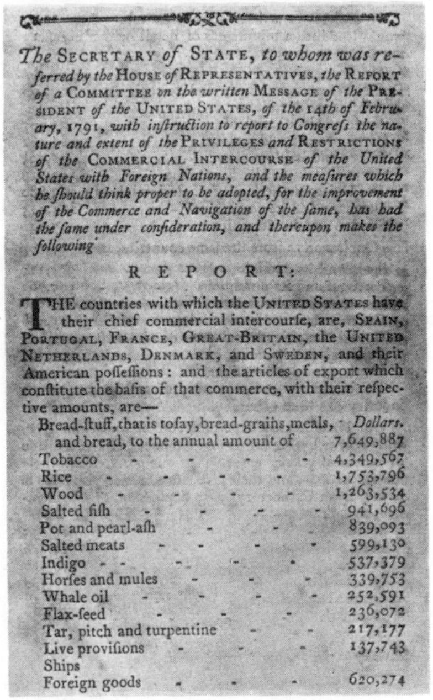

Page from Jefferson's Report on Commerce, *which lists articles of export and their respective amounts*

effects of the adverse party, who counted on the votes of the timid members if forced before they could learn the sense of their constituents. The Interval has produced vast exertions by the British party to mislead the people of the Eastern States. No means have been spared. The most artful & wicked calumnies have been propagated with all the zeal which malice and interest could invent. The blackest of these calumnies, as you may imagine have fallen to the lot of the mover of the Resolutions. The last Boston Paper contains a string of charges framed for the purpose of making the Eastern people believe that he has been the counsellor & abettor of Genet in all his extravagances, and a corrupt tool of France.... It appears however that in spite of all these diabolical manoeuvres, the town of Boston has been so far awakened as to have a Meeting in the town house, & a pretty unanimous vote for a committee to consider the subject & report proper instructions for their members in Congress.... I see by a paper of last evening that even in N. York a meeting of the people has taken place at the instance of the Republican party, and that a committee is appointed for the like purpose. As far as I know the names, the majority is on the right side. One motive for postponing the question so long was the chance of hearing from England, and the probability that the intelligence would strengthen the arguments for retaliation. Letters from Pinkney [Thomas Pinckney, Minister to Great Britain] have accordingly arrived. As yet they are under the seal of confidence but it is in

"House flies plenty" appears to the right on a May 23, 1794, entry in a weather log kept by Madison family.

1794	Therm. at Sun	Wind Rise	Weather at Sun Rise	Thermom. at 2	4	Wind O'Clock	Weather at 4 O'Clock PM.
May 21	60	S.	Fair.	82	85	SW	Fair.
22	66	SW	Fair.	86	91	S.	Fair
23	70	SW	Thin clouds	84	70	NE	Raining & Thunder cloud
24.	68	S.	Fair	84	72	SW	Raining
25	66	NE.	Great fog	80	70	N	Thunder cloud
26	64	E	Overcast	78	79	W	Thunder Cloud
27	58	E.	Overcast		68	NE.	Many clouds.
28	58	NE.	Fair	73	72	NE	Thin Clouds.
29	56	S.	Overcast	70	74	E	Thunder clouds & sprinkle of Rain
30	55	NE	Raining	58	58	NE	Raining
31.	58.	NE.	Raining	64½	64½	NE.	Raining
June 1	61	NE	Misting & thick	68	72	NE	Many clouds, but clearing away
2	60	N	Fair & fog.	78	75	SW	Sprinkling of Rain; & Shower afterwards
3	62	SE.	Fair	80	84	NE	Fair
4	62	NE	Overcast. & then Rain	62	64½	NE.	Overcast
5	60	NE.	Overcast.	74	78	NE	Flying dark clouds
6	58	SE	Fair.	75	76	NE.	Dark cloud at West; & then a small Shower

Rain fallen and when	Quantity Inch.	8ths	
23. Day.		3½	House flies plenty
24 Day		2½	
25 Day.		1½	
Night		¾	
29 Day 3/8 Night 5/8	1	1	
30 Day	1		
Night		4½	
31. Day 3 3/8. Night 1/8		4½	4.25
2 Day		1⅓	
4 Day		2½	
6. afternoon		2¼	5
	3	½	

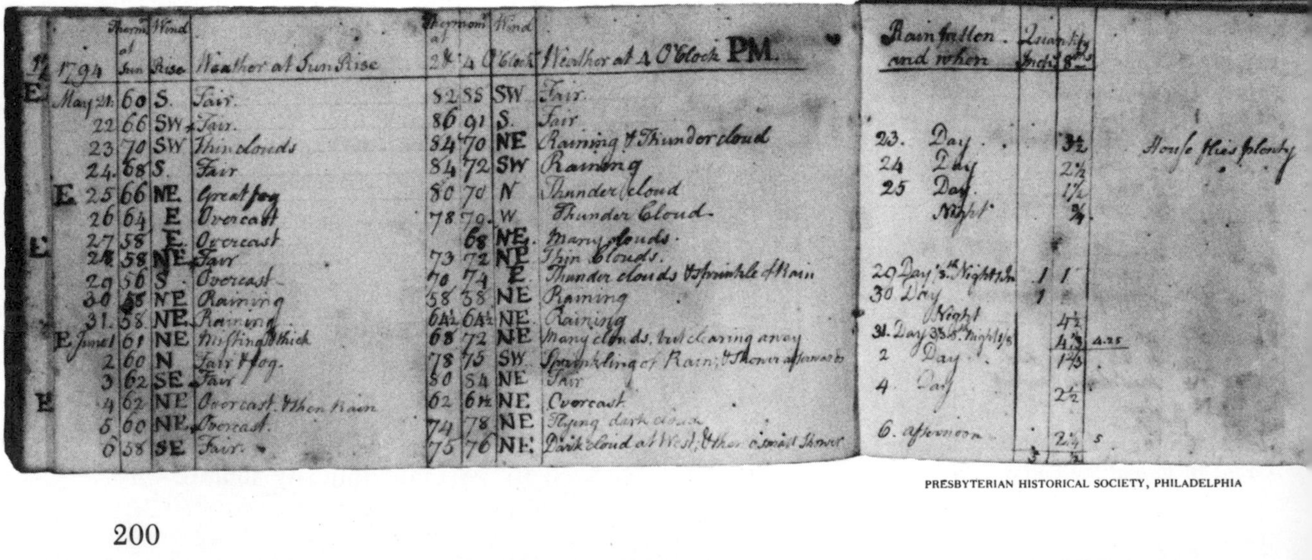

universal conversation that they mark precisely and *more strongly* than ever the unjust & unfriendly features which have characterized the British policy towards the U. States.

Some Political Observations, *which Jefferson ascribed to Madison, justifying the commercial resolutions Madison introduced in 1794*

[Philadelphia,] Mar: 12. 1794. The Merchants, particularly of N. England have had a terrible slam in the W. Indies. About a hundred vessels have been seized by the British for condemnation, on the pretext of enforcing the laws of the Monarchy with regard to the Colony trade. The partizans of England, considering a war as now probable are endeavoring to take the lead in defensive preparations, and to acquire merit with the people by anticipating their wishes. This new symtom of insolence & enmity in Britain, shews rather that she meditates a formal war as so[o]n as she shall have crippled our marine resources, or that she calculates on the pusilanimity of this country & the influence of her party, in a degree that will lead her into aggressions which our love of peace can no longer bear. The commercial propositions are in this state of things, not the precise remedy to be pressed as first in order; but they are in every view & in any event proper to make part of our standing laws till the principle of reciprocity be established by mutual arrangements.

Suddenly "more active medicine"—embargo or non-intercourse—seemed called for, and Madison's resolutions were set aside. The upshot in April, 1794, was the desperate mission of John Jay to negotiate a settlement with Britain. Madison expected no justice from Britain, unless forced by France, and both the Anglicanism of the envoy and Hamilton's ascendancy in the administration added to his misgivings.

While Madison awaited the outcome of Jay's mission, his thoughts turned to more personal matters. An unwilling bachelor at forty-three, his eye had fallen upon the attractive and vivacious Dolley Payne Todd, the twenty-six-year-old widow of a young Quaker lawyer who had died the year before, leaving her with a small son. The Todds had been known in Philadelphia's social and official circles for some time. Now, in the spring following her husband's death, Madison arranged for a formal introduction to the young widow, who wrote excitedly to a friend: "Thou must come to me. Aaron Burr says that the great little Madison has asked to be brought to see me this evening." The meeting was a success and Madison and Dolley were soon embarked on a whirlwind courtship. That summer, while she was recovering from a severe illness near her old home in Hanover County, Virginia, Dolley accepted his proposal of marriage and he replied to her affectionately.

> Orange [Virginia,] Aug: 18. 94:
> I recd some days ago your precious favor from Fredg. I cannot express, but hope you will conceive the joy it gave me. The delay in hearing of your leaving Hanover which I regarded as the only satisfactory proof of your recovery, had filled me with extreme...inquietude, and the consummation of that welcome event was endeared to me by the *stile* in which it was conveyed. I hope you will never have another *deliberation* on that subject. If the sentiments of my heart can guarantee those of yours, they assure me there can never be cause for it.

Madison and Mrs. Todd were married on September 15, 1794, at Harewood, the home of her sister Lucy, near Charles Town in what is now West Virginia. Madison notified his father of the marriage three weeks later, as soon as he could spare his father's servant, Sam.

> Harewood [Virginia,] October 5, 1794
>
> Dear & Hond Sir
> I have detained Sam by whom I send this so much longer than I intended & you expected that many apologies are due for the liberty. I hope it will be a sufficient one that I found him indispensable for a variety of little services, which I did not particularly take into view before I left Orange. These he can himself explain and I therefore leave the task to him; proceeding to the history of what relates to myself. On my arrival here I was able to urge so many conveniences in hastening the event which I solicited that it took place on the 15th ult: on the friday following we set out accompanied by Miss A. Payne, [Dolley's sister] and Miss Harriot Washington, on a visit to my sister Hite, when we arrived the next day, having stopped a night at Winchester with Mr. Bailmain. We had been a day or two only at Mr. Hites, before a slight indisposition which my wife had felt for several days, ended in a regular ague & fever. The fits tho' succeeded by compleat intermissions were so severe that I thought it prudent to call in a Physician from Winchester. Docr Mackay not being in the way Docr Baldwin attended, and by a decisive administration of the Bark soon expelled the complaint.

Dolley Madison as a young woman

Revolutionary Reminiscences of the Old Dominion. . . . BY ALEXANDER BOTELER, 1860

Harewood House, home of Dolley's sister, where Madisons were wed

She has since recovered very fast & I hope notwithstanding a slight indisposition this morning which may be the effect of fatigue & change of weather, that no return is in the least to be apprehended. We left Mr. Hites the day before yesterday. Our time was passed there with great pleasure on our side, and I hope with not less on the other. . . . In 8 or 10 days we expect to set out for Philada—your daughter in law begs you and my mother to accept her best and most respectful affections, which she means to express herself by an early opportunity. She wishes Fanny [Madison's twenty-year-old sister] also be sensible of the pleasure with which a correspondence with her would be carried on. . . .

I remain your affecte son

Js. Madison Jr

When the Madisons returned to Philadelphia for the next meeting of Congress, they moved into the home of James Monroe who had recently been appointed Minister to France. In November, 1794, Jay's Treaty was signed. It exceeded Madison's worst fears. Britain's pledge to evacuate the Northwest posts was the principal point gained, though this obligation descended from the peace of 1783. The treaty assumed American acquiescence in British maritime rule and practice, which had produced the crisis in the first place. Most damaging, in Madison's opinion, was the grant of "most favored nation" status to Britain. Not only was this unreciprocated on her side, but she must now profit freely from any commercial bargain the United States might make with friendly nations. The terms were made public in March, 1795; the Senate consented in June; and a whirlwind of indignation rolled across the land during the summer as the treaty awaited Washington's signature. Madison circulated his views among Republican leaders, including Robert R. Livingston of New York.

Robert R. Livingston

[Orange, Virginia,] Augst. 10. 1795.

Your favor of July 6, having been addressed to Williamsburg instead of *Orange Court House*, did not come to hand till two days ago. Your gloomy picture of the Treaty does not exceed my ideas of it. After yielding terms which would have been scorned by this country in the moment of its greatest embarrassments, & of G. Britains full enjoyment of peace & confidence, it adds to the ruinous bargain with this nation, a disqualification to make a good one with any other. In all our other Treaties it has been carefully stipulated that the nation to be treated as the most favored nations, & to come in for all new privileges that may be granted by the U. States, must pay for them the same or an equivalent price with the grantee. The proposed Treaty with G.B. disregarding this obvious rule of justice & equality, roundly agrees that no duty restriction or prohibition with respect to ships or merchandize shall be applied to G.B. which do not operate on all other nations (see Art. XV). Should any other nation therefore be disposed to give us the most precious & peculiar advantages in their trade, in exchange for the slightest preferences in ours, This article gives G.B. a negative on the transaction; unless it be so modified as to let her in for the favor without paying the price of it. But what nation wd. be willing to buy favors for another; especially when the inducement to buy & the value of the purchase, might depend on the peculiarity of the favor. It must be seen at once that this extraordinary feature would monopolize us to G.B. by precluding any material improvement of our existing Treaties, or the hope of any new ones that would be of much advantage to us. That so insidious an article should have occurred to Lord Grenville's jealousy of the U.S. & his policy of barring their connection with other Countries, and particularly with the French Republic, can surprise no one. The concurrence of the American Envoy in this & several other articles may not be so easily explained; but it seems impossible to screen him from the most illiberal suspicions without referring his conduct to the blindest partiality to the British Nation & Govt. and to the most vindictive sensations towards the French Republic. Indeed the Treaty from one end to the other must be regarded as a demonstration that the Party to which the Envoy belongs & of which he has been more the organ than of the U.S. is a British party, systematically aiming at an exclusive connection with the British Governt. & ready to sacrifice to that object as well the dearest interests of our Commerce, as the most sacred dictates of national honor. This is the true key to this unparalleled proceeding; and can alone explain it to the impartial and discerning part of the public. The leaders of this party stand self-condemned in their efforts to palliate the Treaty by magnifying the necessity of the British commerce to the U.S. and the insufficiency of the U.S. to influence the regulation of it.... It is with much pleasure I can assure you that the sentiment & voice of the people in this state in relation to the attempt to prostrate us to a foreign & unfriendly Nation, are as decided & as loud as could be wished. Many even of those who have hitherto rallied to the most exceptionable party measures, join in the general indignation agst. the Treaty. The few who hold out will soon be under the dilemma of following the example, or of falling under imputations which must disarm them of all injurious influence. You will see by the Newspapers that the City of Richmd. has trodden in the steps of the other Cities by an unanimous address to the President.... With respect to the P. his situation must be a most delicate one for himself, as well as for his Country: and there never was, as you observe, a crisis where the friends of both ought to feel more solicitude, or less reserve. At the same time, I have reasons, which I think good, for doubting the propriety, & of course the utility, of uninvited communications from myself. He cannot, I am persuaded, be a stranger to my opinion on the merits of the Treaty; and I am equally persuaded that the State of the public opinion within my sphere, of information will sufficiently force itself on his attention.

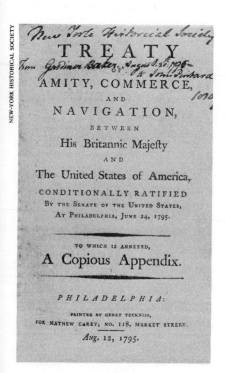

Jay's Treaty

Although the President shed his doubts and approved the treaty, its future still depended on appropriations by the House. The Republican majority set out to stifle the embryo monster, only to be frustrated for three months by Washington's refusal to communicate it. "The situation is truly perplexing," Madison wrote Jefferson. "It is clear that a majority if brought to the merits of the Treaty are agst. it. But as the Treaty is not regularly before the House, & an application to the President brings him personally into the question . . . there is some danger that eno' will fly off to leave the opponents . . . in a minority." Finally, on March 1, 1796, Washington sent the treaty to the House, and after several weeks of maneuver and debate, during which the antitreaty majority slowly wilted, the Republicans suffered mortifying defeat. Madison described the vexatious business to Jefferson.

Philada. May 1. 1796.

The Treaty question was brought to a vote on friday in Come. of whole. Owing to the absence (*certainly* casual & momentary) of one member, & the illness of another, the Committee were divided 49 & 49. The Chairman (Muhlenberg) decided in the affirmative, saying that in the House it would be subject to modification which he wished. In the House yesterday, an Enemy of the Treaty moved a preamble, reciting that altho' the Treaty was highly objectionable, yet considering all circumstances, particularly the duration for two years &c, & confiding in "the efficacy of measures that might be taken for stopping the spoliations & impressments &c," For this ingredient, which you will perceive the scope of, all who meant to persevere agst. the Treaty, with those who only yielded for the reasons expressed in it, ought to have united in voting, as making the pill a bitter one to the Treaty party, as well as less poisonous to the public interest. A few wrongheads however thought fit to separate, whereby the motion was lost by one vote. The main question was then carried in favr. of the Treaty by 51 agst. 48. This revolution was foreseen, and might have been mitigated tho' not prevented, if sooner provided for. But some who were the first to give way to the crisis under its actual pressure, were most averse to prepare for it. The progress of this business throughout has to me been the most worrying & vexatious that I ever encountered; and the more so as the causes lay in the unsteadiness, the follies, the perverseness, & the defections among our friends, more than in the strength or dexterity, or malice of our opponents. It is impossible for me to detail these causes to you now. My consolation under them is in the effect they have in riveting my future purposes. Had the preamble condemning the Treaty on its merits, exercising the discretionary power of the House, and requiring from the Ex. a stoppage of the spoliations &c, been agreed to, I have reason to believe, the Treaty party would have felt it a compleat defeat. You will be informed by the newspapers of the means practised for stirring up petitions &c, in favr. of the Treaty. The plan was laid in this City & circulated by a correspondence thro' the Towns every where. In the mean time the Banks, the British merchts. the insurance Comps. were at work in inflaming individuals, beating down the prices of produce, & sounding the tocksin of foreign war, & domestic convulsions. The success has been such as you would suppose. In several neighbouring districts the people have been so deluded as to constrain their Representatives to renounce their opposition to the Treaty. An appeal to the people on any pending measure, can never be more than an appeal to those in the neighbourhood of the Govt. & to the Banks, the merchts. & the dependents & expectants of the Govt. at a distance.

Philada. May 22. 1796

Congress are hurrying through the remnant of business before them, and will probably adjourn about saturday next. Petitions in favor of the Treaty still come in from distant places. The name of the President & the alarm of war, have had a greater effect, than were apprehended on our side, or expected on the other. A crisis which ought to have been so managed as to fortify the Republican cause, has left it in a very crippled condition; from which its recovery will be the more difficult as the elections in N.Y. Massachusetts & other states, where the prospects were favorable, have taken a wrong turn under the impressions of the moment. Nothing but auspicious contingences abroad or at home can repair the lost ground. Peace in Europe would have a most salutary influence, and accts. just recd. from France revive in some degree the hope of it with the Emperor, which will hasten of course a peace with England. On the other hand, a scene rather gloomy is presented by a letter I have just recd. from Col. M[onroe]. It is dated Feby. 27. The following extracts form the substance of it.

"About a fortnight past I was informed by the minister of foreign affairs that the governmt had at length resolved how to act with us in respect to our treaty with England;

Section of Madison's notes for speaking on Jay's Treaty in 1796

that they considered it as having violated or rather annulled our treaty of alliance with them and taken part with the coalised powers; that they had rather have a open enemy than a perfidious friend; that it was resolved to send an envoy extraordinary to the U.S. to discuss this business with us and whose powers would expire with the execution of the trust. I was astonished with the communication and alarmed with it's probable consequences. I told him it might probably lead to war and thereby separate us which was what our enemies wished and it hasarded much and without a probable gain, that from the moment a person of that character arrived their friends would seem to act under his banner and which circumstance would injure their character and lessen their efforts. In truth I did every thing in my power to prevent this measure and in which I am now told by the minister that I have succeeded. The Directors having resolvd to continue the ordinary course of representation only. But thro' this I hear strong sentiments will be conveyed — the whole of this is made known to the executive by me."

The Jay Treaty was the capstone of the British-centered Federalist system and an astounding defeat for the system of Jefferson and Madison, which was pegged to peace and friendship with France. France, now under the Directory, felt betrayed; and the United States had fled crisis with one power to run into crisis with the other. "It is probable," Madison opined to Jefferson, "that categorical steps on the part of F[rance] toward us are anticipated as a consequence of what has been effected by the British party here, and that such artifice will be practiced by it to charge them in some unpopular form, on its Republican opponents." He was right on both counts: the retaliation of France and the political use the Federalists would make of it.

unsuccessful untill a few days ago

of them which I now inclose. They go

for England, who will either carry

the care of Mr. Adams. I do not yet

the full quantity which you wished

successful as to the seed of the Suga

pursued for the purpose. — I have

allotted for this conveyance, but th

writing in Cypher, and several unse

whether I shall be able to finish i

fear of losing the opportunity for bo